ON FREUD'S
"THE FUTURE OF AN ILLUSION"

CONTEMPORARY FREUD
Turning Points and Critical Issues

General Editor: Leticia Glocer Fiorini

On Freud's "Analysis Terminable and Interminable"
edited by Joseph Sandler

Freud's "On Narcissism: An Introduction"
edited by Joseph Sandler, Ethel Spector Person, Peter Fonagy

On Freud's "Observations on Transference-Love"
edited by Ethel Spector Person, Aiban Hagelin, Peter Fonagy

On Freud's "A Child Is Being Beaten"
edited by Ethel Spector Person

On Freud's "Group Psychology and the Analysis of the Ego"
edited by Ethel Spector Person

On Freud's "Mourning and Melancholia"
edited by Leticia Glocer Fiorini, Thierry Bokanowski, Sergio Lewkowicz

On Freud's "Splitting of the Ego in the Process of Defence"
edited by Thierry Bokanowski, Sergio Lewkowicz

ON FREUD'S "THE FUTURE OF AN ILLUSION"

Edited by
Mary Kay O'Neil & Salman Akhtar

CONTEMPORARY FREUD
Turning Points and Critical Issues

Routledge
Taylor & Francis Group
LONDON AND NEW YORK

Part I: Grateful acknowledgement is made to Sigmund Freud Copyrights, Ltd; the Institute of Psycho-Analysis, London; the Hogarth Press; and BASIC BOOKS, a member of Perseus Books Group, for permission to reprint *The Future of an Illusion* as published in *The Complete Edition of the Psychological Works of Sigmund Freud, Vol. 21,* trans. and ed. James Strachey. All rights reserved 1957. Reproduced by arrangement with Paterson Marsh Ltd., London. And in *The Collected Papers of Sigmund Freud, Vol. 5,* authorized translation under the supervision of Joan Riviere, published by BASIC BOOKS, Inc., a member of Perseus Books Group, by arrangement with the Hogarth Press, Ltd. and the Institute of Psycho-Analysis, London. Reprinted by permission of BASIC BOOKS, a member of Perseus Books Group.

First published 2009 by Karnac Books Ltd.

Published 2019 by Routledge
2 Park Square, Milton Park, Abingdon, Oxon OX14 4RN
52 Vanderbilt Avenue, New York, NY 10017

First issued in hardback 2019

Routledge is an imprint of the Taylor & Francis Group, an informa business

British Library Cataloguing in Publication Data
A C.I.P. for this book is available from the British Library

ISBN 13: 978-0-367-10616-4 (hbk)
ISBN 13: 978-1-85575-627-4 (pbk)

Edited, designed, and produced by Communication Crafts

To the memory of
GEORGE AWAD & MORTIMER OSTOW:
a Toronto-based Palestinian and an Ashkenazi Jew from New York,
both psychoanalysts

CONTENTS

CONTEMPORARY FREUD

IPA Publications Committee

This significant series was founded by Robert Wallerstein and first edited by Joseph Sandler, Ethel Spector Person, and Peter Fonagy; its important contributions have greatly interested psychoanalysts of different latitudes.

The objective of this series is to approach Freud's work from a present and contemporary point of view. On the one hand, this means highlighting the fundamental contributions of his work that constitute the axes of psychoanalytic theory and practice. On the other, it implies the possibility of getting to know and spreading the ideas of present psychoanalysts about Freud's *oeuvre*, both where they coincide and where they differ.

This series considers at least two lines of development: a contemporary reading of Freud that reclaims his contributions and a clarification of the logical and epistemic perspectives from which he is read today.

Freud's theory has branched out, and this has led to a theoretical, technical, and clinical pluralism that has to be worked through. It has therefore become necessary to avoid a snug and uncritical coexistence of concepts in order to consider systems of increasing complexities that take into account both the convergences and the divergences of the categories at play.

Consequently, this project has involved an additional task—that is, gathering psychoanalysts from different geographical regions representing, in addition, different theoretical stances, in order to be able to show their polyphony. This also means an extra effort for the reader that has to do with distinguishing and discriminating, establishing relations or contradictions that each reader will have to eventually work through.

Being able to listen to other theoretical viewpoints is also a way of exercising our listening capacities in the clinical field. This means that the listening should support a space of freedom that would allow us to hear what is new and original.

In this spirit we have brought together authors deeply rooted in the Freudian tradition and others who have developed theories that had not been explicitly taken into account in Freud's work.

The Future of an Illusion reveals Freud's reflections about religion as well as his hope that in the future science will go beyond religion, and reason will replace faith in God. The discussion with an imaginary critic revealed his internal debate, mirroring the debate about this subject in the outside world. However, it also enlightens his way of thinking: deconstructing and constructing at the same time.

The editors, Salman Akhtar and Mary Kay O'Neil, together with the contributors to this volume, accepted the challenge to consider Freudian ideas and their implications nowadays while focusing on the contradictions and gaps in his proposals.

The question of the coexistence between religion and psychoanalysis as well as the place of ideals, belief, illusion, and imagination—and, no less important, the benevolent and destructive aspects of religion—also come into play.

Special thanks are due to the editors and to the contributors to this volume, which enriches the Contemporary Freud's series.

Leticia Glocer Fiorini
Series Editor

ACKNOWLEDGEMENTS

First and foremost, we wish thank the distinguished colleagues who contributed to this volume. We deeply appreciate their efforts, their sacrifice of time, and above all, their patience with our requirements, reminders, and request for revisions. We are grateful to Dr Abigail Ostow, the daughter of the late Dr Mortimer Ostow, for preparing a shorter version of her father's paper for inclusion in this book. With sincerity and affection, we acknowledge the guidance of the members of the current IPA Publications Committee, especially its Chair, Leticia Glocer Fiorini, as well as the editorial counsel of Cesare Sacerdoti, previously the Publications Director of the IPA and an ex-officio member of that committee. We are also thankful to Pippa Hodges for keeping track of all sorts of matters during the book's actual production.

Mary Kay O'Neil & Salman Akhtar

EDITORS AND CONTRIBUTORS

Salman Akhtar was born in India and completed his medical and psychiatric education there. Upon arriving in the United States in 1973, he repeated his psychiatric training at the University of Virginia School of Medicine and then obtained psychoanalytic training from the Philadelphia Psychoanalytic Institute. Currently, he is Professor of Psychiatry at Jefferson Medical College and a training and supervising analyst at the Psychoanalytic Center of Philadelphia. His more than 250 publications include 7 books—*Broken Structures, Quest for Answers, Inner Torment, Immigration and Identity, New Clinical Realms, Objects of Our Desire,* and *Regarding Others*—as well as 25 edited or co-edited volumes in psychiatry and psychoanalysis and 6 collections of poetry. He is also a Scholar-in-Residence at the Inter-Act Theatre Company in Philadelphia.

George A. Awad was born in Acre, Palestine; he became a refugee in Lebanon at the age of 6 years, where he lived for 20 years and obtained his medical education. He trained in psychiatry in the United States and in psychoanalysis in Toronto, Canada, where he lived and practised psychoanalysis and child psychiatry for over 30 years. He was a training analyst at the Toronto Institute for Psychoanalysis and an associate professor of psychiatry at the University of Toronto. He is the author of over 50 articles and chapters in psychiatric and psychoanalytic journals and books. In the mid-1990s he spent two weeks every year for five years in Lebanon, teaching psychodynamic approaches to helping traumatized children and families to front-line mental health workers.

Jennifer Bonovitz received her PhD in Social Work at Bryn Mawr College School of Social Work and Social Research. She is currently a Training and Supervising Analyst in both the child and adult programmes of the Philadelphia Center of Psychoanalysis. Her areas of special interest are early childhood trauma and cross-cultural issues in psychoanalysis.

Sudhir Kakar, psychoanalyst and writer, has a Bachelor's degree in Engineering, and a Master's and PhD in Economics. He has been a Lecturer at Harvard University, visiting professor at the universities of Chicago (1989–93), McGill, Melbourne, Hawaii, and Vienna, Fellow at the Institutes of Advanced Study, Princeton and Berlin, and a Senior Fellow at the Centre for Study of World Religions at Harvard. Dr Kakar is a member of the International Psychoanalytic Association and has been a Training Analyst of the Indian Psychoanalytic Society. He lives in Goa. A leading figure in the fields of cultural psychology and the psychology of religion, Dr Kakar's many honours include the Kardiner Award of Columbia University, Boyer Prize for Psychological Anthropology of the American Anthropological Association, Germany's Goethe Medal, Distinguished Service Award of the Indo–American Psychiatric Association, and the Bhabha, Nehru and National Fellowships of India. He is the author of 15 works of non-fiction and 4 of fiction, of which the latest is *Mad and Divine: Spirit and Psyche in the Modern World.* His books have been translated into 20 languages around the world.

Jonathan Lear is the John U. Nef Distinguished Service Professor at the Committee on Social Thought and the Department of Philosophy at the University of Chicago. He was educated at Yale (BA, History), Cambridge (BA, MA, Philosophy) where he was a Mellon

Fellow, and The Rockefeller University (PhD, Philosophy). He then taught at Cambridge, where he was a Fellow and Director of Studies in Philosophy at Clare College; at Yale, where he was the Kingman Brewster Professor of the Humanities; and now at the University of Chicago. During his time teaching at Yale, he trained as a psychoanalyst at the Western New England Institute for Psychoanalysis. He is currently in private practice and serves on the faculties of the Chicago Institute for Psychoanalysis, the Western New England Institute for Psychoanalysis, and the NYU Institute. His books include: *Aristotle and Logical Theory*; *Aristotle: The Desire to Understand*; *Love and Its Place in Nature: A Philosophical Interpretation of Freudian Psychoanalysis*; *Open Minded: Working out the Logic of the Soul*; *Happiness, Death and the Remainder of Life*; *Therapeutic Action: An Earnest Plea for Irony*; and *Freud*. His most recent book is *Radical Hope: Ethics in the Face of Cultural Devastation*. His writings have been translated into French, German, Italian, Japanese, Portuguese, Spanish, Swedish, and Turkish. In 2009, he will deliver the Tanner Lectures on Human Values at Harvard.

Moisés Lemlij has, among other posts, been Treasurer, Vice-President, and Associate Secretary of the International Psychoanalytical Association; President of the Peruvian Psychoanalytic Society; Director to the Peruvian Institute of Psychoanalysis; and Visiting Professor to the Elliot School of International Affairs at George Washington University and to Guy's Medical School at the University of London. He has been recipient of the Mary S. Sigourney Award and distinguished with the Medal for Exceptional Contributions to Public Health and the Medical Order of the Peruvian College of Physicians. His latest book is *Notas y variaciones sobre temas freudianos* [Notes and variations on Freudian themes]. At present he is Academic Coordinator of the Master's Program on Psychoanalytic Theoretical Studies at the Pontificia Universidad Católica del Perú and Director of the Interdisciplinary Seminar for Andean Studies.

Mary Kay O'Neil, a Supervising and Training Analyst of the Canadian Institute of Psychoanalysis, is in private practice in Montreal, Quebec. Currently, she is Associate Director of the Canadian

Institute of Psychoanalysis (Quebec, English). She completed her PhD at the University of Toronto, where she was on the staff at the University of Toronto Psychiatric Service and Assistant Professor in the Department of Psychiatry. She is author of *The Unsung Psychoanalyst: The Quiet Influence of Ruth Easser* and co-editor of *Confidentiality: Ethical Perspectives and Clinical Dilemmas.* Her research and publications include articles in areas such as depression and young adult development, emotional needs of sole-support mothers and their children, post-analytic contact between analyst and analysand, and psychoanalytic ethics. She has served on psychoanalytic ethics committees at local, national, and international levels, as a reviewer for *JAPA*, the *Canadian Journal of Psychoanalysis,* and, currently, on the North American Editorial Board of the *International Journal of Psychoanalysis.*

Mortimer Ostow was born and raised in New York. After receiving a Master's degree in chemistry from Columbia University, he entered medical school at New York University and graduated in 1941. He was then trained in psychiatry in Washington, DC, and joined the United States Public Health Service. After the Second World War, Dr Ostow resumed his studies, pursuing training in neurology, psychoanalysis, and neurophysiology. His subsequent academic and clinical career spanned over 60 years, and he was widely respected as an analyst, a teacher, and a scientist. He pioneered the coordination of psychopharmacological treatment with psychoanalysis and also the integration of mental health education in the training of Jewish clergy. His nearly 200 scientific publications include 12 books. His last book, *Spirit, Mind, and Brain,* applied neurophysiological insights to what he called man's "religious instinct".

Ethel Spector Person is Professor of Clinical Psychiatry at the College of Physicians and Surgeons, Columbia University, and a Training and Supervising Analyst at the Columbia University Center for Psychoanalytical Training and Research, where she was Director from 1981 until 1991. Her books include *Feeling Strong: The Achievement of Authentic Power*; *The Sexual Century: Selected Papers on Sex and Gender*; *By Force of Fantasy: How We Make Our Lives*; and *Dreams of Love* *and Fateful Encounters: The Power of Romantic Love.* With Catherine Stimpson she co-edited *Women: Sex and Sexuality*, which was given an Award for Excellence in the field of education by Chicago Women Publishing. With Arnold Cooper and Otto Kernberg she co-edited *Psychoanalysis: The Second Century*; and with Arnold Cooper and Glen Gabbard she edited the *APPI Textbook of Psychoanalysis.* She has been active in the American Psychoanalytic Association, where she served both as a Fellow to the Board on Professional Standards and as an elected Councilor to the Executive Council. She was a Vice-President of the International Psychoanalytical Association from 1995 to 1999. Among other awards, she is the recipient of the Sigmund Freud Award from the American Society of Psychoanalytic Physicians; the Section III Recognition Award for her work in women's psychology from Division 39 of The American Psychological Association; and the Award for Distinguished and Meritorious Service to the IPA, 2000. In 2003, she was named the National Woman Psychoanalytic Scholar by the American Psychoanalytic Association. She is at work on a book: *Ah, I Remember It Well: Memories as the Building Blocks of Our Self-Identity.*

Neville Symington is a psychoanalyst in private practice with his psychoanalyst wife in Sydney, Australia. As a young man he took a diploma in Philosophy and then in Theology. He later did a degree in Psychology and took a diploma in Clinical Psychology. He did his psychoanalytic training in London and is a Fellow of the British Psycho-Analytical Society. He held a senior staff position in the Adult Department of the Tavistock Clinic from 1977 to 1985. He was also Chairman of the Psychology Discipline for the Adult and Adolescent Departments at the Tavistock Clinic in London. In 1986 he migrated to Sydney, Australia, where he was Chairman of the Sydney Institute for Psycho-Analysis from 1987 to 1993. He was President of the Australian Psycho-Analytic Society from 1999 to 2002. He is the author of *The Analytic Experience*; *Emotion and Spirit*; *Narcissism: A New Theory*; *The Making of a Psychotherapist*; *The Spirit of Sanity*; *A Pattern of Madness*; *How to Choose a Psychotherapist*; *The Blind Man Sees*; *A Healing Conversation*; and *Becoming a Person through Psycho-Analysis.* He is joint author with Joan Symington of *The Clinical Thinking of Wilfred Bion.* He has lectured in Britain, Norway,

Denmark, Poland, Germany, the United States, Brazil, Israel, India, New Zealand, and Australia.

J. Anderson Thomson, Jr, is a psychiatrist in private practice in Charlottesville, Virginia. He is also a staff psychiatrist at the University of Virginia Elson Student Health Center, Counseling and Psychological Services and the University of Virginia Institute for Law, Psychiatry and Public Policy, as well as the forensic psychiatrist for Region Ten Community Services. He received his BA from Duke University (1970) and his MD from the University of Virginia (1974), and he did his adult psychiatry training at University of Virginia (1974–77). He is an active member of the Virginia Psychoanalytic Society. His private practice is oriented towards individual psychoanalytic psychotherapy, forensic psychiatry, and medication consultation. He was the Assistant Director of the Center for the Study of Mind and Human Interaction at the University of Virginia. Founded by Vamık Volkan, the center conducted interdisciplinary intervention and research in large-group ethnic and political conflict. He has publications on narcissistic personality disorder, PTSD, and the psychology of racism, and psychobiographical essays on Robert E. Lee and Lee Harvey Oswald. His current research interest is in the area of evolutionary psychology, and he used this new lens to write about depression, criminal behaviour, the sexual side-effects of psychotropic medications, religion, and suicide terrorism.

Vamık D. Volkan is an Emeritus Professor of Psychiatry at the University of Virginia, Charlottesville, Virginia, an Emeritus Training and Supervising Analyst at the Washington Psychoanalytic Institute, Washington, DC, and the Senior Erik Erikson Scholar at the Austen Riggs Center in Stockbridge, Massachusetts. He holds Honorary Doctoral Degrees from Kuopio University, Finland, and from Ankara University, Turkey. He has served on the editorial boards of 16 professional journals, including the *Journal of the American Psychoanalytic Association,* has authored or co-authored 30 books, and was the editor or co-editor of 10 more. He has published more than 400 scientific papers or book chapters. Since 1979 he has been involved in a series of unofficial diplomatic negotiations between influential enemy representatives. Currently he is involved in bringing together representatives from the Western and Islamic worlds to examine the existing perceptions and feelings concerning the so-called Western–Islamic world split. He was President of the International Society of Political Psychology, Virginia Psychoanalytic Society, and is President-Elect of the American College of Psychoanalysts.

ON FREUD'S
"THE FUTURE OF AN ILLUSION"

Introduction

Salman Akhtar

The question whether God is a subject for psychoanalysis is something that must be tackled at the very outset of our enterprise. However, as we pay attention to it, the question reveals itself to be the product of a tension that exists between those who believe in the existence of God and those who do not. For the former, God is far beyond human scrutiny, psychoanalytic or otherwise. For the latter, God is an idea evolved by mankind and, like all other fantasies, is a subject for psychoanalysis. Note the paradox: if God actually exists, then He (She or It) is not a subject for psychoanalysis since the discipline deals with intrapsychic phenomena, not with objects in outer reality. As an actual object, God would join the list of chairs, tables, cats and dogs, automobiles, pens, dolls, staircases, rivers and mountains, trees, cigars, grandfather clocks, and other sundry items that populate our external surround. In of themselves, these objects do not constitute topics of psychoanalytic study: ideas, emotions, and behaviours related to them do. Therefore, if God does exist, only the intrapsychic reverberations and elaborations consequent upon this fact would constitute subjects for psychoanalysis. However, if God does not exist and is a psychic creation, then God itself would be a proper subject for psychoanalysis.

Sigmund Freud, by the very act of making God a subject of metapsychological deconstruction, took such a resolutely atheistic position. His pupils and followers adhered "religiously" to the arguments and declarations he made in *The Future of Illusion* (Freud, 1927c) and later in *Civilization and Its Discontents* (1930a). Scientific positivism of the early twentieth century provided a receptive crucible for Freud's debunking of God. He had given voice to what was brewing in the minds of the Western intelligentsia. The unspeakable atrocities that soon followed in the name of religious nationalism in Europe "confirmed" that ethnocentrism and its conceptual twin, religious belief, were dangerous commodities. They led to intoxication with in-group superiority and laid the groundwork for oppression of "others" and even cruelty and genocide. Early European psychoanalysts, themselves the victims of prejudice and violence, wholeheartedly followed the ray of hope offered by Freud's declaration that religion was a hoax and science will sooner or later assure that rationality prevails in the conduct of interpersonal and communal affairs. Atheism and psychoanalysis became inseparable.

Such closure had untoward consequences. First, it discouraged those who believed in God from entering psychoanalytic profession or, if they did enter it, from making their convictions a part of academic discourse; a rich source of theoretical controversy and advance was thus lost. Second, the "religious" and "spiritual" sector of human experience and of the analyst's mind itself—the sector involving Mortimer Ostow's (2001) "religious instinct" and Romain Rolland's (cited in Freud, 1930a) "oceanic feeling"—was sent into intrapsychic exile; displacement to homoethnic idealization, participation in communal rituals with a feigned reluctance, and an occasional death-bed conversion tried to fill this gap, but to little avail. Third, the adulation of Freud's "logically sound" atheism caused inattention towards other important aspects of his *Illusion* book. These included his elucidation of the morality of the oppressed, the ubiquitous human tendency to anthropomorphize nature, and his astonishing exclusion of the role played by the transformative experience a growing child has with his or her mother in the origins of sacred and reverential affects. Finally, focus on the content of the *Illusion* monograph eclipsed the study of its form. To be sure,

Freud had used the literary device of a dialogue with a conceptual opponent elsewhere (e.g. 1916–17) as well, but never with the pervasive force as in this book on religion. The exchange between Freud and his imaginary, God-believing interlocutor fills the pages of *The Future of an Illusion*. But who actually is this religious "friend" of Freud's?

Think for a minute. What conclusion would a practicing analyst draw upon encountering an analysand who constantly talks of a friend with an opinion opposite to his? For instance, what would one think of a philanthropist on the couch who talks incessantly about a selfish and miserly friend of his? Or of a shy academic who does not tire of mocking his exhibitionistic colleagues? What do their preoccupations betray? Now apply the answer to the debate between the self-declared "Godless Jew" and his "religious interlocutor", and you get the following: Freud is arguing with himself. Sheldon Bach's (1977) proposal that a split-off sector of the self invariably shows a "mirror complementarity" with conscious protestations of the individual speaks to this very point. Let me put it bluntly: the *Illusion* monograph is a literary battlefield where "Freud, the Atheist" is involved in a bloody combat with "Freud, the Believer"!

This makes Freud all too human, in my opinion. After all, struggle between theism and atheism is as psychically ubiquitous as the struggles between activity and passivity, spontaneity and restraint, homosexuality and heterosexuality, morality and immorality, and, above all, between living and dying. The debate about God's existence is hardly alien or new. It has raged on throughout mankind's history, and impressive proponents of both sides in this choice are found in Greek and Roman civilizations. Even the Hindus, who are naively portrayed in the West as a God-believing demographic monolith, have had a tradition of arguing about the existence of God that goes back at least to two thousand years before the birth of Christ (Sen, 2005).

With this in mind, Freud appears hardly peculiar for being conflicted about believing—or not believing—in God. It was his keeping the two sides of his ambivalence rigidly apart and professing conscious allegiance to only one side while the other lurked just beneath the surface, that makes him interesting. His *Illusion* book is arresting due to the very tension of such ambivalence. And, frankly, the same conflict is evident in Freud's personal correspondence. He emphatically declares himself to be an atheist in one place and professes gratitude to God in another. The examples of the former include "I am a God-forsaken incredulous Jew" (letter to James Putnam, quoted in Nicholi, 2002, p. 63), "Neither in my private life nor in my writings I have ever made a secret of being an out and out unbeliever" (letter to Charles Singer, quoted in Gay, 1988), and "Why did none of the devout create psychoanalysis? Why did one have to wait for a completely Godless Jew?" (letter to Oscar Pfister, quoted in Gay, 1988). Compare this with what Armand Nicholi, Jr, tells us in his book, *The Question of God*:

> Letters throughout Freud's life are replete with words and phrases such as "I passed my examinations with God's help"; "if God so wills"; "the good Lord"; "taking the Lord to task"; "into the keeping of the Lord"; "until after the Resurrection"; "science seems to demand the existence of God"; "God's judgement"; "God's will"; "God's grace"; "God above"; "if someday we meet above"; "in the next world"; "my secret prayer". In a letter to Oscar Pfister, Freud writes that Pfister was "a true servant of God" and was "in the fortunate position to lead others to God". [Nicholi, 2002, p. 51]

Now it can be asserted that such references to God are not to be taken seriously. They are merely metaphorical and reflect nothing but a manner of speech and a touching affectation. But *that* is precisely my point: namely, that Freud had two pictures of God in mind. One was an anthropomorphized, concrete, and stern but protective father-like presence, which he resolutely defied. The other was a sublime object of wonder, humility, and gratitude, to which he gladly paid homage. The former demanded idolatry, which revolted Freud. The latter evoked humility, which Freud was fearless to experience. Come to think of it, there are two, not one, contradictions in Freud's views on religion. The first contradiction is between his belief and non-belief in God. The second contradiction is between his two visions of divinity. It therefore turns out that what has been taken to be simple and self-evident in Freud's views about religious belief is contradictory, complex, and, frankly, a bit confused and confusing.

With this, we come back full circle. The question raised at the beginning of this discourse—"Is God a subject for psychoanalysis?"—had led to answers that depended upon whether or not one believed in God's existence. Satisfied with that level of inquiry in the beginning, I now feel unease. I want to go further. Now I assert that the question is not whether or not God exists—and even if it were, psychoanalysis could hardly come up with the methodology to answer it—since God, to my mind, both exists and does not exist. The former stance applies to the literal and anthropomorphized version of God and the latter to its metaphorical and subjective version. More correctly, perhaps, the question of God's existence or non-existence is one that is not to be asked. Here Donald Winnicott (1953), who proposed an "intermediate area of experience" where reality and unreality co-exist harmoniously, comes to our rescue. Like literature, games, love, and creativity in general, religious belief belongs in this realm. God is a majestic poem.

A less compromising way is to record what is literal and metaphorical here in separate registers altogether. Albert Einstein's (1950) quip best reflects this spirit (pun unintended). He said that he does not believe in a bearded God sitting up high in the sky, deciding whether he will get to work on time next Thursday, but he does believe in the infinitely complex and mysterious order of the universe that inspires awe and humility in one. Within psychoanalysis, these two views of God can be compared to that in Sigmund Freud's (1927c) *Illusion* book and that implicit in Wilfred Bion's (1965, 1992) concept of "O". Freud's God is "up there". Bion's God is everywhere. Freud's God is sculpted in human terms. Bion's God is painted in the watercolour of wisdom. Freud's God is that of Judeo–Christian and Islamic traditions. Bion's God represents Advaitic Vedantism, which is an antecedent of the modern Hinduism and Zen Buddhism (Vallabhaneni, 2005). Freud's God speaks to the selected few. Bion's God sings through the murmur of the wind and floats on the waves of rivers and oceans. Freud's God can be accepted or refuted, Bion's God is inescapable.

But wait. Didn't I conclude that Freud had two versions of God in mind: one that he rebelled against in the *Illusion* book and another that he thanked profusely in his private correspondence? One way to solve this conundrum is to equate "Freud's God" and

"Bion's God" in the preceding paragraph with these two views held by Freud himself. Fascinating, isn't it?

Even more interesting is that while neither Freud nor Bion mention woman/mother in connection with the origins of God, the foundation of their ideas seems to be in their early mothering experience and its rupture. Freud's traumatic loss of a beloved Catholic nursemaid—who frequently took him to church and in imitation of whom he, as a child, preached to everyone—led to his massive repudiation of religion and music, the two phenomena associated with her memory. Bion's traumatic separation from the Hindu *Aaya* [nanny] of his childhood in rural India led to the split result that he never travelled back to India but incorporated the Sanskrit word *Om* for the Omnipresent Creator in an abbreviated form: "O"—deleting the labial consonant "m", which requires closing the mouth and ending the sound. Both these actions are emblematic of separation—and describe ideas about faith (see also Eigen, 1981; Neri, 2005) that have an unmistakable Eastern ring to them. Both Freud and Bion were responding, albeit in a starkly different manner, to their early "maternal" losses in formulating their ideas about faith and transformative higher powers.

As we put all this together, seven positions *vis-à-vis* religious belief in the psychoanalytic field become evident:

- The mainstream has whole-heartedly concurred with Freud's atheism and, as a result, added little to the psychoanalytic argument in favour of atheism.
- Some psychoanalysts have allowed religion an important structuring role in identity formation (Erikson, 1950, 1959), traced a developmental line of religious belief from its primitive to its mature forms (Loewald, 1953, 1978), and brought in the mother–child relationship to bear upon the genesis of the idea of God (Moloney, 1954). This led to an expanded psychoanalytic view of religious belief.
- A few Christian (Meissner, 1984, 1987, 2001; Rizzuto, 1979, 1998) and Muslim (Ad-Dab'bagh, 2001) psychoanalysts have openly acknowledged their belief in God while also attempting to forge links between religious faith and psychoanalytic metapsychology and practice.

- Still others have brought in the polytheistic (Rao, 2005) and discourse-based Hindu (Rao, 2001; Reddy, 2001, 2005), non-theistic Buddhist (Rubin, 2005), Islamic Sufi (Shafii, 1985), and Jewish mystical (Ostow, 1995) perspectives on religion and thus compounded Freud's argument, which was largely directed at anthropomorphized monotheism.
- A few other psychoanalysts (Bion, 1965, 1992; Grotstein, 2001) have veered away from Freud's idol-like view of God to a de-anthropomorphized view of God as knowledge and order that is spread over the universe like a soft blanket over a sleeping baby: the baby can see, feel, smell, and play with the blanket only if he wakes up from his slumber. Think about it: the Oedipus complex existed before Sophocles and Freud, and *E* was equal to mc^2 long before Einstein.
- Winnicott's (1953) delineation of the "transitional realm" has permitted still other analysts (Akhtar & Parens, 2001) to place God squarely in the area where reality and un-reality co-exist, imagination is born, and paradox reigns supreme. Whether the "transitional area" in a given individual gets populated by God then depends upon vicissitudes of culture, family values, childhood experience, and aesthetic of life idioms. The main issue is, how does the individual use such "belief", and to what intrapsychic and interpersonal advantages or disadvantages?
- Psychoanalysts dealing with large-group psychology and ethnic conflicts (e.g. Volkan, 1997, 2004, 2006) have also stepped clear of the thorny issue of God's existence and focused on the socio-political uses and abuses of religion.

All seven perspectives mentioned above are represented in the pages of this book. Among the contributors to it are robust atheists as well as firm believers. There are also those who seem decidedly uncommitted. They come from different regions of the world, represent different ethno-religious backgrounds, and speak in different psychoanalytic tongues. The questions they raise largely pertain to what literal and metaphorical, conscious and unconscious, adaptive and maladaptive, self-soothing and masochistic, and generous and sadistic uses belief in God can be, has been, and is still being put to? Clearly, Freud's intrapsychic "debate" on whether God exists or not has mushroomed into concerns of much larger scope. Knowing his unflappable willingness to learn, grow, and change his opinions, it is safe to assume that this smorgasbord of conceptual diversity would have been welcomed by Freud, even if he chose to use it for arguing even more forcefully for his avowed position!

PART I

The Future of an Illusion (1927c)

Sigmund Freud

THE FUTURE OF AN ILLUSION

I

When one has lived for quite a long time in a particular civilization[1] and has often tried to discover what its origins were and along what path it has developed, one sometimes also feels tempted to take a glance in the other direction and to ask what further fate lies before it and what transformations it is destined to undergo. But one soon finds that the value of such an enquiry is diminished from the outset by several factors. Above all, because there are only a few people who can survey human activity in its full compass. Most people have been obliged to restrict themselves to a single, or a few, fields of it. But the less a man knows about the past and the present the more insecure must prove to be his judgement of the future. And there is the further difficulty that precisely in a judgement of this kind the subjective expectations of the individual play a part which it is difficult to assess; and these turn out to be dependent on purely personal factors in his own experience, on the greater or lesser optimism of his attitude to life, as it has been dictated for him by his temperament or by his success or failure. Finally, the curious fact makes itself felt that in general people experience their present naïvely, as it were, without being able to form an estimate of its contents; they have first to put themselves at a distance from it—the present, that is to say, must have become the past—before it can yield points of vantage from which to judge the future.

Thus anyone who gives way to the temptation to deliver an opinion on the probable future of our civilization will do well to remind himself of the difficulties I have just pointed out, as well as of the uncertainty that attaches quite generally to any prophecy. It follows from this, so far as I am concerned, that I shall make a hasty retreat before a task that is too great, and shall promptly seek out the small tract of territory which has claimed my attention hitherto, as soon as I have determined its position in the general scheme of things.

Human civilization, by which I mean all those respects in

[1] [See Editor's Note, p. 4.]

which human life has raised itself above its animal status and differs from the life of beasts—and I scorn to distinguish between culture and civilization—, presents, as we know, two aspects to the observer. It includes on the one hand all the knowledge and capacity that men have acquired in order to control the forces of nature and extract its wealth for the satisfaction of human needs, and, on the other hand, all the regulations necessary in order to adjust the relations of men to one another and especially the distribution of the available wealth. The two trends of civilization are not independent of each other: firstly, because the mutual relations of men are profoundly influenced by the amount of instinctual satisfaction which the existing wealth makes possible; secondly, because an individual man can himself come to function as wealth in relation to another one, in so far as the other person makes use of his capacity for work, or chooses him as a sexual object; and thirdly, moreover, because every individual is virtually an enemy of civilization, though civilization is supposed to be an object of universal human interest.[1] It is remarkable that, little as men are able to exist in isolation, they should nevertheless feel as a heavy burden the sacrifices which civilization expects of them in order to make a communal life possible. Thus civilization has to be defended against the individual, and its regulations, institutions and commands are directed to that task. They aim not only at effecting a certain distribution of wealth but at maintaining that distribution; indeed, they have to protect everything that contributes to the conquest of nature and the production of wealth against men's hostile impulses. Human creations are easily destroyed, and science and technology, which have built them up, can also be used for their annihilation.

One thus gets an impression that civilization is something which was imposed on a resisting majority by a minority which understood how to obtain possession of the means to power and coercion. It is, of course, natural to assume that these difficulties are not inherent in the nature of civilization itself but are determined by the imperfections of the cultural forms which have so far been developed. And in fact it is not difficult to

[1] [The hostility of human individuals to civilization plays a large part in the earlier chapters of this work. Freud returned to the subject and discussed it still more fully two years later in his *Civilization and its Discontents* (1930*a*).]

indicate those defects. While mankind has made continual advances in its control over nature and may expect to make still greater ones, it is not possible to establish with certainty that a similar advance has been made in the management of human affairs; and probably at all periods, just as now once again, many people have asked themselves whether what little civilization has thus acquired is indeed worth defending at all. One would think that a re-ordering of human relations should be possible, which would remove the sources of dissatisfaction with civilization by renouncing coercion and the suppression of the instincts, so that, undisturbed by internal discord, men might devote themselves to the acquisition of wealth and its enjoyment. That would be the golden age, but it is questionable if such a state of affairs can be realized. It seems rather that every civilization must be built up on coercion and renunciation of instinct; it does not even seem certain that if coercion were to cease the majority of human beings would be prepared to undertake to perform the work necessary for acquiring new wealth. One has, I think, to reckon with the fact that there are present in all men destructive, and therefore anti-social and anti-cultural, trends and that in a great number of people these are strong enough to determine their behaviour in human society.

This psychological fact has a decisive importance for our judgement of human civilization. Whereas we might at first think that its essence lies in controlling nature for the purpose of acquiring wealth and that the dangers which threaten it could be eliminated through a suitable distribution of that wealth among men, it now seems that the emphasis has moved over from the material to the mental. The decisive question is whether and to what extent it is possible to lessen the burden of the instinctual sacrifices imposed on men, to reconcile men to those which must necessarily remain and to provide a compensation for them. It is just as impossible to do without control of the mass[1] by a minority as it is to dispense with coercion in the work of civilization. For masses are lazy and unintelligent; they have no love for instinctual renunciation, and they are not to be convinced by argument of its inevitability; and the individuals composing them support one another in giving free

[1] ['*Masse.*' The German word has a very wide meaning. It is translated 'group' for special reasons in Freud's *Group Psychology* (1921*c*). See *Standard Ed.*, **18**, 69*n*. Here 'mass' seems more appropriate.]

rein to their indiscipline. It is only through the influence of individuals who can set an example and whom masses recognize as their leaders that they can be induced to perform the work and undergo the renunciations on which the existence of civilization depends. All is well if these leaders are persons who possess superior insight into the necessities of life and who have risen to the height of mastering their own instinctual wishes. But there is a danger that in order not to lose their influence they may give way to the mass more than it gives way to them, and it therefore seems necessary that they shall be independent of the mass by having means to power at their disposal. To put it briefly, there are two widespread human characteristics which are responsible for the fact that the regulations of civilization can only be maintained by a certain degree of coercion—namely, that men are not spontaneously fond of work and that arguments are of no avail against their passions.

I know the objections which will be raised against these assertions. It will be said that the characteristic of human masses depicted here, which is supposed to prove that coercion cannot be dispensed with in the work of civilization, is itself only the result of defects in the cultural regulations, owing to which men have become embittered, revengeful and inaccessible. New generations, who have been brought up in kindness and taught to have a high opinion of reason, and who have experienced the benefits of civilization at an early age, will have a different attitude to it. They will feel it as a possession of their very own and will be ready for its sake to make the sacrifices as regards work and instinctual satisfaction that are necessary for its preservation. They will be able to do without coercion and will differ little from their leaders. If no culture has so far produced human masses of such a quality, it is because no culture has yet devised regulations which will influence men in this way, and in particular from childhood onwards.

It may be doubted whether it is possible at all, or at any rate as yet, at the present stage of our control over nature, to set up cultural regulations of this kind. It may be asked where the number of superior, unswerving and disinterested leaders are to come from who are to act as educators of the future generations, and it may be alarming to think of the enormous amount of coercion that will inevitably be required before these intentions can be carried out. The grandeur of the plan and its importance for the future of human civilization cannot be disputed. It is securely based on the psychological discovery that man is equipped with the most varied instinctual dispositions, whose ultimate course is determined by the experiences of early childhood. But for the same reason the limitations of man's capacity for education set bounds to the effectiveness of such a transformation in his culture. One may question whether, and in what degree, it would be possible for a different cultural environment to do away with the two characteristics of human masses which make the guidance of human affairs so difficult. The experiment has not yet been made. Probably a certain percentage of mankind (owing to a pathological disposition or an excess of instinctual strength) will always remain asocial; but if it were feasible merely to reduce the majority that is hostile towards civilization to-day into a minority, a great deal would have been accomplished—perhaps all that *can* be accomplished.

I should not like to give the impression that I have strayed a long way from the line laid down for my enquiry [p. 5]. Let me therefore give an express assurance that I have not the least intention of making judgements on the great experiment in civilization that is now in progress in the vast country that stretches between Europe and Asia.[1] I have neither the special knowledge nor the capacity to decide on its practicability, to test the expediency of the methods employed or to measure the width of the inevitable gap between intention and execution. What is in preparation there is unfinished and therefore eludes an investigation for which our own long-consolidated civilization affords us material.

[1] [See, however, some remarks in Chapter V of *Civilization and its Discontents* (1930*a*), p. 112 ff. below, and at two points in *Why War?* (1933*b*).]

II

We have slipped unawares out of the economic field into the field of psychology. At first we were tempted to look for the assets of civilization in the available wealth and in the regulations for its distribution. But with the recognition that every civilization rests on a compulsion to work and a renunciation of instinct and therefore inevitably provokes opposition from those affected by these demands, it has become clear that civilization cannot consist principally or solely in wealth itself and the means of acquiring it and the arrangements for its distribution; for these things are threatened by the rebelliousness and destructive mania of the participants in civilization. Alongside of wealth we now come upon the means by which civilization can be defended—measures of coercion and other measures that are intended to reconcile men to it and to recompense them for their sacrifices. These latter may be described as the mental assets of civilization.

For the sake of a uniform terminology we will describe the fact that an instinct cannot be satisfied as a 'frustration', the regulation by which this frustration is established as a 'prohibition' and the condition which is produced by the prohibition as a 'privation'. The first step is to distinguish between privations which affect everyone and privations which do not affect everyone but only groups, classes or even single individuals. The former are the earliest; with the prohibitions that established them, civilization—who knows how many thousands of years ago?—began to detach man from his primordial animal condition. We have found to our surprise that these privations are still operative and still form the kernel of hostility to civilization. The instinctual wishes that suffer under them are born afresh with every child; there is a class of people, the neurotics, who already react to these frustrations with asocial behaviour. Among these instinctual wishes are those of incest, cannibalism and lust for killing. It sounds strange to place alongside one another wishes which everyone seems united in repudiating and others about which there is so much lively dispute in our civilization as to whether they shall be permitted or frustrated; but psychologically it is justifiable to do so. Nor is the attitude of civilization to these oldest instinctual wishes by any means uniform. Cannibalism alone seems to be universally proscribed and—to the non-psycho-analytic view—to have been completely surmounted. The strength of the incestuous wishes can still be detected behind the prohibition against them; and under certain conditions killing is still practised, and indeed commanded, by our civilization. It is possible that cultural developments lie ahead of us in which the satisfaction of yet other wishes, which are entirely permissible to-day, will appear just as unacceptable as cannibalism does now.

These earliest instinctual renunciations already involve a psychological factor which remains important for all further instinctual renunciations as well. It is not true that the human mind has undergone no development since the earliest times and that, in contrast to the advances of science and technology, it is the same to-day as it was at the beginning of history. We can point out one of these mental advances at once. It is in keeping with the course of human development that external coercion gradually becomes internalized; for a special mental agency, man's super-ego, takes it over and includes it among its commandments.[1] Every child presents this process of transformation to us; only by that means does it become a moral and social being. Such a strengthening of the super-ego is a most precious cultural asset in the psychological field. Those in whom it has taken place are turned from being opponents of civilization into being its vehicles. The greater their number is in a cultural unit the more secure is its culture and the more it can dispense with external measures of coercion. Now the degree of this internalization differs greatly between the various instinctual prohibitions. As regards the earliest cultural demands, which I have mentioned, the internalization seems to have been very extensively achieved, if we leave out of account the unwelcome exception of the neurotics. But the case is altered when we turn to the other instinctual claims. Here we observe with surprise and concern that a majority of people obey the cultural prohibitions on these points only under the pressure of external coercion—that is, only where that coercion can make itself effective and so long as it is to be feared. This is also true of what are known as the *moral* demands of civilization, which

[1] [See Chapter III of *The Ego and the Id* (1923*b*), *Standard Ed.*, **19**, 28 ff.]

likewise apply to everyone. Most of one's experiences of man's moral untrustworthiness fall into this category. There are countless civilized people who would shrink from murder or incest but who do not deny themselves the satisfaction of their avarice, their aggressive urges or their sexual lusts, and who do not hesitate to injure other people by lies, fraud and calumny, so long as they can remain unpunished for it; and this, no doubt, has always been so through many ages of civilization.

If we turn to those restrictions that apply only to certain classes of society, we meet with a state of things which is flagrant and which has always been recognized. It is to be expected that these underprivileged classes will envy the favoured ones their privileges and will do all they can to free themselves from their own surplus of privation. Where this is not possible, a permanent measure of discontent will persist within the culture concerned and this can lead to dangerous revolts. If, however, a culture has not got beyond a point at which the satisfaction of one portion of its participants depends upon the suppression of another, and perhaps larger, portion—and this is the case in all present-day cultures—it is understandable that the suppressed people should develop an intense hostility towards a culture whose existence they make possible by their work, but in whose wealth they have too small a share. In such conditions an internalization of the cultural prohibitions among the suppressed people is not to be expected. On the contrary, they are not prepared to acknowledge the prohibitions, they are intent on destroying the culture itself, and possibly even on doing away with the postulates on which it is based. The hostility of these classes to civilization is so obvious that it has caused the more latent hostility of the social strata that are better provided for to be overlooked. It goes without saying that a civilization which leaves so large a number of its participants unsatisfied and drives them into revolt neither has nor deserves the prospect of a lasting existence.

The extent to which a civilization's precepts have been internalized—to express it popularly and unpsychologically: the moral level of its participants—is not the only form of mental wealth that comes into consideration in estimating a civilization's value. There are in addition its assets in the shape of ideals and artistic creations—that is, the satisfactions that can be derived from those sources.

People will be only too readily inclined to include among the psychical assets of a culture its ideals—its estimates of what achievements are the highest and the most to be striven after. It will seem at first as though these ideals would determine the achievements of the cultural unit; but the actual course of events would appear to be that the ideals are based on the first achievements which have been made possible by a combination of the culture's internal gifts and external circumstances, and that these first achievements are then held on to by the ideal as something to be carried further. The satisfaction which the ideal offers to the participants in the culture is thus of a narcissistic nature; it rests on their pride in what has already been successfully achieved. To make this satisfaction complete calls for a comparison with other cultures which have aimed at different achievements and have developed different ideals. On the strength of these differences every culture claims the right to look down on the rest. In this way cultural ideals become a source of discord and enmity between different cultural units, as can be seen most clearly in the case of nations.

The narcissistic satisfaction provided by the cultural ideal is also among the forces which are successful in combating the hostility to culture within the cultural unit. This satisfaction can be shared in not only by the favoured classes, which enjoy the benefits of the culture, but also by the suppressed ones, since the right to despise the people outside it compensates them for the wrongs they suffer within their own unit. No doubt one is a wretched plebeian, harassed by debts and military service; but, to make up for it, one is a Roman citizen, one has one's share in the task of ruling other nations and dictating their laws. This identification of the suppressed classes with the class who rules and exploits them is, however, only part of a larger whole. For, on the other hand, the suppressed classes can be emotionally attached to their masters; in spite of their hostility to them they may see in them their ideals; unless such relations of a fundamentally satisfying kind subsisted, it would be impossible to understand how a number of civilizations have survived so long in spite of the justifiable hostility of large human masses.

A different kind of satisfaction is afforded by art to the participants in a cultural unit, though as a rule it remains inaccessible to the masses, who are engaged in exhausting work and have not enjoyed any personal education. As we discovered long since,[1] art offers substitutive satisfactions for the oldest and still most deeply felt cultural renunciations, and for that reason it serves as nothing else does to reconcile a man to the sacrifices he has made on behalf of civilization. On the other hand, the creations of art heighten his feelings of identification, of which every cultural unit stands in so much need, by providing an occasion for sharing highly valued emotional experiences. And when those creations picture the achievements of his particular culture and bring to his mind its ideals in an impressive manner, they also minister to his narcissistic satisfaction.

No mention has yet been made of what is perhaps the most important item in the psychical inventory of a civilization. This consists in its religious ideas in the widest sense—in other words (which will be justified later) in its illusions.

[1] [Cf., for instance, 'Creative Writers and Day-Dreaming' (1908*e*).]

III

In what does the peculiar value of religious ideas lie?

We have spoken of the hostility to civilization which is produced by the pressure that civilization exercises, the renunciations of instinct which it demands. If one imagines its prohibitions lifted—if, then, one may take any woman one pleases as a sexual object, if one may without hesitation kill one's rival for her love or anyone else who stands in one's way, if, too, one can carry off any of the other man's belongings without asking leave—how splendid, what a string of satisfactions one's life would be! True, one soon comes across the first difficulty: everyone else has exactly the same wishes as I have and will treat me with no more consideration than I treat him. And so in reality only one person could be made unrestrictedly happy by such a removal of the restrictions of civilization, and he would be a tyrant, a dictator, who had seized all the means to power. And even he would have every reason to wish that the others would observe at least one cultural commandment: 'thou shalt not kill'.

But how ungrateful, how short-sighted after all, to strive for the abolition of civilization! What would then remain would be a state of nature, and that would be far harder to bear. It is true that nature would not demand any restrictions of instinct from us, she would let us do as we liked; but she has her own particularly effective method of restricting us. She destroys us—coldly, cruelly, relentlessly, as it seems to us, and possibly through the very things that occasioned our satisfaction. It was precisely because of these dangers with which nature threatens us that we came together and created civilization, which is also, among other things, intended to make our communal life possible. For the principal task of civilization, its actual *raison d'être*, is to defend us against nature.

We all know that in many ways civilization does this fairly well already, and clearly as time goes on it will do it much better. But no one is under the illusion that nature has already been vanquished; and few dare hope that she will ever be entirely subjected to man. There are the elements, which seem to mock at all human control: the earth, which quakes and is torn apart and buries all human life and its works; water, which deluges and drowns everything in a turmoil; storms, which blow everything before them; there are diseases, which we have only recently recognized as attacks by other organisms; and finally there is the painful riddle of death, against which no medicine has yet been found, nor probably will be. With these forces nature rises up against us, majestic, cruel and inexorable; she brings to our mind once more our weakness and helplessness, which we thought to escape through the work of civilization. One of the few gratifying and exalting impressions which mankind can offer is when, in the face of an elemental catastrophe, it forgets the discordancies of its civilization and all its internal difficulties and animosities, and recalls the great common task of preserving itself against the superior power of nature.

For the individual, too, life is hard to bear, just as it is for mankind in general. The civilization in which he participates imposes some amount of privation on him, and other men bring him a measure of suffering, either in spite of the precepts of his civilization or because of its imperfections. To this are added the injuries which untamed nature—he calls it Fate—inflicts on him. One might suppose that this condition of things would result in a permanent state of anxious expectation in him and a severe injury to his natural narcissism. We know already how the individual reacts to the injuries which civilization and other men inflict on him: he develops a corresponding degree of resistance to the regulations of civilization and of hostility to it. But how does he defend himself against the superior powers of nature, of Fate, which threaten him as they threaten all the rest?

Civilization relieves him of this task; it performs it in the same way for all alike; and it is noteworthy that in this almost all civilizations act alike. Civilization does not call a halt in the task of defending man against nature, it merely pursues it by other means. The task is a manifold one. Man's self-regard, seriously menaced, calls for consolation; life and the universe must be robbed of their terrors; moreover his curiosity, moved, it is true, by the strongest practical interest, demands an answer.

A great deal is already gained with the first step: the humanization of nature. Impersonal forces and destinies cannot be approached; they remain eternally remote. But if the elements have passions that rage as they do in our own souls, if death itself is not something spontaneous but the violent act of an evil Will, if everywhere in nature there are Beings around us of a kind that we know in our own society, then we can breathe freely, can feel at home in the uncanny and can deal by psychical means with our senseless anxiety. We are still defenceless, perhaps, but we are no longer helplessly paralysed; we can at least react. Perhaps, indeed, we are not even defenceless. We can apply the same methods against these violent supermen outside that we employ in our own society; we can try to adjure them, to appease them, to bribe them, and, by so influencing them, we may rob them of a part of their power. A replacement like this of natural science by psychology not only provides immediate relief, but also points the way to a further mastering of the situation.

For this situation is nothing new. It has an infantile prototype, of which it is in fact only the continuation. For once before one has found oneself in a similar state of helplessness: as a small child, in relation to one's parents. One had reason to fear them, and especially one's father; and yet one was sure of his protection against the dangers one knew. Thus it was natural to assimilate the two situations. Here, too, wishing played its part, as it does in dream-life. The sleeper may be seized with a presentiment of death, which threatens to place him in the grave. But the dream-work knows how to select a condition that will turn even that dreaded event into a wish-fulfilment: the dreamer sees himself in an ancient Etruscan grave which he has climbed down into, happy to find his archaeological interests satisfied.[1] In the same way, a man makes the forces of nature not simply into persons with whom he can associate as he would with his equals—that would not do justice to the overpowering impression which those forces make on him—but he gives them the character of a father. He turns them into gods, following in this, as I have tried to show,[2] not only an infantile prototype but a phylogenetic one.

In the course of time the first observations were made of regularity and conformity to law in natural phenomena, and with this the forces of nature lost their human traits. But man's

[1] [This was an actual dream of Freud's, reported in Chapter VI (G) of *The Interpretation of Dreams* (1900*a*), *Standard Ed.*, **5**, 454–5.]

[2] [See Section 6 of the fourth essay in *Totem and Taboo* (1912–13), *Standard Ed.*, **13**, 146 ff.]

helplessness remains and along with it his longing for his father, and the gods. The gods retain their threefold task: they must exorcize the terrors of nature, they must reconcile men to the cruelty of Fate, particularly as it is shown in death, and they must compensate them for the sufferings and privations which a civilized life in common has imposed on them.

But within these functions there is a gradual displacement of accent. It was observed that the phenomena of nature developed automatically according to internal necessities. Without doubt the gods were the lords of nature; they had arranged it to be as it was and now they could leave it to itself. Only occasionally, in what are known as miracles, did they intervene in its course, as though to make it plain that they had relinquished nothing of their original sphere of power. As regards the apportioning of destinies, an unpleasant suspicion persisted that the perplexity and helplessness of the human race could not be remedied. It was here that the gods were most apt to fail. If they themselves created Fate, then their counsels must be deemed inscrutable. The notion dawned on the most gifted people of antiquity that Moira [Fate] stood above the gods and that the gods themselves had their own destinies. And the more autonomous nature became and the more the gods withdrew from it, the more earnestly were all expectations directed to the third function of the gods—the more did morality become their true domain. It now became the task of the gods to even out the defects and evils of civilization, to attend to the sufferings which men inflict on one another in their life together and to watch over the fulfilment of the precepts of civilization, which men obey so imperfectly. Those precepts themselves were credited with a divine origin; they were elevated beyond human society and were extended to nature and the universe.

And thus a store of ideas is created, born from man's need to make his helplessness tolerable and built up from the material of memories of the helplessness of his own childhood and the childhood of the human race. It can clearly be seen that the possession of these ideas protects him in two directions—against the dangers of nature and Fate, and against the injuries that threaten him from human society itself. Here is the gist of the matter. Life in this world serves a higher purpose; no doubt it is not easy to guess what that purpose is, but it certainly signifies a perfecting of man's nature. It is probably the spiritual part of man, the soul, which in the course of time has so slowly and unwillingly detached itself from the body, that is the object of this elevation and exaltation. Everything that happens in this world is an expression of the intentions of an intelligence superior to us, which in the end, though its ways and byways are difficult to follow, orders everything for the best—that is, to make it enjoyable for us. Over each one of us there watches a benevolent Providence which is only seemingly stern and which will not suffer us to become a plaything of the over-mighty and pitiless forces of nature. Death itself is not extinction, is not a return to inorganic lifelessness, but the beginning of a new kind of existence which lies on the path of development to something higher. And, looking in the other direction, this view announces that the same moral laws which our civilizations have set up govern the whole universe as well, except that they are maintained by a supreme court of justice with incomparably more power and consistency. In the end all good is rewarded and all evil punished, if not actually in this form of life then in the later existences that begin after death. In this way all the terrors, the sufferings and the hardships of life are destined to be obliterated. Life after death, which continues life on earth just as the invisible part of the spectrum joins on to the visible part, brings us all the perfection that we may perhaps have missed here. And the superior wisdom which directs this course of things, the infinite goodness that expresses itself in it, the justice that achieves its aim in it—these are the attributes of the divine beings who also created us and the world as a whole, or rather, of the one divine being into which, in our civilization, all the gods of antiquity have been condensed. The people which first succeeded in thus concentrating the divine attributes was not a little proud of the advance. It had laid open to view the father who had all along been hidden behind every divine figure as its nucleus. Fundamentally this was a return to the historical beginnings of the idea of God. Now that God was a single person, man's relations to him could recover the intimacy and intensity of the child's relation to his father. But if one had done so much for one's father, one wanted to have a reward, or at least to be his only beloved child, his Chosen People. Very much later, pious America laid claim to being 'God's own Country'; and, as regards one of the shapes in which men worship the deity, the claim is undoubtedly valid.

The religious ideas that have been summarized above have of course passed through a long process of development and have been adhered to in various phases by various civilizations. I have singled out one such phase, which roughly corresponds to the final form taken by our present-day white Christian civilization. It is easy to see that not all the parts of this picture tally equally well with one another, that not all the questions that press for an answer receive one, and that it is difficult to dismiss the contradiction of daily experience. Nevertheless, such as they are, those ideas—ideas which are religious in the widest sense—are prized as the most precious possession of civilization, as the most precious thing it has to offer its participants. It is far more highly prized than all the devices for winning treasures from the earth or providing men with sustenance or preventing their illnesses, and so forth. People feel that life would not be tolerable if they did not attach to these ideas the value that is claimed for them. And now the question arises: what are these ideas in the light of psychology? Whence do they derive the esteem in which they are held? And, to take a further timid step, what is their real worth?

IV

An enquiry which proceeds like a monologue, without interruption, is not altogether free from danger. One is too easily tempted into pushing aside thoughts which threaten to break into it, and in exchange one is left with a feeling of uncertainty which in the end one tries to keep down by over-decisiveness. I shall therefore imagine that I have an opponent who follows my arguments with mistrust, and here and there I shall allow him to interject some remarks.[1]

I hear him say: 'You have repeatedly used the expressions "civilization creates these religious ideas", "civilization places them at the disposal of its participants". There is something about this that sounds strange to me. I cannot myself say why, but it does not sound so natural as it does to say that civilization has made rules about distributing the products of labour or about rights concerning women and children.'

I think, all the same, that I am justified in expressing myself in this way. I have tried to show that religious ideas have arisen from the same need as have all the other achievements of civilization: from the necessity of defending oneself against the crushingly superior force of nature. To this a second motive was added—the urge to rectify the shortcomings of civilization which made themselves painfully felt. Moreover, it is especially apposite to say that civilization gives the individual these ideas, for he finds them there already; they are presented to him ready-made, and he would not be able to discover them for himself. What he is entering into is the heritage of many generations, and he takes it over as he does the multiplication table, geometry, and similar things. There is indeed a difference in this, but that difference lies elsewhere and I cannot examine it yet. The feeling of strangeness that you mention may be partly due to the fact that this body of religious ideas is usually put forward as a divine revelation. But this presentation of it is itself a part of the religious system, and it entirely ignores the

[1] [Freud had adopted the same method of presentation in his recent discussion of lay analysis (1926*e*) and also, though in somewhat different circumstances, a quarter of a century earlier in his paper on 'Screen Memories' (1899*a*).]

known historical development of these ideas and their differences in different epochs and civilizations.

'Here is another point, which seems to me to be more important. You argue that the humanization of nature is derived from the need to put an end to man's perplexity and helplessness in the face of its dreaded forces, to get into a relation with them and finally to influence them. But a motive of this kind seems superfluous. Primitive man has no choice, he has no other way of thinking. It is natural to him, something innate, as it were, to project his existence outwards into the world and to regard every event which he observes as the manifestation of beings who at bottom are like himself. It is his only method of comprehension. And it is by no means self-evident, on the contrary it is a remarkable coincidence, if by thus indulging his natural disposition he succeeds in satisfying one of his greatest needs.'

I do not find that so striking. Do you suppose that human thought has no practical motives, that it is simply the expression of a disinterested curiosity? That is surely very improbable. I believe rather that when man personifies the forces of nature he is again following an infantile model. He has learnt from the persons in his earliest environment that the way to influence them is to establish a relation with them; and so, later on, with the same end in view, he treats everything else that he comes across in the same way as he treated those persons. Thus I do not contradict your descriptive observation; it is in fact natural to man to personify everything that he wants to understand in order later to control it (psychical mastering as a preparation for physical mastering); but I provide in addition a motive and a genesis for this peculiarity of human thinking.

'And now here is yet a third point. You have dealt with the origin of religion once before, in your book *Totem and Taboo* [1912–13]. But there it appeared in a different light. Everything was the son–father relationship. God was the exalted father, and the longing for the father was the root of the need for religion. Since then, it seems, you have discovered the factor of human weakness and helplessness, to which indeed the chief role in the formation of religion is generally assigned, and now you transpose everything that was once the father complex into terms of helplessness. May I ask you to explain this transformation?'

With pleasure. I was only waiting for this invitation. But is it really a transformation? In *Totem and Taboo* it was not my purpose to explain the origin of religions but only of totemism. Can you, from any of the views known to you, explain the fact that the first shape in which the protecting deity revealed itself to men should have been that of an animal, that there was a prohibition against killing and eating this animal and that nevertheless the solemn custom was to kill and eat it communally once a year? This is precisely what happens in totemism. And it is hardly to the purpose to argue about whether totemism ought to be called a religion. It has intimate connections with the later god-religions. The totem animals become the sacred animals of the gods; and the earliest, but most fundamental moral restrictions—the prohibitions against murder and incest—originate in totemism. Whether or not you accept the conclusions of *Totem and Taboo*, I hope you will admit that a number of very remarkable, disconnected facts are brought together in it into a consistent whole.

The question of why in the long run the animal god did not suffice, and was replaced by a human one, was hardly touched on in *Totem and Taboo*, and other problems concerning the formation of religion were not mentioned in the book at all. Do you regard a limitation of that kind as the same thing as a denial? My work is a good example of the strict isolation of the particular contribution which psycho-analytic discussion can make to the solution of the problem of religion. If I am now trying to add the other, less deeply concealed part, you should not accuse me of contradicting myself, just as before you accused me of being one-sided. It is, of course, my duty to point out the connecting links between what I said earlier and what I put forward now, between the deeper and the manifest motives, between the father-complex and man's helplessness and need for protection.

These connections are not hard to find. They consist in the relation of the child's helplessness to the helplessness of the adult which continues it. So that, as was to be expected, the motives for the formation of religion which psycho-analysis revealed now turn out to be the same as the infantile contribution to the *manifest* motives. Let us transport ourselves into the mental life of a child. You remember the choice of object according to the anaclitic [attachment] type, which psycho-analysis talks of?[1]

[1] [See Freud's paper on narcissism (1914*c*), *Standard Ed.*, **14**, 87.]

The libido there follows the paths of narcissistic needs and attaches itself to the objects which ensure the satisfaction of those needs. In this way the mother, who satisfies the child's hunger, becomes its first love-object and certainly also its first protection against all the undefined dangers which threaten it in the external world—its first protection against anxiety, we may say.

In this function [of protection] the mother is soon replaced by the stronger father, who retains that position for the rest of childhood. But the child's attitude to its father is coloured by a peculiar ambivalence. The father himself constitutes a danger for the child, perhaps because of its earlier relation to its mother. Thus it fears him no less than it longs for him and admires him. The indications of this ambivalence in the attitude to the father are deeply imprinted in every religion, as was shown in *Totem and Taboo*. When the growing individual finds that he is destined to remain a child for ever, that he can never do without protection against strange superior powers, he lends those powers the features belonging to the figure of his father; he creates for himself the gods whom he dreads, whom he seeks to propitiate, and whom he nevertheless entrusts with his own protection. Thus his longing for a father is a motive identical with his need for protection against the consequences of his human weakness. The defence against childish helplessness is what lends its characteristic features to the adult's reaction to the helplessness which *he* has to acknowledge—a reaction which is precisely the formation of religion. But it is not my intention to enquire any further into the development of the idea of God; what we are concerned with here is the finished body of religious ideas as it is transmitted by civilization to the individual.

V

LET us now take up the thread of our enquiry.[1] What, then, is the psychological significance of religious ideas and under what heading are we to classify them? The question is not at all easy to answer immediately. After rejecting a number of formulations, we will take our stand on the following one. Religious ideas are teachings and assertions about facts and conditions of external (or internal) reality which tell one something one has not discovered for oneself and which lay claim to one's belief. Since they give us information about what is most important and interesting to us in life, they are particularly highly prized. Anyone who knows nothing of them is very ignorant; and anyone who has added them to his knowledge may consider himself much the richer.

There are, of course, many such teachings about the most various things in the world. Every school lesson is full of them. Let us take geography. We are told that the town of Constance lies on the Bodensee.[2] A student song adds: 'if you don't believe it, go and see.' I happen to have been there and can confirm the fact that that lovely town lies on the shore of a wide stretch of water which all those who live round it call the Bodensee; and I am now completely convinced of the correctness of this geographical assertion. In this connection I am reminded of another, very remarkable, experience. I was already a man of mature years when I stood for the first time on the hill of the Acropolis in Athens, between the temple ruins, looking out over the blue sea. A feeling of astonishment mingled with my joy. It seemed to say: 'So it really *is* true, just as we learnt at school!' How shallow and weak must have been the belief I then acquired in the real truth of what I heard, if I could be so astonished now! But I will not lay too much stress on the significance of this experience; for my astonishment could have had another explanation, which did not occur to me at the time and which is of a wholly subjective nature and has to do with the special character of the place.[3]

[1] [From the end of Chapter III, p. 20.]

[2] [The German name for what we call the Lake of Constance.]

[3] [This had happened in 1904, when Freud was almost fifty. He wrote

All teachings like these, then, demand belief in their contents, but not without producing grounds for their claim. They are put forward as the epitomized result of a longer process of thought based on observation and certainly also on inferences. If anyone wants to go through this process himself instead of accepting its result, they show him how to set about it. Moreover, we are always in addition given the source of the knowledge conveyed by them, where that source is not self-evident, as it is in the case of geographical assertions. For instance, the earth is shaped like a sphere; the proofs adduced for this are Foucault's pendulum experiment,[1] the behaviour of the horizon and the possibility of circumnavigating the earth. Since it is impracticable, as everyone concerned realizes, to send every schoolchild on a voyage round the world, we are satisfied with letting what is taught at school be taken on trust; but we know that the path to acquiring a personal conviction remains open.

Let us try to apply the same test to the teachings of religion. When we ask on what their claim to be believed is founded, we are met with three answers, which harmonize remarkably badly with one another. Firstly, these teachings deserve to be believed because they were already believed by our primal ancestors; secondly, we possess proofs which have been handed down to us from those same primaeval times; and thirdly, it is forbidden to raise the question of their authentication at all. In former days anything so presumptuous was visited with the severest penalties, and even to-day society looks askance at any attempt to raise the question again.

This third point is bound to rouse our strongest suspicions. After all, a prohibition like this can only be for one reason—that society is very well aware of the insecurity of the claim it makes on behalf of its religious doctines. Otherwise it would certainly be very ready to put the necessary data at the disposal of anyone who wanted to arrive at conviction. This being so, it is with a feeling of mistrust which it is hard to allay that we pass on to an examination of the other two grounds of proof. We ought to believe because our forefathers believed. But these

a full account of the episode in an open letter to Romain Rolland some ten years after the present work (1936*a*).]

[1] [J. B. L. Foucault (1819–68) demonstrated the diurnal motion of the earth by means of a pendulum in 1851.]

ancestors of ours were far more ignorant than we are. They believed in things we could not possibly accept to-day; and the possibility occurs to us that the doctrines of religion may belong to that class too. The proofs they have left us are set down in writings which themselves bear every mark of untrustworthiness. They are full of contradictions, revisions and falsifications, and where they speak of factual confirmations they are themselves unconfirmed. It does not help much to have it asserted that their wording, or even their content only, originates from divine revelation; for this assertion is itself one of the doctrines whose authenticity is under examination, and no proposition can be a proof of itself.

Thus we arrive at the singular conclusion that of all the information provided by our cultural assets it is precisely the elements which might be of the greatest importance to us and which have the task of solving the riddles of the universe and of reconciling us to the sufferings of life—it is precisely those elements that are the least well authenticated of any. We should not be able to bring ourselves to accept anything of so little concern to us as the fact that whales bear young instead of laying eggs, if it were not capable of better proof than this.

This state of affairs is in itself a very remarkable psychological problem. And let no one suppose that what I have said about the impossibility of proving the truth of religious doctrines contains anything new. It has been felt at all times—undoubtedly, too, by the ancestors who bequeathed us this legacy. Many of them probably nourished the same doubts as ours, but the pressure imposed on them was too strong for them to have dared to utter them. And since then countless people have been tormented by similar doubts, and have striven to suppress them, because they thought it was their duty to believe; many brilliant intellects have broken down over this conflict, and many characters have been impaired by the compromises with which they have tried to find a way out of it.

If all the evidence put forward for the authenticity of religious teachings originates in the past, it is natural to look round and see whether the present, about which it is easier to form judgements, may not also be able to furnish evidence of the sort. If by this means we could succeed in clearing even a single portion of the religious system from doubt, the whole of it would gain enormously in credibility. The proceedings of the spiritualists meet us at this point; they are convinced of the survival of the individual soul and they seek to demonstrate to us beyond doubt the truth of this one religious doctrine. Unfortunately they cannot succeed in refuting the fact that the appearance and utterances of their spirits are merely the products of their own mental activity. They have called up the spirits of the greatest men and of the most eminent thinkers, but all the pronouncements and information which they have received from them have been so foolish and so wretchedly meaningless that one can find nothing credible in them but the capacity of the spirits to adapt themselves to the circle of people who have conjured them up.

I must now mention two attempts that have been made—both of which convey the impression of being desperate efforts—to evade the problem. One, of a violent nature, is ancient; the other is subtle and modern. The first is the '*Credo quia absurdum*' of the early Father of the Church.[1] It maintains that religious doctrines are outside the jurisdiction of reason—are above reason. Their truth must be felt inwardly, and they need not be comprehended. But this *Credo* is only of interest as a self-confession. As an authoritative statement it has no binding force. Am I to be obliged to believe *every* absurdity? And if not, why this one in particular? There is no appeal to a court above that of reason. If the truth of religious doctrines is dependent on an inner experience which bears witness to that truth, what is one to do about the many people who do not have this rare experience? One may require every man to use the gift of reason which he possesses, but one cannot erect, on the basis of a motive that exists only for a very few, an obligation that shall apply to everyone. If one man has gained an unshakable conviction of the true reality of religious doctrines from a state of ecstasy which has deeply moved him, of what significance is that to others?

The second attempt is the one made by the philosophy of 'As if'. This asserts that our thought-activity includes a great number of hypotheses whose groundlessness and even absurdity we fully realize. They are called 'fictions', but for a variety of practical reasons we have to behave 'as if' we believed in these fictions. This is the case with religious doctrines because of their incomparable importance for the maintenance of human

[1] ['I believe because it is absurd.' This is attributed to Tertullian.]

society.[1] This line of argument is not far removed from the '*Credo quia absurdum*'. But I think the demand made by the 'As if' argument is one that only a philosopher could put forward. A man whose thinking is not influenced by the artifices of philosophy will never be able to accept it; in such a man's view, the admission that something is absurd or contrary to reason leaves no more to be said. It cannot be expected of him that precisely in treating his most important interests he shall forgo the guarantees he requires for all his ordinary activities. I am reminded of one of my children who was distinguished at an early age by a peculiarly marked matter-of-factness. When the children were being told a fairy story and were listening to it with rapt attention, he would come up and ask: 'Is that a true story?' When he was told it was not, he would turn away with a look of disdain. We may expect that people will soon behave in the same way towards the fairy tales of religion, in spite of the advocacy of 'As if'.

But at present they still behave quite differently; and in past times religious ideas, in spite of their incontrovertible lack of authentication, have exercised the strongest possible influence on mankind. This is a fresh psychological problem. We must ask where the inner force of those doctrines lies and to what it is that they owe their efficacy, independent as it is of recognition by reason.

[1] I hope I am not doing him an injustice if I take the philosopher of 'As if' as the representative of a view which is not foreign to other thinkers: 'We include as fictions not merely indifferent theoretical operations but ideational constructs emanating from the noblest minds, to which the noblest part of mankind cling and of which they will not allow themselves to be deprived. Nor is it our object so to deprive them—for as *practical fictions* we leave them all intact; they perish only as *theoretical truths*.' (Hans Vaihinger, 1922, 68 [C. K. Ogden's translation, 1924, 48–9].)

VI

I THINK we have prepared the way sufficiently for an answer to both these questions. It will be found if we turn our attention to the psychical origin of religious ideas. These, which are given out as teachings, are not precipitates of experience or end-results of thinking: they are illusions, fulfilments of the oldest, strongest and most urgent wishes of mankind. The secret of their strength lies in the strength of those wishes. As we already know, the terrifying impression of helplessness in childhood aroused the need for protection—for protection through love—which was provided by the father; and the recognition that this helplessness lasts throughout life made it necessary to cling to the existence of a father, but this time a more powerful one. Thus the benevolent rule of a divine Providence allays our fear of the dangers of life; the establishment of a moral world-order ensures the fulfilment of the demands of justice, which have so often remained unfulfilled in human civilization; and the prolongation of earthly existence in a future life provides the local and temporal framework in which these wish-fulfilments shall take place. Answers to the riddles that tempt the curiosity of man, such as how the universe began or what the relation is between body and mind, are developed in conformity with the underlying assumptions of this system. It is an enormous relief to the individual psyche if the conflicts of its childhood arising from the father-complex—conflicts which it has never wholly overcome—are removed from it and brought to a solution which is universally accepted.

When I say that these things are all illusions, I must define the meaning of the word. An illusion is not the same thing as an error; nor is it necessarily an error. Aristotle's belief that vermin are developed out of dung (a belief to which ignorant people still cling) was an error; so was the belief of a former generation of doctors that *tabes dorsalis* is the result of sexual excess. It would be incorrect to call these errors illusions. On the other hand, it was an illusion of Columbus's that he had discovered a new sea-route to the Indies. The part played by his wish in this error is very clear. One may describe as an illusion the assertion made by certain nationalists that the Indo-

Germanic race is the only one capable of civilization; or the belief, which was only destroyed by psycho-analysis, that children are creatures without sexuality. What is characteristic of illusions is that they are derived from human wishes. In this respect they come near to psychiatric delusions. But they differ from them, too, apart from the more complicated structure of delusions. In the case of delusions, we emphasize as essential their being in contradiction with reality. Illusions need not necessarily be false—that is to say, unrealizable or in contradiction to reality. For instance, a middle-class girl may have the illusion that a prince will come and marry her. This is possible; and a few such cases have occurred. That the Messiah will come and found a golden age is much less likely. Whether one classifies this belief as an illusion or as something analogous to a delusion will depend on one's personal attitude. Examples of illusions which have proved true are not easy to find, but the illusion of the alchemists that all metals can be turned into gold might be one of them. The wish to have a great deal of gold, as much gold as possible, has, it is true, been a good deal damped by our present-day knowledge of the determinants of wealth, but chemistry no longer regards the transmutation of metals into gold as impossible. Thus we call a belief an illusion when a wish-fulfilment is a prominent factor in its motivation, and in doing so we disregard its relations to reality, just as the illusion itself sets no store by verification.

Having thus taken our bearings, let us return once more to the question of religious doctrines. We can now repeat that all of them are illusions and insusceptible of proof. No one can be compelled to think them true, to believe in them. Some of them are so improbable, so incompatible with everything we have laboriously discovered about the reality of the world, that we may compare them—if we pay proper regard to the psychological differences—to delusions. Of the reality value of most of them we cannot judge; just as they cannot be proved, so they cannot be refuted. We still know too little to make a critical approach to them. The riddles of the universe reveal themselves only slowly to our investigation; there are many questions to which science to-day can give no answer. But scientific work is the only road which can lead us to a knowledge of reality outside ourselves. It is once again merely an illusion to expect anything from intuition and introspection; they can give us nothing but particulars about our own mental life, which are hard to interpret, never any information about the questions which religious doctrine finds it so easy to answer. It would be insolent to let one's own arbitrary will step into the breach and, according to one's personal estimate, declare this or that part of the religious system to be less or more acceptable. Such questions are too momentous for that; they might be called too sacred.

At this point one must expect to meet with an objection. 'Well then, if even obdurate sceptics admit that the assertions of religion cannot be refuted by reason, why should I not believe in them, since they have so much on their side—tradition, the agreement of mankind, and all the consolations they offer?' Why not, indeed? Just as no one can be forced to believe, so no one can be forced to disbelieve. But do not let us be satisfied with deceiving ourselves that arguments like these take us along the road of correct thinking. If ever there was a case of a lame excuse we have it here. Ignorance is ignorance; no right to believe anything can be derived from it. In other matters no sensible person will behave so irresponsibly or rest content with such feeble grounds for his opinions and for the line he takes. It is only in the highest and most sacred things that he allows himself to do so. In reality these are only attempts at pretending to oneself or to other people that one is still firmly attached to religion, when one has long since cut oneself loose from it. Where questions of religion are concerned, people are guilty of every possible sort of dishonesty and intellectual misdemeanour. Philosophers stretch the meaning of words until they retain scarcely anything of their original sense. They give the name of 'God' to some vague abstraction which they have created for themselves; having done so they can pose before all the world as deists, as believers in God, and they can even boast that they have recognized a higher, purer concept of God, notwithstanding that their God is now nothing more than an insubstantial shadow and no longer the mighty personality of religious doctrines. Critics persist in describing as 'deeply religious' anyone who admits to a sense of man's insignificance or impotence in the face of the universe, although what constitutes the essence of the religious attitude is not this feeling but only the next step after it, the reaction to it which seeks a remedy for it. The man who goes no further, but humbly acquiesces in the small part which human beings play in the great world—such a man is, on the contrary, irreligious in the truest sense of the word.

To assess the truth-value of religious doctrines does not lie within the scope of the present enquiry. It is enough for us that we have recognized them as being, in their psychological nature, illusions. But we do not have to conceal the fact that this discovery also strongly influences our attitude to the question which must appear to many to be the most important of all. We know approximately at what periods and by what kind of men religious doctrines were created. If in addition we discover the motives which led to this, our attitude to the problem of religion will undergo a marked displacement. We shall tell ourselves that it would be very nice if there were a God who created the world and was a benevolent Providence, and if there were a moral order in the universe and an after-life; but it is a very striking fact that all this is exactly as we are bound to wish it to be. And it would be more remarkable still if our wretched, ignorant and downtrodden ancestors had succeeded in solving all these difficult riddles of the universe.

VII

HAVING recognized religious doctrines as illusions, we are at once faced by a further question: may not other cultural assets of which we hold a high opinion and by which we let our lives be ruled be of a similar nature? Must not the assumptions that determine our political regulations be called illusions as well? and is it not the case that in our civilization the relations between the sexes are disturbed by an erotic illusion or a number of such illusions? And once our suspicion has been aroused, we shall not shrink from asking too whether our conviction that we can learn something about external reality through the use of observation and reasoning in scientific work—whether this conviction has any better foundation. Nothing ought to keep us from directing our observation to our own selves or from applying our thought to criticism of itself. In this field a number of investigations open out before us, whose results could not but be decisive for the construction of a '*Weltanschauung*'. We surmise, moreover, that such an effort would not be wasted and that it would at least in part justify our suspicion. But the author does not dispose of the means for undertaking so comprehensive a task; he needs must confine his work to following out one only of these illusions—that, namely, of religion.

But now the loud voice of our opponent brings us to a halt. We are called to account for our wrong-doing:

'Archaeological interests are no doubt most praiseworthy, but no one undertakes an excavation if by doing so he is going to undermine the habitations of the living so that they collapse and bury people under their ruins. The doctrines of religion are not a subject one can quibble about like any other. Our civilization is built up on them, and the maintenance of human society is based on the majority of men's believing in the truth of those doctrines. If men are taught that there is no almighty and all-just God, no divine world-order and no future life, they will feel exempt from all obligation to obey the precepts of civilization. Everyone will, without inhibition or fear, follow his asocial, egoistic instincts and seek to exercise his power; Chaos, which we have banished through many thousands of years of the work of civilization, will come again. Even if we knew, and could prove, that religion was not in possession of the truth, we ought to conceal the fact and behave in the way prescribed by the philosophy of "As if"—and this in the interest of the preservation of us all. And apart from the danger of the undertaking, it would be a purposeless cruelty. Countless people find their one consolation in religious doctrines, and can only bear life with their help. You would rob them of their support, without having anything better to give them in exchange. It is admitted that so far science has not achieved much, but even if it had advanced much further it would not suffice for man. Man has imperative needs of another sort, which can never be satisfied by cold science; and it is very strange—indeed, it is the height of inconsistency—that a psychologist who has always insisted on what a minor part is played in human affairs by the intelligence as compared with the life of the instincts—that such a psychologist should now try to rob mankind of a precious wish-fulfilment and should propose to compensate them for it with intellectual nourishment.'

What a lot of accusations all at once! Nevertheless I am ready with rebuttals for them all; and, what is more, I shall assert the view that civilization runs a greater risk if we maintain our present attitude to religion than if we give it up.

But I hardly know where to begin my reply. Perhaps with the assurance that I myself regard my undertaking as completely harmless and free of risk. It is not I who am overvaluing the intellect this time. If people are as my opponents describe them —and I should not like to contradict them—then there is no danger of a devout believer's being overcome by my arguments and deprived of his faith. Besides, I have said nothing which other and better men have not said before me in a much more complete, forcible and impressive manner. Their names are well known, and I shall not cite them, for I should not like to give an impression that I am seeking to rank myself as one of them. All I have done—and this is the only thing that is new in my exposition—is to add some psychological foundation to the criticisms of my great predecessors. It is hardly to be expected that precisely this addition will produce the effect which was denied to those earlier efforts. No doubt I might be asked here what is the point of writing these things if I am certain that they will be ineffective. But I shall come back to that later.

The one person this publication may injure is myself. I shall have to listen to the most disagreeable reproaches for my shallowness, narrow-mindedness and lack of idealism or of understanding for the highest interests of mankind. But on the one hand, such remonstrances are not new to me; and on the other, if a man has already learnt in his youth to rise superior to the disapproval of his contemporaries, what can it matter to him in his old age when he is certain soon to be beyond the reach of all favour or disfavour? In former times it was different. Then utterances such as mine brought with them a sure curtailment of one's earthly existence and an effective speeding-up of the opportunity for gaining a personal experience of the after-life. But, I repeat, those times are past and to-day writings such as this bring no more danger to their author than to their readers. The most that can happen is that the translation and distribution of his book will be forbidden in one country or another—and precisely, of course, in a country that is convinced of the high standard of its culture. But if one puts in any plea at all for the renunciation of wishes and for acquiescence in Fate, one must be able to tolerate this kind of injury too.

The further question occurred to me whether the publication of this work might not after all do harm. Not to a person, however, but to a cause—the cause of psycho-analysis. For it cannot be denied that psycho-analysis is my creation, and it has met with plenty of mistrust and ill-will. If I now come forward with such displeasing pronouncements, people will be only too ready to make a displacement from my person to psycho-analysis. 'Now we see,' they will say, 'where psycho-analysis leads to. The mask has fallen; it leads to a denial of God and of a moral ideal, as we always suspected. To keep us from this discovery we have been deluded into thinking that psycho-analysis has no *Weltanschauung* and never can construct one.'[1]

An outcry of this kind will really be disagreeable to me on account of my many fellow-workers, some of whom do not by any means share my attitude to the problems of religion. But psycho-analysis has already weathered many storms and now it must brave this fresh one. In point of fact psycho-analysis is a method of research, an impartial instrument, like the infinitesimal calculus, as it were. If a physicist were to discover with the latter's help that after a certain time the earth would be

[1] [See some remarks at the end of Chapter II of *Inhibitions, Symptoms and Anxiety* (1926*d*), *Standard Ed.*, **20**, 95–6.]

destroyed, we would nevertheless hesitate to attribute destructive tendencies to the calculus itself and therefore to proscribe it. Nothing that I have said here against the truth-value of religions needed the support of psycho-analysis; it had been said by others long before analysis came into existence. If the application of the psycho-analytic method makes it possible to find a new argument against the truths of religion, *tant pis* for religion; but defenders of religion will by the same right make use of psycho-analysis in order to give full value to the affective significance of religious doctrines.

And now to proceed with our defence. Religion has clearly performed great services for human civilization. It has contributed much towards the taming of the asocial instincts. But not enough. It has ruled human society for many thousands of years and has had time to show what it can achieve. If it had succeeded in making the majority of mankind happy, in comforting them, in reconciling them to life and in making them into vehicles of civilization, no one would dream of attempting to alter the existing conditions. But what do we see instead? We see that an appallingly large number of people are dissatisfied with civilization and unhappy in it, and feel it as a yoke which must be shaken off; and that these people either do everything in their power to change that civilization, or else go so far in their hostility to it that they will have nothing to do with civilization or with a restriction of instinct. At this point it will be objected against us that this state of affairs is due to the very fact that religion has lost a part of its influence over human masses precisely because of the deplorable effect of the advances of science. We will note this admission and the reason given for it, and we shall make use of it later for our own purposes; but the objection itself has no force.

It is doubtful whether men were in general happier at a time when religious doctrines held unrestricted sway; more moral they certainly were not. They have always known how to externalize the precepts of religion and thus to nullify their intentions. The priests, whose duty it was to ensure obedience to religion, met them half-way in this. God's kindness must lay a restraining hand on His justice. One sinned, and then one made a sacrifice or did penance and then one was free to sin once more. Russian introspectiveness has reached the pitch of concluding that sin is indispensable for the enjoyment of all the blessings of divine grace, so that, at bottom, sin is pleasing to God. It is no secret that the priests could only keep the masses submissive to religion by making such large concessions as these to the instinctual nature of man. Thus it was agreed: God alone is strong and good, man is weak and sinful. In every age immorality has found no less support in religion than morality has. If the achievements of religion in respect to man's happiness, susceptibility to culture[1] and moral control are no better than this, the question cannot but arise whether we are not overrating its necessity for mankind, and whether we do wisely in basing our cultural demands upon it.

Let us consider the unmistakable situation as it is to-day. We have heard the admission that religion no longer has the same influence on people that it used to. (We are here concerned with European Christian civilization.) And this is not because its promises have grown less but because people find them less credible. Let us admit that the reason—though perhaps not the only reason—for this change is the increase of the scientific spirit in the higher strata of human society. Criticism has whittled away the evidential value of religious documents, natural science has shown up the errors in them, and comparative research has been struck by the fatal resemblance between the religious ideas which we revere and the mental products of primitive peoples and times.

The scientific spirit brings about a particular attitude towards worldly matters; before religious matters it pauses for a little, hesitates, and finally there too crosses the threshold. In this process there is no stopping; the greater the number of men to whom the treasures of knowledge become accessible, the more widespread is the falling-away from religious belief—at first only from its obsolete and objectionable trappings, but later from its fundamental postulates as well. The Americans who instituted the 'monkey trial' at Dayton[2] have alone shown themselves consistent. Elsewhere the inevitable transition is accomplished by way of half-measures and insincerities.

[1] [The nature of 'susceptibility to culture' had been discussed by Freud in the first section of his paper on 'War and Death' (1915*b*), *Standard Ed.*, **14**, 283.]

[2] [A small town in Tennessee where, in 1925, a science teacher was prosecuted for breach of a State law by teaching that 'man is descended from the lower animals'.]

Civilization has little to fear from educated people and brain-workers. In them the replacement of religious motives for civilized behaviour by other, secular motives would proceed unobtrusively; moreover, such people are to a large extent themselves vehicles of civilization. But it is another matter with the great mass of the uneducated and oppressed, who have every reason for being enemies of civilization. So long as they do not discover that people no longer believe in God, all is well. But they will discover it, infallibly, even if this piece of writing of mine is not published. And they are ready to accept the results of scientific thinking, but without the change having taken place in them which scientific thinking brings about in people. Is there not a danger here that the hostility of these masses to civilization will throw itself against the weak spot that they have found in their task-mistress? If the sole reason why you must not kill your neighbour is because God has forbidden it and will severely punish you for it in this or the next life—then, when you learn that there is no God and that you need not fear His punishment, you will certainly kill your neighbour without hesitation, and you can only be prevented from doing so by mundane force. Thus either these dangerous masses must be held down most severely and kept most carefully away from any chance of intellectual awakening, or else the relationship between civilization and religion must undergo a fundamental revision.

VIII

One might think that there would be no special difficulties in the way of carrying out this latter proposal. It is true that it would involve a certain amount of renunciation, but more would perhaps be gained than lost, and a great danger would be avoided. Everyone is frightened of it, however, as though it would expose civilization to a still greater danger. When St. Boniface[1] cut down the tree that was venerated as sacred by the Saxons the bystanders expected some fearful event to follow upon the sacrilege. But nothing happened, and the Saxons accepted baptism.

When civilization laid down the commandment that a man shall not kill the neighbour whom he hates or who is in his way or whose property he covets, this was clearly done in the interest of man's communal existence, which would not otherwise be practicable. For the murderer would draw down on himself the vengeance of the murdered man's kinsmen and the secret envy of others, who within themselves feel as much inclined as he does for such acts of violence. Thus he would not enjoy his revenge or his robbery for long, but would have every prospect of soon being killed himself. Even if he protected himself against his single foes by extraordinary strength and caution, he would be bound to succumb to a combination of weaker men. If a combination of this sort did not take place, the murdering would continue endlessly and the final outcome would be that men would exterminate one another. We should arrive at the same state of affairs between individuals as still persists in Corsica between families, though elsewhere only between nations. Insecurity of life, which is an equal danger for everyone, now unites men into a society which prohibits the individual from killing and reserves to itself the right to communal killing of anyone who violates the prohibition. Here, then, we have justice and punishment.

But we do not publish this rational explanation of the prohibition against murder. We assert that the prohibition has been issued by God. Thus we take it upon ourselves to guess His intentions, and we find that He, too, is unwilling for men

[1] [The eighth-century, Devonshire-born, 'Apostle of Germany'.]

to exterminate one another. In behaving in this way we are investing the cultural prohibition with a quite special solemnity, but at the same time we risk making its observance dependent on belief in God. If we retrace this step—if we no longer attribute to God what is our own will and if we content ourselves with giving the social reason—then, it is true, we have renounced the transfiguration of the cultural prohibition, but we have also avoided the risk to it. But we gain something else as well. Through some kind of diffusion or infection, the character of sanctity and inviolability—of belonging to another world, one might say—has spread from a few major prohibitions on to every other cultural regulation, law and ordinance. But on these the halo often looks far from becoming: not only do they invalidate one another by giving contrary decisions at different times and places, but apart from this they show every sign of human inadequacy. It is easy to recognize in them things that can only be the product of short-sighted apprehensiveness or an expression of selfishly narrow interests or a conclusion based on insufficient premisses. The criticism which we cannot fail to level at them also diminishes to an unwelcome extent our respect for other, more justifiable cultural demands. Since it is an awkward task to separate what God Himself has demanded from what can be traced to the authority of an all-powerful parliament or a high judiciary, it would be an undoubted advantage if we were to leave God out altogether and honestly admit the purely human origin of all the regulations and precepts of civilization. Along with their pretended sanctity, these commandments and laws would lose their rigidity and unchangeableness as well. People could understand that they are made, not so much to rule them as, on the contrary, to serve their interests; and they would adopt a more friendly attitude to them, and instead of aiming at their abolition, would aim only at their improvement. This would be an important advance along the road which leads to becoming reconciled to the burden of civilization.

But here our plea for ascribing purely rational reasons to the precepts of civilization—that is to say, for deriving them from social necessity—is interrupted by a sudden doubt. We have chosen as our example the origin of the prohibition against murder. But does our account of it tally with historical truth? We fear not; it appears to be nothing but a rationalistic construction. With the help of psycho-analysis, we have made a study of precisely this piece of the cultural history of mankind,[1] and, basing ourselves on it, we are bound to say that in reality things happened otherwise. Even in present-day man purely reasonable motives can effect little against passionate impulsions. How much weaker then must they have been in the human animal of primaeval times! Perhaps his descendants would even now kill one another without inhibition, if it were not that among those murderous acts there was one—the killing of the primitive father—which evoked an irresistible emotional reaction with momentous consequences. From it arose the commandment: Thou shalt not kill. Under totemism this commandment was restricted to the father-substitute; but it was later extended to other people, though even to-day it is not universally obeyed.

But, as was shown by arguments which I need not repeat here, the primal father was the original image of God, the model on which later generations have shaped the figure of God. Hence the religious explanation is right. God actually played a part in the genesis of that prohibition; it was His influence, not any insight into social necessity, which created it. And the displacement of man's will on to God is fully justified. For men knew that they had disposed of their father by violence, and in their reaction to that impious deed, they determined to respect his will thenceforward. Thus religious doctrine tells us the historical truth—though subject, it is true, to some modification and disguise—whereas our rational account disavows it.

We now observe that the store of religious ideas includes not only wish-fulfilments but important historical recollections. This concurrent influence of past and present must give religion a truly incomparable wealth of power. But perhaps with the help of an analogy yet another discovery may begin to dawn on us. Though it is not a good plan to transplant ideas far from the soil in which they grew up, yet here is a conformity which we cannot avoid pointing out. We know that a human child cannot successfully complete its development to the civilized stage without passing through a phase of neurosis sometimes of greater and sometimes of less distinctness. This is because so many instinctual demands which will later be

[1] [Cf. the fourth essay in *Totem and Taboo* (1912-13).]

unserviceable cannot be suppressed by the rational operation of the child's intellect but have to be tamed by acts of repression, behind which, as a rule, lies the motive of anxiety. Most of these infantile neuroses are overcome spontaneously in the course of growing up, and this is especially true of the obsessional neuroses of childhood. The remainder can be cleared up later still by psycho-analytic treatment. In just the same way, one might assume, humanity as a whole, in its development through the ages, fell into states analogous to the neuroses,[1] and for the same reasons—namely because in the times of its ignorance and intellectual weakness the instinctual renunciations indispensable for man's communal existence had only been achieved by it by means of purely affective forces. The precipitates of these processes resembling repression which took place in prehistoric times still remained attached to civilization for long periods. Religion would thus be the universal obsessional neurosis of humanity; like the obsessional neurosis of children, it arose out of the Oedipus complex, out of the relation to the father. If this view is right, it is to be supposed that a turning-away from religion is bound to occur with the fatal inevitability of a process of growth, and that we find ourselves at this very juncture in the middle of that phase of development. Our behaviour should therefore be modelled on that of a sensible teacher who does not oppose an impending new development but seeks to ease its path and mitigate the violence of its irruption. Our analogy does not, to be sure, exhaust the essential nature of religion. If, on the one hand, religion brings with it obsessional restrictions, exactly as an individual obsessional neurosis does, on the other hand it comprises a system of wishful illusions together with a disavowal[2] of reality, such as we find in an isolated form nowhere else but in amentia,[3] in a state of blissful hallucinatory confusion. But these are only analogies, by the help of which we endeavour to understand a social phenomenon; the pathology of the individual does not supply us with a fully valid counterpart.

It has been repeatedly pointed out (by myself and in

[1] [Freud returned to this question at the end of his *Civilization and its Discontents* (1930*a*), p. 144 below, and in Part I of Chapter III of *Moses and Monotheism* (1939*a*).]

[2] [See the paper on 'Fetishism' (1927*e*), p. 153 below.]

[3] ['Meynert's amentia': a state of acute hallucinatory confusion.]

particular by Theodor Reik[1]) in how great detail the analogy between religion and obsessional neurosis can be followed out, and how many of the peculiarities and vicissitudes in the formation of religion can be understood in that light. And it tallies well with this that devout believers are safeguarded in a high degree against the risk of certain neurotic illnesses; their acceptance of the universal neurosis spares them the task of constructing a personal one.[2]

Our knowledge of the historical worth of certain religious doctrines increases our respect for them, but does not invalidate our proposal that they should cease to be put forward as the reasons for the precepts of civilization. On the contrary! Those historical residues have helped us to view religious teachings, as it were, as neurotic relics, and we may now argue that the time has probably come, as it does in an analytic treatment, for replacing the effects of repression by the results of the rational operation of the intellect. We may foresee, but hardly regret, that such a process of remoulding will not stop at renouncing the solemn transfiguration of cultural precepts, but that a general revision of them will result in many of them being done away with. In this way our appointed task of reconciling men to civilization will to a great extent be achieved. We need not deplore the renunciation of historical truth when we put forward rational grounds for the precepts of civilization. The truths contained in religious doctrines are after all so distorted and systematically disguised that the mass of humanity cannot recognize them as truth. The case is similar to what happens when we tell a child that new-born babies are brought by the stork. Here, too, we are telling the truth in symbolic clothing, for we know what the large bird signifies. But the child does not know it. He hears only the distorted part of what we say, and feels that he has been deceived; and we know how often his distrust of the grown-ups and his refractoriness actually take their start from this impression. We have become convinced that it is better to avoid such symbolic disguisings of the truth in what we tell children and not to withhold from them a

[1] [Cf. Freud, 'Obsessive Actions and Religious Practices' (1907*b*) and Reik (1927).]

[2] [Freud had often made this point before: e.g. in a sentence added in 1919 to his study on Leonardo da Vinci (1910*c*), *Standard Ed.*, **11**, 123.]

knowledge of the true state of affairs commensurate with their intellectual level.[1]

[1] [Freud later drew a distinction between what he termed 'material' and 'historical' truth in several passages. See, in particular, Section G of Part II of Chapter III of *Moses and Monotheism* (1939*a*). Cf. also an Editor's footnote on the subject in Chapter XII (C) of *The Psychopathology of Everyday Life* (1901*b*), *Standard Ed.*, **6**, 256.]

IX

'You permit yourself contradictions which are hard to reconcile with one another. You begin by saying that a piece of writing like yours is quite harmless: no one will let himself be robbed of his faith by considerations of the sort put forward in it. But since it is nevertheless your intention, as becomes evident later on, to upset that faith, we may ask why in fact you are publishing your work? In another passage, moreover, you admit that it may be dangerous, indeed very dangerous, for someone to discover that people no longer believe in God. Hitherto he has been docile, but now he throws off his obedience to the precepts of civilization. Yet your whole contention that basing the commandments of civilization on religious grounds constitutes a danger for civilization rests on the assumption that the believer can be turned into an unbeliever. Surely that is a complete contradiction.

'And here is another. On the one hand you admit that men cannot be guided through their intelligence, they are ruled by their passions and their instinctual demands. But on the other hand you propose to replace the affective basis of their obedience to civilization by a rational one. Let who can understand this. To me it seems that it must be either one thing or the other.

'Besides, have you learned nothing from history? Once before an attempt of this kind was made to substitute reason for religion, officially and in the grand manner. Surely you remember the French Revolution and Robespierre? And you must also remember how short-lived and miserably ineffectual the experiment was? The same experiment is being repeated in Russia at the present time, and we need not feel curious as to its outcome. Do you not think we may take it for granted that men cannot do without religion?

'You have said yourself that religion is more than an obsessional neurosis. But you have not dealt with this other side of it. You are content to work out the analogy with a neurosis. Men, you say, must be freed from a neurosis. What else may be lost in the process is of no concern to you.'

The appearance of contradiction has probably come about

because I have dealt with complicated matters too hurriedly. But we can remedy this to some extent. I still maintain that what I have written is quite harmless in one respect. No believer will let himself be led astray from his faith by these or any similar arguments. A believer is bound to the teachings of religion by certain ties of affection. But there are undoubtedly countless other people who are not in the same sense believers. They obey the precepts of civilization because they let themselves be intimidated by the threats of religion, and they are afraid of religion so long as they have to consider it as a part of the reality which hems them in. They are the people who break away as soon as they are allowed to give up their belief in the reality-value of religion. But they too are unaffected by arguments. They cease to fear religion when they observe that others do not fear it; and it was of them that I asserted that they would get to know about the decline of religious influence even if I did not publish my work. [Cf. p. 39.]

But I think you yourself attach more weight to the other contradiction which you charge me with. Since men are so little accessible to reasonable arguments and are so entirely governed by their instinctual wishes, why should one set out to deprive them of an instinctual satisfaction and replace it by reasonable arguments? It is true that men are like this; but have you asked yourself whether they *must* be like this, whether their innermost nature necessitates it? Can an anthropologist give the cranial index of a people whose custom it is to deform their children's heads by bandaging them round from their earliest years? Think of the depressing contrast between the radiant intelligence of a healthy child and the feeble intellectual powers of the average adult. Can we be quite certain that it is not precisely religious education which bears a large share of the blame for this relative atrophy? I think it would be a very long time before a child who was not influenced began to trouble himself about God and things in another world. Perhaps his thoughts on these matters would then take the same paths as they did with his forefathers. But we do not wait for such a development; we introduce him to the doctrines of religion at an age when he is neither interested in them nor capable of grasping their import. Is it not true that the two main points in the programme for the education of children to-day are retardation of sexual development and premature religious influence? Thus by the time the child's intellect awakens, the doctrines of religion have already become unassailable. But are you of opinion that it is very conducive to the strengthening of the intellectual function that so important a field should be closed against it by the threat of Hell-fire? When a man has once brought himself to accept uncritically all the absurdities that religious doctrines put before him and even to overlook the contradictions between them, we need not be greatly surprised at the weakness of his intellect. But we have no other means of controlling our instinctual nature but our intelligence. How can we expect people who are under the dominance of prohibitions of thought to attain the psychological ideal, the primacy of the intelligence? You know, too, that women in general are said to suffer from 'physiological feeble-mindedness'[1]—that is, from a lesser intelligence than men. The fact itself is disputable and its interpretation doubtful, but one argument in favour of this intellectual atrophy being of a secondary nature is that women labour under the harshness of an early prohibition against turning their thoughts to what would most have interested them—namely, the problems of sexual life. So long as a person's early years are influenced not only by a sexual inhibition of thought but also by a religious inhibition and by a loyal inhibition[2] derived from this, we cannot really tell what in fact he is like.

But I will moderate my zeal and admit the possibility that I, too, am chasing an illusion. Perhaps the effect of the religious prohibition of thought may not be so bad as I suppose; perhaps it will turn out that human nature remains the same even if education is not abused in order to subject people to religion. I do not know and you cannot know either. It is not only the great problems of this life that seem insoluble at the present time; many lesser questions too are difficult to answer. But you must admit that here we are justified in having a hope for the future—that perhaps there is a treasure to be dug up capable of enriching civilization and that it is worth making the experiment of an irreligious education. Should the experiment prove unsatisfactory I am ready to give up the reform and to return

[1] [The phrase was used by Moebius (1903). Cf. Freud's early paper on 'civilized' sexual morality (1908*d*), *Standard Ed.*, **9**, 199, where the present argument is anticipated.]

[2] [I.e. in regard to the Monarchy.]

to my earlier, purely descriptive judgement that man is a creature of weak intelligence who is ruled by his instinctual wishes.

On another point I agree with you unreservedly. It is certainly senseless to begin by trying to do away with religion by force and at a single blow. Above all, because it would be hopeless. The believer will not let his belief be torn from him, either by arguments or by prohibitions. And even if this did succeed with some it would be cruelty. A man who has been taking sleeping draughts for tens of years is naturally unable to sleep if his sleeping draught is taken away from him. That the effect of religious consolations may be likened to that of a narcotic is well illustrated by what is happening in America. There they are now trying—obviously under the influence of petticoat government—to deprive people of all stimulants, intoxicants, and other pleasure-producing substances, and instead, by way of compensation, are surfeiting them with piety. This is another experiment as to whose outcome we need not feel curious [p. 46].[1]

Thus I must contradict you when you go on to argue that men are completely unable to do without the consolation of the religious illusion, that without it they could not bear the troubles of life and the cruelties of reality. That is true, certainly, of the men into whom you have instilled the sweet—or bitter-sweet—poison from childhood onwards. But what of the other men, who have been sensibly brought up? Perhaps those who do not suffer from the neurosis will need no intoxicant to deaden it. They will, it is true, find themselves in a difficult situation. They will have to admit to themselves the full extent of their helplessness and their insignificance in the machinery of the universe; they can no longer be the centre of creation, no longer the object of tender care on the part of a beneficent Providence. They will be in the same position as a child who has left the parental house where he was so warm and comfortable. But surely infantilism is destined to be surmounted. Men cannot remain children for ever; they must in the end go out into 'hostile life'. We may call this '*education to reality*'. Need I confess to you that the sole purpose of my book is to point out the necessity for this forward step?

[1] [This was written in the middle of the period of National Prohibition in the United States (1920–33).]

You are afraid, probably, that they will not stand up to the hard test? Well, let us at least hope they will. It is something, at any rate, to know that one is thrown upon one's own resources. One learns then to make a proper use of them. And men are not entirely without assistance. Their scientific knowledge has taught them much since the days of the Deluge, and it will increase their power still further. And, as for the great necessities of Fate, against which there is no help, they will learn to endure them with resignation. Of what use to them is the mirage of wide acres in the moon, whose harvest no one has ever yet seen? As honest smallholders on this earth they will know how to cultivate their plot in such a way that it supports them. By withdrawing their expectations from the other world and concentrating all their liberated energies into their life on earth, they will probably succeed in achieving a state of things in which life will become tolerable for everyone and civilization no longer oppressive to anyone. Then, with one of our fellow-unbelievers, they will be able to say without regret:

Den Himmel überlassen wir
Den Engeln und den Spatzen.[1]

[1] ['We leave Heaven to the angels and the sparrows.' From Heine's poem *Deutschland* (Caput I). The word which is here translated 'fellow-unbelievers'—in German '*Unglaubensgenossen*'—was applied by Heine himself to Spinoza. It had been quoted by Freud as an example of a particular kind of joke-technique in his book on jokes (1905*c*), *Standard Ed.*, **8**, 77.]

X

'That sounds splendid! A race of men who have renounced all illusions and have thus become capable of making their existence on earth tolerable! I, however, cannot share your expectations. And that is not because I am the obstinate reactionary you perhaps take me for. No, it is because I am sensible. We seem now to have exchanged roles: you emerge as an enthusiast who allows himself to be carried away by illusions, and I stand for the claims of reason, the rights of scepticism. What you have been expounding seems to me to be built upon errors which, following your example, I may call illusions, because they betray clearly enough the influence of your wishes. You pin your hope on the possibility that generations which have not experienced the influence of religious doctrines in early childhood will easily attain the desired primacy of the intelligence over the life of the instincts. This is surely an illusion: in this decisive respect human nature is hardly likely to change. If I am not mistaken—one knows so little about other civilizations—there are even to-day peoples which do not grow up under the pressure of a religious system, and yet they approach no nearer to your ideal than the rest. If you want to expel religion from our European civilization, you can only do it by means of another system of doctrines; and such a system would from the outset take over all the psychological characteristics of religion—the same sanctity, rigidity and intolerance, the same prohibition of thought—for its own defence. You have to have something of the kind in order to meet the requirements of education. And you cannot do without education. The path from the infant at the breast to the civilized man is a long one; too many human young would go astray on it and fail to reach their life-tasks at the proper time if they were left without guidance to their own development. The doctrines which had been applied in their upbringing would always set limits to the thinking of their riper years—which is exactly what you reproach religion with doing to-day. Do you not observe that it is an ineradicable and innate defect of our and every other civilization, that it imposes on children, who are driven by instinct and weak in intellect, the making of decisions which only the mature intelligence of adults can vindicate? But civilization cannot do otherwise, because of the fact that mankind's age-long development is compressed into a few years of childhood; and it is only by emotional forces that the child can be induced to master the task set before it. Such, then, are the prospects for your "primacy of the intellect".

'And now you must not be surprised if I plead on behalf of retaining the religious doctrinal system as the basis of education and of man's communal life. This is a practical problem, not a question of reality-value. Since, for the sake of preserving our civilization, we cannot postpone influencing the individual until he has become ripe for civilization (and many would never become so in any case), since we are obliged to impose on the growing child some doctrinal system which shall operate in him as an axiom that admits of no criticism, it seems to me that the religious system is by far the most suitable for the purpose. And it is so, of course, precisely on account of its wish-fulfilling and consolatory power, by which you claim to recognize it as an "illusion". In view of the difficulty of discovering anything about reality—indeed, of the doubt whether it is possible for us to do so at all—we must not overlook the fact that human needs, too, are a piece of reality, and, in fact, an important piece and one that concerns us especially closely.

'Another advantage of religious doctrine resides, to my mind, in one of its characteristics to which you seem to take particular exception. For it allows of a refinement and sublimation of ideas, which make it possible for it to be divested of most of the traces which it bears of primitive and infantile thinking. What then remains is a body of ideas which science no longer contradicts and is unable to disprove. These modifications of religious doctrine, which you have condemned as half-measures and compromises, make it possible to avoid the cleft between the uneducated masses and the philosophic thinker, and to preserve the common bond between them which is so important for the safeguarding of civilization. With this, there would be no need to fear that the men of the people would discover that the upper strata of society "no longer believe in God". I think I have now shown that your endeavours come down to an attempt to replace a proved and emotionally valuable illusion by another one, which is unproved and without emotional value.'

You will not find me inaccessible to your criticism. I know how difficult it is to avoid illusions; perhaps the hopes I have confessed to are of an illusory nature, too. But I hold fast to one distinction. Apart from the fact that no penalty is imposed for not sharing them, my illusions are not, like religious ones, incapable of correction. They have not the character of a delusion. If experience should show—not to me, but to others after me, who think as I do—that we have been mistaken, we will give up our expectations. Take my attempt for what it is. A psychologist who does not deceive himself about the difficulty of finding one's bearings in this world, makes an endeavour to assess the development of man, in the light of the small portion of knowledge he has gained through a study of the mental processes of individuals during their development from child to adult. In so doing, the idea forces itself upon him that religion is comparable to a childhood neurosis, and he is optimistic enough to suppose that mankind will surmount this neurotic phase, just as so many children grow out of their similar neurosis. These discoveries derived from individual psychology may be insufficient, their application to the human race unjustified, and his optimism unfounded. I grant you all these uncertainties. But often one cannot refrain from saying what one thinks, and one excuses oneself on the ground that one is not giving it out for more than it is worth.

And there are two points that I must dwell on a little longer. Firstly, the weakness of my position does not imply any strengthening of yours. I think you are defending a lost cause. We may insist as often as we like that man's intellect is powerless in comparison with his instinctual life, and we may be right in this. Nevertheless, there is something peculiar about this weakness. The voice of the intellect is a soft one, but it does not rest till it has gained a hearing. Finally, after a countless succession of rebuffs, it succeeds. This is one of the few points on which one may be optimistic about the future of mankind, but it is in itself a point of no small importance. And from it one can derive yet other hopes. The primacy of the intellect lies, it is true, in a distant, distant future, but probably not in an *infinitely* distant one. It will presumably set itself the same aims as those whose realization you expect from your God (of course within human limits—so far as external reality, *'Ανάγκη*, allows it), namely the love of man and the decrease of suffering. This being so, we may tell ourselves that our antagonism is only a temporary one and not irreconcilable. We desire the same things, but you are more impatient, more exacting, and—why should I not say it?—more self-seeking than I and those on my side. You would have the state of bliss begin directly after death; you expect the impossible from it and you will not surrender the claims of the individual. Our God, *Λόγος*,[1] will fulfil whichever of these wishes nature outside us allows, but he will do it very gradually, only in the unforeseeable future, and for a new generation of men. He promises no compensation for us, who suffer grievously from life. On the way to this distant goal your religious doctrines will have to be discarded, no matter whether the first attempts fail, or whether the first substitutes prove to be untenable. You know why: in the long run nothing can withstand reason and experience, and the contradiction which religion offers to both is all too palpable. Even purified religious ideas cannot escape this fate, so long as they try to preserve anything of the consolation of religion. No doubt if they confine themselves to a belief in a higher spiritual being, whose qualities are indefinable and whose purposes cannot be discerned, they will be proof against the challenge of science; but then they will also lose their hold on human interest.

And secondly: observe the difference between your attitude to illusions and mine. You have to defend the religious illusion with all your might. If it becomes discredited—and indeed the threat to it is great enough—then your world collapses. There is nothing left for you but to despair of everything, of civilization and the future of mankind. From that bondage I am, we are, free. Since we are prepared to renounce a good part of our infantile wishes, we can bear it if a few of our expectations turn out to be illusions.

Education freed from the burden of religious doctrines will not, it may be, effect much change in men's psychological nature. Our god *Λόγος* is perhaps not a very almighty one, and he may only be able to fulfil a small part of what his predecessors have promised. If we have to acknowledge this we shall accept it with resignation. We shall not on that account lose our interest in the world and in life, for we have one sure support

[1] The twin gods *Λόγος* [*Logos:* Reason] and *'Ανάγκη* [*Ananke:* Necessity] of the Dutch writer Multatuli. [Cf. an Editor's footnote to 'The Economic Problem of Masochism' (1924*c*), *Standard Ed.*, **19**, 168.]

which you lack. We believe that it is possible for scientific work to gain some knowledge about the reality of the world, by means of which we can increase our power and in accordance with which we can arrange our life. If this belief is an illusion, then we are in the same position as you. But science has given us evidence by its numerous and important successes that it is no illusion. Science has many open enemies, and many more secret ones, among those who cannot forgive her for having weakened religious faith and for threatening to overthrow it. She is reproached for the smallness of the amount she has taught us and for the incomparably greater field she has left in obscurity. But, in this, people forget how young she is, how difficult her beginnings were and how infinitesimally small is the period of time since the human intellect has been strong enough for the tasks she sets. Are we not all at fault, in basing our judgements on periods of time that are too short? We should make the geologists our pattern. People complain of the unreliability of science—how she announces as a law to-day what the next generation recognizes as an error and replaces by a new law whose accepted validity lasts no longer. But this is unjust and in part untrue. The transformations of scientific opinion are developments, advances, not revolutions. A law which was held at first to be universally valid proves to be a special case of a more comprehensive uniformity, or is limited by another law, not discovered till later; a rough approximation to the truth is replaced by a more carefully adapted one, which in turn awaits further perfectioning. There are various fields where we have not yet surmounted a phase of research in which we make trial with hypotheses that soon have to be rejected as inadequate; but in other fields we already possess an assured and almost unalterable core of knowledge. Finally, an attempt has been made to discredit scientific endeavour in a radical way, on the ground that, being bound to the conditions of our own organization, it can yield nothing else than subjective results, whilst the real nature of things outside ourselves remains inaccessible. But this is to disregard several factors which are of decisive importance for the understanding of scientific work. In the first place, our organization—that is, our mental apparatus—has been developed precisely in the attempt to explore the external world, and it must therefore have realized in its structure some degree of expediency; in the second place, it is itself a constituent part of the world which we set out to investigate, and it readily admits of such an investigation; thirdly, the task of science is fully covered if we limit it to showing how the world must appear to us in consequence of the particular character of our organization; fourthly, the ultimate findings of science, precisely because of the way in which they are acquired, are determined not only by our organization but by the things which have affected that organization; finally, the problem of the nature of the world without regard to our percipient mental apparatus is an empty abstraction, devoid of practical interest.

No, our science is no illusion. But an illusion it would be to suppose that what science cannot give us we can get elsewhere.

PART II

Discussion of *The Future of an Illusion*

1

Deconstructing Freud's *The Future of an Illusion*: eight conceptual strands

Ethel Spector Person

> . . . the less a man knows about the past and the present the more insecure must prove to be his judgment of the future.
>
> Sigmund Freud, *The Future of an Illusion* (1927c), p. 5

The editor's note at the beginning of Volume 21 of the collected works of Freud, which features both *The Future of an Illusion* (1927c) and *Civilization and Its Discontents* (1930a), remarks on what Freud described as "a significant change from his writings of the previous decade. He observes that "after making a long detour through the natural sciences, medicine and psychotherapy", he has turned to the cultural problems that had fascinated him in his youth. The editor notes that the piece that marked the beginning of this venture was *The Future of an Illusion.* But *Future of an Illusion* is in many ways a transitional paper. As I have read and re-read this paper, which has many defects, I would suggest that it served its purpose by leading into the more complex rendition of culture as depicted in *Civilization and Its Discontents.*

The "illusion" under discussion addresses the limitations that sometimes shackle us by curtailing an individual's scope of thought. This paper is pivotal insofar as it is a first step in Freud's segué into charting the interdigitation of culture and psyche. In fact, one of the most cogent things Freud says about *The Future of an Illusion* is a remark he makes about it in *Civilization and Its Discontents*:

> In my *Future of an Illusion* I was concerned much less with the deepest sources of the religious feeling than with what the common man understands with his religion—with the system of doctrines and promises which, on the one hand, explains to him the riddles of this world with enviable completeness, and, on the other, assures him that a careful Providence will watch over his life and will compensate him in a future existence for any frustrations he suffers here. The common man cannot imagine that Providence otherwise than in the figure of an enormously exalted father. . . . The whole thing is so patently infantile, so foreign to reality, that to anyone with a friendly attitude to humanity it is painful to think that the great majority of mortals will never be able to rise above this new view of life. It is still more humiliating to discover how large a number of people living today, who cannot but see that this religion is not tenable, nevertheless try to defend it piece by piece in a series of pitiful rearguard actions. One would like to mix among the ranks of the believers in order to meet these philosophers, who think they can rescue the God of religion by replacing him by an impersonal, shadowy and abstract principle, and to address them with the warning words: "Thou shalt not take the lord of thy God in vain!" [Freud, 1930a, p. 74]

Freud quotes Goethe in a footnote: "He who possesses science and art also has religion; but he who possesses neither of these two, let him have religion!"

I will briefly address the position Freud takes in his eight sections of *The Future of an Illusion.* God, of course, has a major role, but certainly not an idealized one, in that text.

What is civilization?

Freud opens his investigation by observing two characteristics of civilization:

> When one has lived for quite a long time in a particular civilization and has often tried to discover what its origins were and along what path it has developed, one sometimes also feels

> tempted to take a glance in the other direction and to ask what further fate lies before it and what transformations it is destined to undergo [1927c, p. 5]

But because of the complexities involved, this is difficult if not impossible to do. Only a few people can look at the broad aspects of human activity. Freud posits "the less a man knows the past and the present the more insecure must prove to be his judgement of the future" (p. 5). He notes that the present must become the past before you can count on it as a vantage point from which to extrapolate about the future. Thus, he decides to scale his discussion down to two characteristics of civilization.

For Freud, civilization has acquired

> all the knowledge and capacity that men have acquired in order to control the forces of nature and extract its wealth for the satisfaction of human needs and (too), on the other hand, all the regulation that is necessary in order to adjust the relations of men to one another and especially the distribution of the available wealth. . . mutual relations of men are profoundly influenced by the amount of instinctual satisfaction which the existing wealth makes possible; secondly because an individual man can himself come to function as wealth in relation to another one, insofar as the other person makes use of the capacity for work or chooses him as a sexual object; and thirdly moreover because every individual is virtually an enemy of civilization, though civilization is suppose to be an object of universal human interest [1927c, pp. 5–6]

He suggests that these trends are interdependent. His argument is that civilization must be defended against the individual and that the aims must be

> not only at effecting a certain distribution of wealth but at maintaining that distribution; indeed, they have to protect everything that contributes to the conquest of nature and the production of wealth against men's hostile impulses. Human creations are easily destroyed, and science and technology which built them up, can also can be used for their annihilation [p. 6]

Freud concludes that

> every civilization must be built up on coercion and renunciation of instinct; it does not even seem certain that if coercion

> were to cease the majority of human beings would be prepared to undertake to perform the work necessary for acquiring new wealth. [p. 7]

He views masses as largely lazy and unintelligent insofar as "they have no love for instinctual renunciation, and they are not to be convinced by argument of its inevitability; and the individuals composing them support one another in giving free reign to their indiscipline" (pp. 7–8). They need to have an example of a leader and thus be induced to "perform the work and undergo the renunciations on which the existence of civilization depends" (p. 8).

The power of religious ideas

Freud addresses his central question: "In what does the peculiar value of religious ideas lie?" (1927c, p. 15). He acknowledges that he has slipped unawares out of the economic field, to turn to psychology. He says that

> for the sake of a uniform terminology we will describe the fact that an instinct cannot be satisfied as a "frustration", the regulation by which this frustration is established as a "prohibition" and the condition which is produced by the prohibition as a "privation". The first step is to distinguish between privations which affect everyone and privations which do not affect everyone but only groups, classes, or even single individuals. [1927c, p. 10]

Freud proposes that he is looking directly at psychology rather than at economics. He addresses "the means by which civilization can be defended—measures of coercion and other measures that are intended to reconcile men to it are to recompense them for their sacrifices. These latter may be described as the mental assets of civilization" (p. 10). What is entailed is the necessary renunciation of acting on certain instincts.

Freud notes that when an infant cannot be satisfied, this results in a frustration, the regulation of which takes the form of "a prohibition" (p. 10). The condition that is produced by the prohibition is a privation. He sees privations as having lasted for thousands of years before it was possible for man to "detach himself from his primordial animal condition" (p. 10). Nonetheless, such privations can still be operative, which he judges as the "kernel of hostility to civilization" (p. 10). Each generation of children is subject to feeling such privations. And as they grow up, some people will act upon their frustrations through asocial behaviour.

Among the instinctual wishes Freud lists are those of incest, cannibalism, and the lust for killing. He notes that cannibalism alone seems to be universally proscribed. On the other hand, he points out that "the strength of the incestuous wishes can still be detected behind the prohibitions against them; and under certain conditions killing is still practiced, and indeed commanded" (p. 11). But Freud also predicted that some currently acceptable practices would become unacceptable in later generations.

Freud speaks to the psychology of instinctual renunciations, pointing out that "external coercion gradually becomes internalized; for a special mental agency, man's super-ego, takes it over and includes it among its commandments" (p. 11). One can see this transformation as it takes place over time as the child gradually becomes a "moral and social being" (p. 11). Freud emphasizes that the superego "is a most precious cultural asset in the psychological field" (p. 11). The wider the population in which this asset is viable, the more secure is the culture.

Freud turns out to be a culturalist as well as a psychoanalyst. What he points out is that

> if. . . a culture has not got beyond a point in which the satisfaction of one portion of its participants depends upon the suppression of another, and perhaps larger portion—and this is the case in all present-day cultures—it is understandable that the suppressed people should develop an intense hostility toward a culture whose existence they make possible by their work, but in whose wealth they have too small a share. [p. 12]

Therefore, that part of the population will likely not have internalized what the cultural prohibitions are. In turn, Freud notes that the higher social strata may have their own hostility towards the lower classes. He suggests that "the narcissistic satisfaction provided by the cultural ideal is also among the forces which are successful in combating the hostility to culture within the cultural unit" (p. 13). Such cultural ideals points out that even if one is in a lowly position, one can make up for it, if, for example, during Roman times one is a Roman citizen. Freud also speculates that the suppressed classes are often emotionally attached to their masters. He notes, too, that art is a satisfaction to participants in a cultural unit, even though it often excludes the masses.

The value of religious ideas

Freud opens this section by asking the question: "In what does the value of religious ideas lie? (p. 15). He sees the raison d'être of civilization to defend us against nature. He had already spoken of the "hostility to civilization which is produced by the pressure that civilization exercises, the renunciation of instincts which it demands" (p. 15). But if prohibitions were lifted, dire things might occur, among them that a man would be free to "take any woman that one pleases as a sexual object, if one may without hesitation kill one rival for her love or anyone else who stands in one's way, if, too, one can carry off any of the man's belongings without asking leave—how splendid, what a string of satisfactions one's life would be!" (p. 15). But, consequently, anyone else who fostered the very same desires would treat him with no more consideration. Only a tyrant or a dictator who had seized all means to power could be unrestrictedly happy in such a situation . What civilization does is to protect us, to some degree, from the forces of both nature and fate. Freud quickly points out that "no one is under the illusion that nature has already been vanquished; and few dare hope that she will ever be entirely subjected to man" (p. 15). Moreover, there are many threats to human control, some of them elemental, some of them personal inflictions or injuries—fate, as it were. It is here that civilization enters the picture. For Freud: "Man's self-regard, seriously menaced, calls for consolation" (p. 16). And so, we often try to appease nature. Freud sees this as analogous to an infantile prototype, in which the small child finds himself in a similar state of helplessness. He proposes that, just as one relied on the father, dream-work has the possibility of creating ease:

> The sleeper may be seized with a presentiment of death, which threatens to place him in the grave. But the dream-work knows how to select a condition that will turn even that dreaded event

> into a wish-fulfilment: the dreamer sees himself in an ancient Etruscan grave, which he has climbed down into, happy to find his archaeological interests satisfied. [p. 17]

It turns out that Freud himself had dreamed of himself in an ancient Etruscan grave, into which he had climbed, happy to find his archaeological interests satisfied (see *The Interpretation of Dreams*, 1900a, pp. 454–455). Here Freud acts to put us at ease, endorsing those wishful fantasies that we turn to our advantage in pushing fear away.

As Freud puts it, by worshiping the powerful gods and appealing to their oversight, we feel protected from the dangers of both fate and nature: "Over each one of us there watches a benevolent Providence which is only seemingly stern and which will not suffer us to become a plaything of the over-mighty and pitiless forces of nature" (p. 19). Further than this, death itself no longer means extinction but, rather, "the beginning of a new kind of existence which lies on the path of development to something higher" (p. 19). Freud observes that religious ideas have been structured differently over the course of generations and civilizations, but he is referring here to "one such phase, which roughly corresponds to the final form taken by our present-day white Christian civilization" (p. 20). Even given the fact that "the parts of this picture" do not "tally equally well with one another". . . "those ideas. . . which are religious in the widest sense—are prized as the most precious possession of civilization, as the most precious thing it has to offer to its participants" (p. 20). But he is also setting up the fundamental question: ". . . to take a further step, what is their real worth?" (p. 20).

The origins of religious ideas

It is, of course, Freud's strategy to propose that religious ideas stem from the same origins as do all other aspects of our civilization. They are designed to protect us against those forces of nature which can devastate or even destroy us. But there is also a second motive: "The urge to rectify the shortcomings of civilization, which made themselves painfully felt" (p. 21). Freud observes that each of us enters into the heritage of earlier generations and incorporates as we do "the multiplication table, geometry, and similar things".

Religious ideas are put forward as divine revelations (p. 21), as part of a religious doctrine that ignores what we know of "the historical development of these ideas and their differences in different epochs and civilizations" (p. 22). We personify things in order to master them, both psychically and physically. As Freud points out, we personify the forces of nature by virtue of following an infantile model, having learned from the people who surround us. Just as we influence those around us so as to form a relationship to them, later on and with the same aspirations, we treat those who cross our way just as we treated people earlier in our lives.

One question Freud raises is why an animal god proved insufficient and needed to be replaced by a human one. He says "you should not accuse me of contradicting myself, just as before you accused me of being one-sided. . . . What I said earlier and what I put forward now, between the deeper and the manifest motives, between the father-complex and man's helplessness and need for protection" (p. 23). For Freud, such connections are easily at hand, consisting, as they do, of the "relation of the child's helplessness to the helplessness of the adult which continues it" (p. 23).

Because it is the mother who satisfies the child's hunger, she is the child's first love object as well as its "first protection against all the defined dangers which threaten it in the external world—nonetheless the mother is soon replaced by the stronger father which retains that position for the rest of childhood" (p. 24). In Freud's culture, in which women had no equality, the mother makes but a brief appearance. However, the child's attitude to the father is ambivalent, since the father himself constitutes a potential danger. The child admires his father but also fears him. In addition, he cannot lean on the father forever; consequently, "he creates for himself the gods whom he dreads, whom he seeks to propitiate, and whom he nevertheless entrusts with his own protection" (p. 24).

The psychological significance of religious ideas

Freud raises the question of the psychological significance of religious ideas and how one might classify them: "Religious ideas are teachings and assertions about facts and conditions of external (or internal) reality which tell one something one has not discovered for oneself and which lay claim to one's belief" (p. 25). He contrasts graphical assertions to the teaching of a religion. As to the teachings of religion, it is often felt that these "deserve to be believed because they were already believed by our primal ancestors", because "we possess proofs which have been handed down to us from those same primeval times", and because "it is forbidden to raise the questions of their authentication at all" (p. 26). Here Freud sneaks in the snake, as it were, pointing out that there is but one reason for such a prohibition: that we are "very well aware of the insecurity of the claim [the church] makes on behalf of the religious doctrines" (p. 26). Such proofs often prove to be contradictory, filled with revisions and falsifications. That which should be of the greatest importance to us is less well authenticated than in almost any other realm. Freud necessarily criticizes the church's tradition that "religious doctrines are outside the jurisdiction of reason—are above reason" (p. 28). Such a belief system is consolidated in the mode of "we have to behave 'as if' we believe in these fictions. Such is the state of religious doctrines because of their incomparable importance for the maintenance of human society" (p. 29). Freud labelled this conundrum a psychological problem.

The illusory nature of religious ideas

Freud suggests at the start of chapter VI that one might answer some unanswered questions of the previous chapter by turning one's attention to the "psychical origin of religious ideas" (p. 30). He regards such ideas as illusions—hence his title, *The Future of an Illusion.* Such illusions find their strength in humankind's wishes and hopes. Freud relates this to the protection we first sought through love, which was our first experience in the family. Such a necessity, as "to cling to the existence of a father", gradually changes itself into the need to lean on an even more powerful father—God himself. These illusions, however, are not to be understood as errors. Freud analogizes them to the example of Columbus, who believed that he had discovered a new sea route to the Indies. He remarks that the part played by Columbus's error was founded on his wish, his desire, to have made it to the Indies. As another example, Freud describes an illusion as an assertion made by certain nationalists that the Indo–Germanic race is the only one capable of civilization. What might also be one of his favourite examples of illusion is the parental idea that children are creatures without sexuality. Freud stresses how illusions are the product of our all-too-human wishes. He regards them as coming "near to psychiatric delusions". He wittily proposes that "while a middle-class girl may have the illusion that a prince will come and marry her, it is possible. To say that the Messiah will come and found a golden age is much less likely" (p. 31). For Freud, "it would be very nice if there were a God who created the world and was a benevolent Providence, and if there were a moral order in the universe and an after-life, but it is a very striking fact that all this is exactly as we are bound to wish it to be" (p. 33).

Illusions of civilization

Freud addresses other potential illusions that arise in civilization. He tries to give religion its due, writing that "it has clearly performed great services for human civilization" (p. 37.) But he also argues that these have been inadequate: "those historical residues have helped us to view religious teachings, as it were, as neurotic relics, and we may now argue that the time has probably come as it does in an analytic treatment, for replacing the effects of repression by the results of the rational operation of the intellect" (p. 37). Freud makes the point that while religion has clearly performed great services for individual humans, particularly in its taming of asocial instincts, it has nonetheless failed to show what it can actually achieve. In essence, he is arguing that religion no longer has the same impact on people as before. For Freud: "So long as 'the people' do not discover that [they] no longer believe in God, all is well" (p. 39). Here he is measuring scientific thinking compared to religious thinking. Freud compares religion to the practice of telling children they were brought by the stork. He asks what the merit is of closing off the mind with threats of hell-fire. He suggests that one might experiment with irreligious education, while his critics plead on behalf of religious training. Claiming a distinction between the illusions of God and his illusions, Freud says, "My illusions are not like religious ones, incapable of correction." Freud believes in a system that is based on laws and proofs. He views himself as being on the side of science.

Science and illusions of religion

In this chapter Freud suggests that having identified religious doctrines as illusions, still other assets "by which we let our lives be ruled [may] be of a similar nature" (p. 34). This should raise several questions, for example, whether the relations between the sexes are disturbed by illusions, and whether our political regulations might also be illusions. (I am particularly impressed here that he understands some possible disconnection between the sexes, but perhaps without understanding the reasons for it.)

Regarding religion, Freud notes the agitation these ideas might bring to the public. As Freud puts it: "The doctrines of religion are a subject to scribble about like any other" (p. 34). He addresses why this might be believed to lead to chaos. He feels prepared to confront that problem. Freud is for giving up religion, but "modestly" acknowledges the difficulties in propounding such a view and how he might well be maligned. Nonetheless, he argues his case. As he puts it: "If it [religion] succeeded in making the majority of mankind happy, in comforting them, in reconciling them to life, no one would dream of attempting to alter the existing conditions" (p. 37). But—and here he goes on to critique the culture and declare how many disaffected people there are—religion has clearly not worked. Freud wants to embolden the scientific spirit and its place in our lives. His argument is that the replacement of religious motives by secular ones would proceed unobtrusively.

It is astonishing that this brilliant, creative man was so overcome by what I would speculate was a moment of grandiosity. But the interesting thing is that he could go to the edge and come back, as was later demonstrated in *Civilization and Its Discontents* (1930a), which followed quickly upon the publication of *The Future of an Illusion.*

Discussion

Freud viewed religion as an off-shoot of the father-complex. He saw it as representing man's helplessness in the world and his need for countering the ultimate fate of death, the struggle of civilization, and the forces of nature. For Freud, the obedience to God was comparable to a childlike longing for a father.

What Freud proposed is that:

> Having recognized religious doctrines as illusions, we are at once faced by a further question: may not other cultural assets of which we hold a high opinion and by which we let our lives be ruled be of a similar nature? Must not the assumptions that determine our political regulations be called illusions as well? and is it not the case that in our civilization the relations between the sexes are disturbed by an erotic illusion or a number of such illusions? [1927c, p. 34]

This, of course, is where Freud nods at the existence of women, but without detailing their status.

Freud argues that "nothing ought to keep us from directing our observation to our own selves or from applying our thought to criticism of itself" (p. 34). He interrupts his argument to strengthen it by going *mano á mano* with God. He is, of course, more than sufficiently brilliant to present the culture's reasons and rationalizations, as he understands them, for God worship. In explanation, he observes that the child's "terrifying impression of helplessness" gave rise to the desire for an all-powerful, protective, and just father. He believed that religious ideas were based on this desire and were essentially disconnected from reality. He reduces religion as a balm for man's neediness.

For Freud:

> Our civilization is built upon [the doctrine of religion], and the maintenance of human society is based on the majority of men's believing in the truth of those doctrines. If men are taught that there is no almighty and all-just God, no divine world-order, and no future life, they will feel exempt from all obligations to obey the precepts of civilization. Everyone will, without inhibition or fear, follow his asocial egoistic instincts and seek to exercise his power; Chaos, which we have banished through many thousands of years of the work of civilization, will come again. Even

> if we knew, and could prove, that religion was not in possession of the truth, we ought to conceal the fact and behave in the way prescribed by the philosophy of "As if"—and this is in the interest of the preservation of us all. [pp. 34–35]

Of course what Freud is trying to do here is to revive what I would view as a dead horse. Freud's argument is that "civilization runs a greater risk if we maintain our present attitude to religion than if we give it up" (p. 35). He argues that many have made this case before him, and that if he has anything new, it is "to add some psychological foundation to the criticisms of my great predecessors" (p. 35). For Freud, illusions were close kin to delusions, both derived from deeply felt wishes.

Freud pauses for a moment to wonder whether the paper he was writing would have any antithetical effect on psychoanalysis—since, as he puts it, "it cannot be denied that psycho-analysis is my creation, and it has met with plenty of mistrust and ill-will" (p. 36). Here, he is experiencing himself as a brave warrior indeed by insisting that he is placing himself in a position for significant criticism. He is arguing that religion has not made the majority of mankind happy. And he is quick to express his fears about writing in this vein:

> The further question occurred to me whether the publication of this work might not after all do harm. Not to a person, however, but to a cause—the cause of psycho-analysis. For it cannot be denied that psycho-analysis is my creation, and it has met with plenty of mistrust and ill-will. If I now come forward with such displeasing pronouncements, people will only be too ready to make a displacement from my person to psycho-analysis. "Now we see", they will say "where psycho-analysis leads to. The mask has fallen; it leads to a denial of God and of a moral ideal, as we always suspected. To keep us from this discovery we have been deluded into thinking that psycho-analysis has no *Weltanschauung* and never can construct one". [p. 36]

Freud asserts that such an outcry would be disagreeable to him, but only because of the problems it might cause his many fellow workers, some of whom, he acknowledges, did not share his feelings about religion. Freud has often been described as a conquistador, and it appears to be the way he identified himself. In discussing whether or not his lack of God worship might hurt his cause, he says that

> psycho-analysis has already weathered many storms and now it must brave this fresh one. In point of fact, psycho-analysis is a method of research, an impartial instrument, like the infinitesimal calculus, as it were. If a physicist were to discover with the latter's help that after a certain time the earth would be destroyed, we would nevertheless hesitate to attribute destructive tendencies to the calculus itself and therefore to prescribe it. Nothing that I have said here against the truth-value of religions needed the support of psycho-analysis; it had been said by others long before analysis came into existence. If the application of the psycho-analytic method makes it possible to find a new arrangement against the truths of religion, *tant pis* for religion; but defenders of religion will by the same right make use of psycho-analysis in order to give full value to the affective significance of religious doctrines. [pp. 36–37]

Freud then segues into what he calls "our" defence. Here I assume "our" refers to psychoanalysts, some of whom, however, did not share his appraisal of religion. He remarks that religion has performed great services for human civilizations, contributing much towards taming asocial instincts—"But not enough" (p. 37).

It is in reading *The Future of an Illusion* several times that I have a take on Freud that is different from the one I had before. There is, at the very least, some measure of grandiosity that surfaced. In the moment when he appears to be appreciating the immense success of psychoanalysis, he is also measuring himself against the Godhead. I believe that to be an unfortunate detour—though, fortunately, as it turned out, a relatively short one. He goes so far as to propose that

> Russian introspectiveness has reached the pitch of concluding that sin is indispensable for the enjoyment of all the blessings of divine grace, so that, at bottom, it is seen as pleasing to God. It is no secret that the priests could only keep the masses submissive to religion by making such large concessions as these to the instinctual measure of man. Thus it was agreed that God alone is strong and good, man is weak and sinful. In every age immorality has found no less support in religion than morality has. [pp. 37–38]

In some strange way he seems to be going *mano á mano* with God. He argues that while the scientific spirit is able to bring about a particular attitude towards worldly matters, before religious matters it passes for little.

This is Freud, probably at the height of his pride in psychoanalysis. He appears almost too certain of some things that a number of educated people of his own day would fail to agree with him about. I am not speaking only of religious people, but also of agnostics, who would claim it impossible to know the truth of humankind's origins—whether it came about through an act of God or some click in the far distant past that brought animal and then human life into being.

Part of the problem with *The Future of an Illusion* is that Freud strayed far outside the traditional field of psychoanalysis that he had himself created. He appears to have been trying to re-order culture and civilization. Here he is at a great distance from dealing with any one individual's neurosis or conflicts. In large part, I am very grateful for the bend in the road that he took. The topic of culture and civilization is obviously an important one to explore. But, unfortunately, Freud was not only observing the culture. He was also trying to implement a new social structure, but he lacked the necessary fire power to accomplish his dream. While I remain a great admirer of Freud, I find *The Future of an Illusion* somewhat problematic. Interestingly enough, the fact is that Freud continues to question the piece even as he is writing it.

As a creative and brilliant man, Freud positioned psychoanalysis as a major method of helping people. But in *The Future of an Illusion* he came perilously close to positioning it as an alternative belief system to religion. I should make it clear that I am not writing from a religious point of view but, quite the contrary, from a pragmatic one. I do not believe that bringing negative ideas about religion into psychoanalysis was prudent then, nor is it today. Nonetheless, Freud was agile enough to go back to the source of his authentic genius and to continue his explorations of the role of psychoanalysis in treating people (and in writing a brilliant exposition of the changing tides of life). It may be true that those few souls who, like Freud, are extremely brilliant in one way or another, temporarily move beyond their gift, great though it might be, in order to have a shot at reconstituting the world. However, Freud, to his credit, did not get stuck there. He did what he needed to do, which was to expand on his original ideas and flesh out the importance of psychoanalysis, both for its treatment capabilities and for its major insights into the pleasures and pains, the hearts and souls, of men and women.

Perhaps, one might best view *The Future of an Illusion* as the stepping stone to *Civilization and Its Discontents*, which I deem as one of Freud's important contributions to psychoanalytic thinking. Very little is said of women in *Future of an Illusion*. That Freud was limited to some extent by the structure in which he lived, and in which women were generally deemed less competent than men, should not come as surprise. It is the fate of us all to be limited by the ethos of the culture in which we live. Some few of us can transcend it, but that is more likely to happen when we are members of a group that is being denied its own voice.

However, there is an important interpretation of *The Future of an Illusion* that needs to be acknowledged. It is interesting that it has remained relatively underprivileged in comparison to many of Freud's works, which are deemed essential. I believe that Ernest Wallwork (2007) has provided something interesting about Freud in relationship to *The Future of an Illusion*. Wallwork proposes that one misinterpretation of Freud that impacts on current attitudes towards ethics is derived from the potentially relativistic implications of the concept of the superego:

> If the superego is synonymous with morality, as Freud sometimes indicates, nothing more than a set of purely arbitrary standards that the individual has internalized by introjecting the prohibitions and ideals of his or her parents and other authority figures, then nothing can be said in defence of moral standards other than that they are standards one happens to have. [Wallwork, 2007, p. 286]

What Wallwork is arguing is that to the extent that Freud's position is valid, there can be

> no principled basis for choosing one set of ethical norms over another as guides for action—no grounds for reasoning that might persuade in the presence of conflict—other than egoistic strategies for obtaining rewards and avoiding external punishments and internal guilt or shame. [p. 286]

But Wallwork suggests that this was not really Freud's position. He believes that Freud resisted the "pull of ethical relativism by arguing that there [were] certain reasonable moral guidelines that can be defended" (p. 286). He also suggests that this aspect of Freud's work has failed to be sufficiently appreciated by virtue of the fact that it is a subtext, and not the major text, in Freud's all-out attack on religion in *The Future of an Illusion*:

> Freud's sub rosa point is that weakening the religious grounds for morality poses dangers to society and requires new rational justifications—the main task of ethics. Against ethical relativism, Freud declares that the time has come to "put forward rational grounds for the precepts of civilization [Freud, 1927c, p. 44]

"The challenge to contemporary analysts is to locate these grounds" (Wallwork, 2007, pp. 286–287).

Wallwork goes on to say:

> Although Freud never directly addressed the "rational bases" for morality, much can be adduced about the deep ethic in his work from what he says about happiness as the goal of life, the primacy of love of and respect for others as natural dispositions, the good of community, and the value of shared rules. This deep ethic continues to inform psychoanalysis today. [Wallwork, 2007, p. 287]

Wallwork argues that Freud's alternative ethic to the moralism of the superego is often missed because it is drowned out by the negativity of his critique of religion as duty-oriented—particularly Kantian—ethics. As he puts it:

> Readers are unprepared for the Aristotelian form of ethics (oriented toward achieving personal happiness) that informs Freud's thinking, including his critique of superego moralism. Instead of viewing ethics as seeking an ahistorical, perspectiveless set of universal principles legitimated by reason alone, without reference to local commitments or particular experiences and affects, Freud sees ethics (at least when he is thinking constructively) primarily as dealing with the question of how it is best to live our lives. Here ethical deliberation is not about fining and applying a meta-decision-making procedure, such as Kant's categorical imperative or Bentham's utilitarian calculus,

> to resolve moral dilemmas. Rather, ethics is a matter of negotiating or straddling multiple incommensurate conscious and unconscious responsibilities and values that emerge out of "thick" reasoning, supportive of the most fitting moral judgement for the agent(s) in some specific context. [p. 287]

What Wallwork is, in large part, aiming to do is to bridge the connection between *The Future of an Illusion* and *Civilization and Its Discontents*. I believe that this is the correct way to understand and evaluate *The Future of an Illusion*—that is, as a necessary predecessor to *Civilization and Its Discontents*, which is one of Freud's great works. It is also an act of courage to confront what we see about us, and judge, as Freud did in *The Future of an Illusion*, but not to get so stuck in it as to overlook the brilliance of all that was still to come.

2

The illusion of a future: the rhetoric of Freud's critique of religious belief

Jonathan Lear

1. Freud took himself to have a psychoanalytically valid argument against the honest viability of religious belief. By *psychoanalytically valid* I mean an argument that ought to convince anyone who accepts the basic principles of psychoanalytic explanation and interpretation. Thus, while the argument was not meant to persuade those who did not already believe in psychoanalytic diagnoses, the claim was nevertheless a strong one: namely, that no one who properly understood psychoanalytic insights could legitimately find a way also to embrace religious belief. (I take "proper understanding" to imply living in the light of that understanding.) If Freud's argument was as strong as he claimed it to be, it would mean that anyone who, in the face of his interpretation, continued to adhere to religious conviction would thereby reveal him- or herself as to some degree psychoanalytically unfit—that is, they would thereby show themselves to be clinging to infantile wishes. As a social fact, Freud's argument had a significant effect on the development of psychoanalysis in the twentieth century: though there were a few exceptions, his argument provided an orientation for analysts towards analysands who professed religious conviction, and it played

an important role in who was allowed to train to be an analyst (for some notable exceptions, see, e.g., Loewald, 1953; Meissner, 1984; Rizzuto, 1998). This is one reason why a careful examination of Freud's argument is not an arcane matter: people were excluded from the psychoanalytic profession, and analysands were regularly regarded as psychically unhealthy, based on the assumption that Freud's argument was sound. By way of comparison: the American Psychoanalytic Association has officially distanced itself from Freud's arguments that homosexuality is a form of psychic ill health. Indeed, such a view is now taken to be a form of discrimination (APA, 1992). Is it not at least possible that Freud's argument against religious belief fosters a similar discrimination (not yet recognized as such) against religious believers?

It is characteristic of prejudice that those who suffer from it tend not to recognize it as such. (It is easy enough to recognize it in others.) So if one is on the lookout for discrimination in one's own practice or profession, one must proceed cautiously, looking for signs and symptoms. One sign is the way that the antireligious view could be propped up by rhetorical gestures that fall sort of genuine argument. To take one example, in *A Godless Jew,* the historian Peter Gay wrote, "it is certain—and I am devoting the rest of this book to demonstrating this argument—that if Freud had been a [religious] believer . . . he would not have developed psychoanalysis" (1987, pp. 30–31).[1] According to Gay, the very existence of psychoanalysis depends on Freud having had the courage to reject religious belief. But if one looks for the purported demonstration, one looks in vain. Look for yourself, and you will see that there is no *argument* there. What one finds instead is the repetition of stock phrases—notably that "religious ideas are incorrigible, scientific ideas corrigible"—mixed in with historical anecdotes about Freud (p. 32). Gay never tells us what he means by his claim that "religious ideas are incorrigible"; and even if we only consider the Jewish tradition in which Freud was raised, there are obvious counterexamples. Maimonides' twelfth-century *Guide of the Perplexed* (1963) argues for a massive revision in the interpretation of the Torah, in part to reconcile it with the Hellenistic science and philosophy of his day. The mythic stories of the Bible, according to Maimonides, should not to be accepted as literally true but, rather, as a guide for the young and immature. (I return to Maimonides later in this chapter.) Of Spinoza, who was both influenced by and critical of Maimonides, Gay writes, "As early as the seventeenth century, Spinoza, one of the two or three philosophers Freud ever professed to admire, had laid it down that one must read the Bible as one reads all other books: critically" (Gay, 1987, p. 46). Fine; but Gay does not notice that he here provides compelling evidence against his own thesis. Spinoza's claim that the Bible should be read critically—just as one reads other books, including scientific ones—is itself an instance of the corrigibility of religious ideas. Spinoza did not give up professing religious belief; rather, he argued for a radical revision in how God should be conceived (see Spinoza, 1992, 2001).[2] And even if, as some suspect, Spinoza was not sincere in his profession, that does not matter for the issue at hand: all that matters is that he *might* have been sincere. Indeed, if one takes him at his word, the very corrigibility of science should be understood as a process by which we better come to understand the divine. What is this, if not an attempt to correct religious ideas? The important point here is not to criticize Gay's "argument"; it is to note that in the second half of the twentieth century, the fact that genuine argument was missing was not particularly noticed. Why not? I suspect that the "psychoanalytically informed" reader of the day did not notice because he did not feel the need for argument: it was common knowledge that "religious belief is illusion". Whatever the truth of this last claim, these are the dynamics of professionally shared prejudice. If we wish to reassure ourselves that we are free of its lingering residues, it is imperative to return to Freud's argument and determine just how good an argument it is.

2. Freud famously argued that religious belief is illusion. He meant this in a precise sense: a belief is an illusion if it is caused by a wish (Freud, 1927c, p. 31). This would typically be a misfire in the process of belief-formation. For if we take the paradigmatic case, it is inherent in the very idea of belief that it takes itself to be caused, in a truth-preserving way, by that which it is about. If I believe that there is a cat on the mat, it is because, for example, I take myself to be seeing a cat on the mat, and I take the actual cat's presence on the mat to be causing—in the right sorts of ways—both my perceptual experience and the formation of a propositional belief.

Obviously, there are other legitimate routes to my belief: I might take Carol's word for it; and she might have taken Ted's word for it, and so on. But, roughly, I accept this chain of testimony because I believe that there is a causal chain leading back to that cat on the mat and that cat on the mat's causing all of our beliefs in the right sorts of ways. If, by contrast, my belief that there is a cat on the mat is caused not by any cat's being on any mat but, rather, by a wishful impulse—perhaps cats are unconsciously linked to my mother, and I have a wish to see her stretched out there on an imaginary mat—then I am mistaking a dreamlike experience for an experience of reality. My attempts to live within the truth, such as they are, are short-circuited.

To take a more salient example: consider the belief that God gave Moses the Ten Commandments at Mount Sinai. How could someone come to have such a belief? In the paradigm cases at least, it is constituent of the very idea of belief that one has some idea, however hazy, of how one has come to have it. And the idea of how it came about ought at least to lend credence to the belief's being true. If, when asked why one believes that Moses received the Law, someone says, "I was holding a chewing-gum wrapper and I folded it into a paper airplane. I resolved that if I could fly it to the far wall, I would believe that God gave Moses the Ten Commandments. The plane hit the wall."—by his very account of how the purported belief came about, it is thereby impugned. Obviously, his belief would be impugned even if God did give Moses the Ten Commandments. In that case, his belief would be true, but it would not have been acquired in the right sort of way. We all recognize that beliefs like this call for an account, however hazy, of how they appropriately have come about. In this case, a typical answer would be: "God did give Moses the Ten Commandments on Mount Sinai. Moses came down and reported this to the Israelites and gave them the Commandments. The account of this event was recorded in the Torah, and it has been passed on from generation to generation until the present day." Whether or not this account is true, it is the *sort* of answer that would legitimate having the belief. And it would seem that the very idea of having a factual belief—that is, a belief about how the world is, was, or will be—requires that one have some such account of how one has come to have it. If, when asked why he believes this, he says, "I have no idea; I just do"—then, although he may be in a significant psychological and epistemic state, his claim to factual belief is impugned.

So, Freud's claim that religious belief is illusion seems to be threatening from inside the perspective of religious belief itself. To stick with the current example: if I were to come to see that my purported belief that God gave Moses the Ten Commandments was ultimately caused by wishes of mine—or perhaps also the wishes of others—that *ought* to impugn my belief. And if it does not, that reveals a problem about me and my epistemic relations to the world. The essential problem with illusion is that we are mistaken about the basis of our commitment to it. We take it to be a belief based on responsiveness to the world; in fact, it is primarily held in place by unconscious wishes. And if, when this is pointed out to us, we continue to cling to the religious belief, we thereby manifest a kind of pig-headedness. Rather than being rational animals, swayed in response to the way things are as well as to good arguments, we would show ourselves to be stubbornly clinging to wishful illusions. If that were all there was to be said about the matter, there would be reason to object to training any such person to be a psychoanalyst. There would also be reason to think that the analysis of any such person, persisting unabated in an illusion, was—to use an expression that was common in the last century and has its own wishfulness—"incomplete".

3. Freud argues that religious belief is an illusion by offering an account of the wish that causes it. Religious belief, he argues, arises from infantile experiences of helplessness (Freud, 1927c, pp. 15–19). Religion emerges as a cultural elaboration of childhood fantasies whose function is to protect us against a sense of utter vulnerability. According to Freud, we wishfully imagine that the world is ordered according to a higher purpose, and we each have a proper role within it.

> Over each one of us there watches a benevolent Providence which is only seemingly stern and which will not suffer us to become a plaything of the over-mighty and pitiless force of nature. Death itself is not extinction, is not a return to inorganic lifelessness, but the beginning of a new kind of existence which lies on the path of development to something higher. [Freud, 1927c, pp. 18–19]

Freud diagnoses this as a manifestation in adult life of an infantile longing for a protective father—a powerful figure who was on one's side and who could ensure that the world was overall just (Freud, 1927c, p. 33). This is why Freud thinks that religion is illusion: it is held in place by "the oldest, strongest and most urgent wishes of mankind". The secret of their strength lies in the strength of those wishes. His judgement is merciless:

> The whole thing is so patently infantile, so foreign to reality, that to anyone with a friendly attitude to humanity it is painful to think that the great majority of mortals will never be able to rise above this view of life [Freud, 1930a, p. 74]

Even more pathetic, Freud thinks, are those educated people who ought to know better but still try to defend religion "in a series of pitiful rearguard actions".

4. How good is Freud's argument? This is a difficult question to answer because it is not entirely clear what kind of an argument it is meant to be. So, for instance, it does not seem even to be trying to be a logically valid proof—in the sense of an argument that begins with clearly true premises and then moves by rules of inference that are necessarily truth-preserving to a conclusion that therefore must be true. The argument is not aspiring to that kind of rigour; so to criticize it for lacking it would miss the mark. But, then, what kind of an argument is it?

Freud's argument seems to work along the lines of an interpretation: he is *pointing something out* for those who are ready and able to see it. In offering an interpretation, Freud is ostensibly supplying the concept (illusion) with which a phenomenon (religious belief) can be properly understood. This kind of argument is, as such, impeccable. The question, then, is how well it is being deployed in this case. This is not at all an easy question to answer. Overall, Freud's argument seems to have the shape of a de-legitimating genealogy.[3] Typically, genealogies are used to valorize and to legitimate.[4] So, to take a relevant case: the Israelites' claim to have a special relation with God is meant to be legitimated by a genealogy that goes back to a special relation that God established with Abraham. Freud substitutes a subversive genealogy: the *story* of Abraham's special relation with God goes back to primordial wishes among the ancient Israelites that they should have such a relationship. (It may also go back to a series of all-too-human crimes that are subsequently covered over in myth—see also Freud, 1939a). This story is preserved through the generations not only by the Torah and its associated rituals, but by the same primordial wishes re-arising in each generation, fuelling this whole network of belief and ritual. So Freud's argument seems to have the form of a transformation of genealogies. He takes a pre-existing genealogy that is supernatural and legitimating and puts in its place one that is thoroughly naturalistic and de-legitimating.

But if Freud is in effect offering a counter-genealogy, there ought to be a way to evaluate it. After all, Freud is himself claiming that his genealogy is better than those offered in traditional religious genealogies. His is purportedly true, the others are false. We need to consider three interrelated issues: First, on what basis could one judge that Freud's genealogy is true? This is a question of the *epistemic ground* of this account. Second, how does Freud's argument persuade? This is a question about the *rhetoric* of Freud's argument. Rhetoric studies not only how an argument leads the psyche along in the direction of being persuaded, but also whether the form of persuasion is legitimate. For even if Freud's analysis is ultimately correct, there is a further question of how we might legitimately come to grasp it. By way of analogy: in a logically valid proof, it is not enough that the conclusion be true. One needs to see it as following from true premises according to rules of inference that are obviously truth-preserving. In this way, the proof offers an account of how a reasonable inquirer could come to see the truth as true. In the case of Freud's counter-genealogy, it could conceivably be the case that, on the one hand, his overall analysis of religious belief as illusion is correct, but, on the other hand, he has persuaded us via bullying, crowd-pleasing, narcissistically gratifying wish-fulfilling fantasy. In other words, he could be right about his conclusion, but persuade by gratifying our own wishes. In which case, what we believed might be true, but our minds would nevertheless be stuffed with illusions. So even if we agree with Freud's conclusion—especially if we agree with it—we need to see how we have earned the right to believe what we believe. The third and final issue we need to consider is the *scope* or generality of the conclusion. Freud thought he had shown not merely that some people use religion to gratify infantile needs—that is hardly news—but that illusion is what religious belief ultimately amounts to. How does he attain such a far-reaching conclusion?

5. I said earlier that Freud writes as though he is pointing something out. We have learned both from philosophy and from psychoanalysis that an enormous amount is involved in the ostensibly simple act of pointing something out. Philosophically speaking, for an act of pointing to succeed, there needs to be a shared background of understanding, a shared form of life, between the person doing the pointing and the person who is being invited to see what is being pointed out (Davidson, 1984; Wittgenstein, 1978). (What gestures count as pointing? Is the person pointing to the wall, its shape, colour, or the writing upon it?) Psychoanalytically speaking, if we consider an individual analysis and think of an interpretation as a more sophisticated form of pointing something out, the question of the analysand's readiness to hear it is all-important. The history of psychoanalytic technique can be seen as unfolding from Freud's realization that simply speaking the truth to the analysand—in effect, pointing out the repressed memory or the unconscious conflict—is not sufficient for cure. Psychoanalytic technique is meant to facilitate a process by which the analysand can come to see the hitherto unconscious conflict for himself. Ideally, an interpretation comes at a time when the analysand is *ready* to see what the interpretation is talking about. So, in a broad context, the study of psychoanalytic technique can be seen as a branch of rhetoric: it studies how an interpretation can genuinely succeed in pointing something out.

It would seem that when it comes to large-scale cultural interpretation—in this case, an analysis of the general phenomenon of religious commitment—there ought to be a similar account of readiness. After all, if Freud's interpretation is true—if religious belief is illusion—then we ought to expect it to be held in place by powerful psychic forces that resist recognizing it as such. If religious commitment is illusion, how is it that we could come to see it in those terms?

As we have seen, Freud thought that "the great majority of mortals" will never be able to rise above their infantile attachments—and thus they will never be able to see that religious belief is illusion. His argument is clearly not for them. The argument thus seems designed for (those whom Freud regarded to be) a psychological elite: those who are able to separate themselves from the pervasive illusions of humankind and face the truth. Freud seems to think that this psychological elite forms a historical vanguard. He grasps that he is writing in a historical period of secularization, and his critique is meant to contribute to that process. His argument seems to be directed either at those who have already abandoned religious belief or are already wavering in agnosticism or those who are insipidly going through the empty social forms of religious participation. For such readers, the argument is meant to facilitate their journey towards a non-religious life—by giving them an interpretation that vindicates it. In this way, Freud takes himself to be helping the historical process of secularization along by offering an interpretation that justifies it. There is thus a question of the legitimacy of such historical interpretation.

Freud thought that there were parallels between individual and historical development. If we look to individual development, he says, we see that a person develops through psychological stages. In particular, the inevitable oedipal crisis of childhood is eventually outgrown and falls away.

> In just the same way, one might assume, humanity as a whole, in its development through the ages, fell into stages analogous to the neuroses, and for the same reasons. . . . Religion would thus be the universal obsessional neurosis of humanity; like the obsessional neurosis of children, it arose out of the Oedipus complex, out of the relation to the father. If this view is right, it is to be supposed that a turning-away from religion is bound to occur with the *fatal inevitability* of a process of growth and that we find ourselves at this very juncture in the middle of that phase of development. [Freud, 1927c, p. 43; emphasis added]

On Freud's account, then, his interpretation will be persuasive to those who are attuned to the march of history: those who are historically ready to put up with this "fatal inevitability" and face the truth. Freud does not give an account of what it is about the psychological make-up of this historical vanguard that makes them ready and able to do this. And, with hindsight, his view of history seems to have its own kernel of wishfulness. He gives us no reason to believe that the history of civilization proceeds "in just the same way" as the development of an individual. He imagines a conversation with a religious interlocutor that, read today, looks like a heroic fantasy.[5]

> We desire the same things, but you are more impatient, more exacting, and—why should I not say it?—more self-seeking than I and those on my side. You would have the state of bliss begin directly after death; you expect the impossible from it, and you will not surrender the claims of the individual. Our God *Λogos* [Logos] will fulfil whichever of these wishes nature outside us allows, but he will do it very gradually, only in the unforeseeable future, and for a new generation of men. He promises no compensation for us, who suffer grievously from life. On the way to this distant goal your religious doctrines will have to be discarded, no matter whether the first attempts fail, or whether the first substitutes prove to be untenable. You know why: in the long run nothing can withstand reason and experience, and the contradiction which religion offers to both is all too palpable. Even purified religious ideas cannot escape this fate, so long as they try to preserve anything of the consolation of religion. [p. 54]

Whatever one thinks about religious belief—even if one ultimately agrees with Freud that it is illusion—one should by now see that this passage at least gives less the future of an illusion than the illusion of a future. History is assumed to be progressive, inexorably unfolding and ultimately truth-revealing. This is a triumphal story of human progress in which one can play a role if one is willing and able to participate in the triumph.

Suppose we turn away from Freud's progressivist image of history. There does not, then, seem to be an account of why anyone should be ready to grasp and accept Freud's interpretation. Even if we grant, for the sake of argument, that religious belief is illusion, why should we think that we should be able to see it as such simply by being invited to do so? In the absence of an account of why certain people are ready to face the truth, there seems to be no explanation of why this interpretation of religious belief, even if true, should have the right sort of effect on those who are exposed to it. Given the complexity of offering and receiving interpretations in the case of an individual analysis, this is a significant lacuna. In the individual case, by contrast, it is by now beyond question that not only must an interpretation be true, but an analysand must be ready to hear it. It is not an exaggeration to say that there has been a hundred years of painstaking study of what it is for an interpretation to be formulated and delivered in an appropriate way and at an appropriate time for the analysand. It would seem that an analogous question of readiness ought to arise when it comes to large-scale cultural interpretations delivered to the culture at large. This is a serious rhetorical issue, and it raises a question about the value of such interpretations (I discuss this issue in Lear, 2007). Since psychoanalytic insight is so difficult to acquire in individual case, what good could large-scale cultural critique serve? To be sure: it might be true that religious belief is illusion; and it might be true that we are ready to grasp it as such if someone like Freud would point it out. But we need an account of what this readiness consists in.

On the surface, the claim that religious belief is illusion would seem to be self-undermining. If such belief is a powerful illusion, it would seem that I ought to be in the grip of it. And if I were in its grip, I would not be able to see it as such. Freud's own account of the painful historical process of enlightenment, where we are slowly weaned from this illusory attachment, gives one sort of answer. But if we abjure recourse to that type of answer, it is unclear what could take its place. Suppose we are persuaded by Freud's argument that religious belief is illusion. It would seem that a certain healthy scepticism is in order about how we came to be persuaded. For, in such a situation, we would not typically be diagnosing ourselves as suffering from illusion, but diagnosing others as suffering from an illusion from which we were free. It would seem incumbent on a psychoanalytically minded person who found himself in this position to enquire whether this interpretation—which in effect does look down on others—is providing narcissistic gratifications, or relieving anxiety, of which he might be unaware.

One solid answer could be: "In my own individual analysis I have come to see over time that religion has played a wishful, illusory role in my life." This could be part of, or even the conclusion of, a process of working through the role of religious engagement in an individual analysand's life. One might come to a similar conclusion through the painstaking analysis of another. In each case, the analysis would show how one might come to know that religious belief is—at least in this individual's case—illusion. The theories of how the mind works that justify psychoanalytic technique would thereby serve to legitimate the conclusion. This would provide what I have called the epistemic ground of claim that religious belief was illusion: it would give the reason for thinking the claim is true. One might even come to think that this is a typical use to which religious beliefs can be put. For example, one might gather data from a number of analyses, or come to think that what one has discovered in the individual case has a paradigmatic structure, and so on. However, if this is the route of discovery, then there is a question about the scope or generality of what one has discovered.

6. Freud wanted to make a stronger claim than that religious belief could be put to wishful use: he wanted to claim that it was constitutive of religious belief that it was wishful. The claim of psychoanalytic validity implies that there is *no way* one can both (a) believe in the principles of psychoanalysis and live according to them *and* (b) live a life that embodies religious commitment. The idea would be that in coming to recognize religious belief as illusion (in a psychoanalytically appropriate way), one would thereby be in the process of giving it up. One would be working through the illusion and finding less illusory ways to live. Thus, in order to impugn Freud's argument—that is, to show that it is psychoanalytically *invalid* to claim that religious belief is illusion—one needs to show that there is a genuine possibility of someone fulfilling both conditions (a) and (b)—that is, one needs to establish that it is at least possible for someone to believe in and live according to psychoanalytic principles (including especially those regarding the nature of illusion) and also to live a religiously committed life.

It is not easy to understand how one argues for a possibility. Typically, when logicians want to establish a possibility, they construct a model. So, for instance, when they want to show that a certain form of argument is invalid, they construct a model in which the premises are true and the conclusion is false. This is meant to establish that it is at least possible for the premises to be true and the conclusion false. And the model need not be actually true: it need only be possible. In the present case, we are concerned not with forms of argument, but with forms of life: the possibility of a person living a life that is both psychoanalytically self-aware and religiously committed. Along the lines of constructing a model, we need to see if we can reasonably imagine such a person.

One needs to imagine someone for whom illusion does not exhaust or give the fundamental basis of their life of religious commitment. And it seems to me we need a plausible example, not just some weird counterexample. Freud purports to give us an account of what religious belief consists in. His argument would not be seriously impugned if we can imagine some utter oddball who is a wild exception to all of life's normal rules. On the other hand, we do not need to account for all religious believers: all we need to show is that the religious commitment of a plausible and serious person need not be illusion. So, a psychoanalytically minded person might accept, even welcome, the idea that there was an illusory dimension to her religious engagement. She might accept that, given the vagaries of infantile development, it is no surprise that her own initial engagements with religious ideas had an infantile, wishful aspect. And, following Freud, she might accept that there are aspects of infantile life that persist in adult life. Still, for her, these infantile forms of engagement were stepping-stones for deeper forms of religious engagement in adult life. Such a person, for instance, could be a serious reader of Maimonides (English translation, 1963).[6] Writing almost a millennium before Freud, Maimonides basically agrees with Freud that the stories in the Torah are wishful—but he does so in the service of deepening religious belief, not of debunking it. For Maimonides, the stories in the Bible are myths that are meant to attract and grab the young or religiously immature reader; but, properly interpreted, they could lead a serious reader in the right direction. The stories are there for the sake of growing beyond them. *A guide of the perplexed* is an extended account of how one might properly use the Torah so as to grow beyond literal belief in its stories. But this growth was meant to be religious growth. Contra Freud, Maimonides saw that there were sophisticated ways of living with these stories other than forming straightforward empirical beliefs about their literal truth. This does not mean that the issue of truth need not arise (Blass, 2004). But it need not arise in the form Freud thought it must. Maimonides, as I understand him, was committed to a robust form of religious truth—for him, God exists—but the problem of forming a non-idolatrous conception of God's existence was not only extraordinarily difficult: it was itself a religious task. It is an attempt to overcome idolatry—in the sense of overcoming rigid adherence to religious images and myths—that is itself a way of worshipping God. From a Maimonidean perspective, although God really does exist, there is no way adequately to grasp this from the perspective of a detached empirical observer—*à la* Freud's nineteenth-century image of the inquiring scientist. And unless one is still in the grip of a tired and outworn positivism, it should no longer seem surprising or objectionable that there are genuine truths that elude such a stance.[7] Obviously, it is beyond the scope of this essay to discuss Maimonides' conception of God in any detail, but I think enough has been said to show that Freud's critique of religious belief does not really touch it. And I do not see why there could not be room in the contemporary world for a psychoanalytic Maimonides: someone who believes that childish religious belief is illusion, but who also thought that that recognition was a step in overcoming idolatry, not a step in overcoming religious commitment.

Obviously, none of these considerations impugns the thought that religious belief can and does function as illusion. But they do impugn the idea that religious belief always and everywhere has to function that way. Of course, someone might think that, as a matter of fact, religion does always and everywhere function as illusion. But I do not see that there are any distinctively psychoanalytic considerations that support such a conclusion. Nor do I think there is anything in Freud's argument that establishes a claim of such broad scope. And that points us in the direction of an outlook that is, I think, more in tune with the overall spirit of Freudian psychoanalysis: that if one wants to grasp the role of religious belief in a given individual's life, there is no substitute for the analysis of that individual. Religious belief can play various roles in people's lives—and, no doubt, there is room to speculate about typical uses to which religious belief can be put—but Freud's one-size-fits-all diagnosis flattens differences that ought to make a difference.

NOTES

I am indebted to Gabriel Lear and Hans Loewald for extended conversations on the topics discussed in this paper.

1. See also Gay, 1987, p. 41, where the claim is repeated.
2. Especially Spinoza, 1992, part I, "Concerning God". For an intro-

duction to Spinoza's thought, see Nadler, 1999, 2001, and Allison, 1987, especially chapter 3, "God".

3. This essay is a development of ideas I began to formulate in Lear, 2005.

4. For two excellent accounts of the functions of genealogies, see Geuss, 1999, and Williams, 2002.

5. The psychoanalytically imaginative reader might want to speculate on what split-off part of Freud's own psyche this "religious interlocutor" represents.

6. I am indebted to Leon Wieseltier for a seminar he gave on this text at the Committee on Social Thought.

7. For an introduction, see, e.g., Cartwright, 1983, 1989, 1999; Galison, 1987, 1997; Hacking, 1981, 1983; Kuhn, 1962, 1987, 1997. For a paradigm of the positivism that had such a deleterious effect on psychoanalytic thinking about religion in the twentieth century, see Gay, 1987.

3

The past of an illusion: an evolutionary perspective on religious belief

J. Anderson Thomson, Jr

Biology is truly a land of unlimited possibilities. We may expect it to give us the most surprising information, and we cannot guess what answers it will return in a few dozen years to the questions we have put to it. They may be of a kind which will blow away the whole of our artificial structure of hypotheses.

Sigmund Freud, *Beyond the Pleasure Principle* (1920g), p. 60

We do not have the option of "choosing" absolute truth or faith. We only have the right to say, of those who *do* claim to know the truth of revelation, that they are deceiving themselves and attempting to deceive—or to intimidate—others. Of course, it is better and healthier for the mind to "choose" the path of skepticism and inquiry in any case, because only by continual exercise of these faculties can we hope to achieve anything. Whereas religions are merely "fossilized philosophies" or philosophy with the questions left out. To "choose" dogma and faith over doubt and experiment is to throw out the ripening vintage and to reach greedily for the Kool-Aid.

Christopher Hitchens, *God Is Not Great* (2007), p. 278

Four score years after Sigmund Freud published *The Future of an Illusion* (1927c), the world still needs its fierce wisdom, its insistence on an objective analysis of religion, and its rousing defence of science. Today we witness young men and women willingly kill themselves and countless others in the name of God. Fundamentalists of all stripes advocate murder, misogyny, suspension of civil liberties, prohibitions on life-saving medical research, and early "godly" education that amounts to child abuse. Will the world ever awaken from its long nightmare of religious belief (Weinberg, 2006)?

To see where we are today, and how Freud's ideas stand the test of time, it is necessary to lay out the most significant development in psychology since Freud: the merger of the cognitive neurosciences, depth psychology, palaeontology, anthropology, and evolutionary biology. It is only through this new lens of evolutionary psychology that the origins and functions of religious belief can be seen in their fine details.

Basics

We are our minds, and the mind is what the brain does (Pinker, 1997, 2002). The human brain is a complex conglomeration of neural networks, shaped over millions of years by natural selection to tell us how to survive—how to solve the adaptive problems faced by our mammalian, primate, australopithecine, and ancient Homo ancestors—problems that stood in the way of replicating the genome. Adaptive problems included finding food, friends, mates, and shelter and surviving climate, predators, and enemies. Sexuality, because it is so crucial to reproductive success, received particular attention by the sculpting of natural selection. Romantic love and sex comprise a myriad complex adaptations biologically forged in that crucible of time before history.

We are "risen apes, not fallen angels" (Allman, 1994). We are, more specifically, a risen African ape, a hominid who emerged in Pleistocene savannahs less than 200,000 years ago. Our different races, ethnicities, and religions mask an essential truth—that underneath our skin we are all Africans, the sons and daughters of small bands of hunter–gatherers who arose on that continent and conquered the world by adapting and surviving (Stringer & McKie, 1996).

Our most immediate ancestors, the primates, arose 65 million years ago, when dinosaurs disappeared. The social apes appeared some 35 million years ago. Changes in the climate led to greater seasonal patterns, cooling and drying, which particularly affected the area of Africa known as the Great Rift Valley, which runs from Ethiopia to South Africa. We should think of it as the birth canal of the human species. With these climate shifts, the movement of geological plates closed the Isthmus of Panama and drove the Indian subcontinent into Asia, thus giving rise to the Himalayas and changing the environment on the eastern side of the Rift Valley from rainforests to woodlands to savannas. The apes that survived were those that began to move upright and could manage to forage over a greater distance. What made us originally human was bipedalism—upright walking.

We began to change from a small-brained bipedal ape to something new. In fact, two million years ago there were at least four human-like species still alive in Africa. Even 100,000 years ago, there were probably three species, one each in Africa, Europe, and East Asia (Stringer & Andrews, 2005). Now we are a species alone, and human narcissism wants to believe we were predestined to succeed, shaped by a human-like god. Too many of our identities are based on the mistaken belief that we were somehow "chosen". Chance climate changes could have readily derailed our evolution and those cherished identities.

Who are we now?

Christian fundamentalists, jihadists, creationists, and "intelligent design" theorists all use modern electronic devices. Yet they choose to ignore that the same science that dictates the flow of electrons in cell phones and computers reveals how the universe really works. Modern electronics is part of the same science that confirms natural selection and reveals our origins and evolutionary history from primates, monkeys, apes, and early hominids. It leaves no room for divine intervention, a 6,000-year-old earth, or a world built in a week by a divine *Naumeister* (Folger, 2004). Darwin's theory, now established, is the only workable explanation we have for the remarkable fact of our own existence, the vast diversity of plant and animal life, the compelling illusion of design in nature, and the architecture of the human mind (Dawkins, 1985, 2004).

Any behaviour implies the presence of underlying psychological mechanisms. Any mechanism postulated implies a causal process that shaped it and an environment in which it was formed. Natural selection is the only process we know that designs and maintains functional mechanisms. In essence, there is no such thing as a non-evolutionary psychology, psychoanalysis, or theory of behaviour (Edward Hagen, personal communication, 2004). Yet all of this knowledge floats freely in front of the denying eyes of most of humanity and modern psychoanalytic theory, despite Freud's clear anticipation of it.

Time

It is important to adjust our view to several new lenses: huge time spans and a gene-centred view of life. Life is four billion years old. The legacy of that original replicating RNA-like molecule resides in all of us, on chromosome 1 (Ridley, 2000). For 90%+ of our existence as a species, fully formed Homo sapiens, we lived in an environment far different from the one we occupy today. That environment, known as the EEA (the environment of evolutionary adaptation) is the one for which we are still designed, lacking the evolutionary time to have moved much beyond it (Bowlby, 1982). Other than ourselves, we have no direct records of the EEA. Its shape can only be discerned by inference, from its echoes in our psychology and the few preliterate peoples who survive. In a sense our modern skulls contain Stone Age brains (Allman, 1994). We are adapted to the task demands of a hunter–gatherer life that to us seems long since gone but really resides in the evolutionarily immediate past and has dominated our species for the bulk of our history. We may be changing rapidly in the sense of cultural time, but to our own still somewhat primitive brains we are nearly standing still. If we are to glean a clear understanding of human nature and religious belief, this EEA is one of the lenses through which we must view ourselves and our psyches.

Cognitive mechanisms underlying religion

The mildest criticism of religion remains the most radical and devastating. Religion is entirely man-made (Hitchens, 2007). Whether humanity wants to accept it or not, through a combination of evolutionary psychology, psychoanalysis, the new cognitive sciences, and anthropology, we now know more about why religion appeared, why particular religious ideas emerged, why they are widespread, why they are recurrent features of human minds and human societies, why they are attractive to human minds, and how and why they are related to survival and deadly violence (Atran, 2002; Barrett, 2004; Boyer, 1994, 2001; Burkett, 1996; Dawkins, 2006; Dennett, 1997, 2005; Freud, 1927c; Guthrie, 1993; Harris, 2004, 2006; Hartung, 1995; Humphrey, 1996; Kirkpatrick, 1999, 2004; Kriegman & Kriegman, 1998).

Science, the science that Freud predicted and extolled in *The Future of an Illusion*, has illuminated the foundations of religious belief. All religious beliefs, not just those of the predominant three modern monotheistic religions, have the common denominator of crediting nature with some human capacity for symbolic action. Religion is always a human concept with alterations. There is perhaps one violation of our intuitive assumptions, which is arresting and demands our attention, but then many that confirm our intuitive assumptions to structure the belief and ultimately bring it back to a human form (Boyer, 2001). For example, God resides "everywhere" but has all the human sensory features. He is a man who sees your actions, hears your prayers, thinks, plans, and speaks.

All individuals are vulnerable to religious beliefs. What makes us human can also make us religious. Human minds produce religious ideas and are vulnerable to believing them (Atran, 2002; Boyer, 2001). At the individual level, religion and a religious identity are the cultural byproducts of many different cognitive mechanisms that evolved to solve other problems and to promote survival and reproductive success in ancestral environments.

1. A partial list of these cognitive devices begins with the mechanism of *decoupled cognition*. This ability arises in childhood and is seen vividly in pretend play. A child might say a bottle cap is a flying saucer. The child knows that it is a cap to a bottle but can decouple his or her cognition and think of it as a flying saucer,

with the attributes imagined and related to as such. Theatre and filmgoers use such "suspension of disbelief" all the time. They know that what is happening on the stage or screen is not real. Yet, when watching it, they choose to believe that it is, that the people on the stage really live in Shakespearean England, or that the car on the screen really is blown to smithereens while the driver survives, and so on. This mechanism easily comes into play in religion when one suspends disbelief. Is that not the definition of faith? Interaction in our minds with unseen others makes gods and ancestor worship quite easy.

2. The *attachment system* plays a central role in religion (Kirkpatrick, 1999, 2004). When distressed, we instinctively turn towards a caretaker—usually a parent or parent substitute. When there is no suitable attachment figure, we create one. A god or ancestor to whom a religious person appeals is usually a caretaker figure. Prayer is unique to our species and arises from our prolonged, neotonous developmental history. We beseech the supernatural to change the distress caused by the natural world. Gods are super parents who provide reassurance beyond any mortal parent (Humphrey, 1996).

3. The concept of *transference* is particularly useful in understanding certain aspects of religion. First, we must understand why the capacity for transference evolved in the human mind. What problems does it solve? What adaptive function does it serve? Early relationship strategies form stable personality characteristics. Early relationships are the grammar for conducting later relationships. Imagine what it would be like if we had to learn anew how to relate to people with each new relationship as our lives unfolded. Basing present relationships on past relationships—real, imagined, or wished-for—are an efficient way of anticipating outcomes.

The capacity for transference evolved as a crucial aspect of the human mind (Nesse & Lloyd, 1992). In psychoanalysis and analytically based therapy, we see how disturbed early relationships distort present relationships. When that transference is repeated in psychoanalytic therapy, the details of the transference itself become the arena for treatment. Think of all the potential transferences mobilized by religious beliefs between believers and their gods:

God the father, Mary the mother, and so on, and all that we may bring of our personal relationships with our fathers, mothers, and significant objects into religious beliefs and identities.

Treatment of religious individuals often unmasks transference relationships contributing to the patient's religious beliefs. To give a stark example, a young woman had been physically, emotionally, and verbally abused by her father. She sought in religion a considerate father who would love her and accept her love in a way unquestionably different from her own father. She would ask for guidance from "God" for life decisions, talk to God as a young adult would to a supportive and knowledgeable parent, and worry about God's reaction as a young woman would fret about a father's reaction.

4. Humans are born with exquisite mechanisms to recognize and relate to *kin*. That is crucial to not just our survival, but to the survival of copies of our genes that reside in our kin. We evolved to favour those with our genes over those without. Religions evoke our kin emotions. Roman Catholicism offers an example. The nuns are "sisters" or even "Mother Superior", the priests are "fathers", the monks are "brothers", and the Pope is the "Holy Father". Exploitation of kin emotions is central to the recruitment of today's suicide bombers (Atran, 2003, 2006; McDermott, 2005; Pedahzur, 2005; Sageman, 2004; Thomson, 2006).

5. *Reciprocal altruism* is essential to cognitive ability. Humans have complex cognitive software for reciprocal exchange. What one gives and what one receives are kept in strict account. Sacrificial offerings are just one place where this capacity is used by religions: for example, sacrificing a pig to bring a good harvest. Often prayer is an explicit plea for reciprocity. If the supplicant promises something, he hopes to be rewarded in return.

6. Humans have *moral feeling systems*. One frequent argument that favours religion is that morality requires it. Not so. We might not have formal explicit moral systems, but we are all born with moral inferential systems (Alexander, 1987; Hauser, 2006). This is clear in young children who know the fundamental difference between right and wrong long before being introduced to religion.

We need to dismantle the idea that morality requires religion.

Consider: is there any single ethical statement made or ethical action performed by a religious person that could not be spoken or accomplished by a nonbeliever? Yet it is easy to come up with a vicious statement made or an evil action taken *because* of religious faith (Hitchens, 2007). Genuine morality is doing what is right, regardless of what we are told. Religious morality is doing what we are told, regardless of whether it is right.

We need look no further than the dominant faith in the West, Christianity. As Christopher Hitchens (with whom I strongly agree) notes, is it moral to tell children, to tell anyone, that their sins can be forgiven because of a human sacrifice in which they had no say? Is it moral to preach that because of the dreadful public torture and death of a preacher two thousand years ago, all will be pardoned? Is it moral or abject masochism to tell children that they are sinful, guilty creatures responsible for sins committed before they were born and could not influence, and their only chance to be freed of those burdens is to take part, symbolically, in a ritual of crucifixion? Is it moral to frighten children with hell and eternal punishment? Is it moral to make an implicit appeal to totalitarianism—they can never know right from wrong unless they are the property of a celestial dictator whom they must love and fear? Is Christianity a source of moral guidance? Or does it instil by subtle psychic coercion not just irrationality, but immorality (Hitchens, 2007, pp. 208–210). If God wanted to forgive mankind's sins, why not just forgive them? Why have Jesus tortured and executed in payment, which condemned future generations of Jews to persecution as "Christ-killers"? In order to impress himself, God/Jesus had himself tortured and executed, in vicarious punishment for a symbolic sin committed by a non-existent Adam (Dawkins, 2006). The sado-masochism embedded in this morality should spark the interest of psychoanalysts.

7. Human minds contain *natural kinds modules* or "living-thing describers" that permit us to distinguish animate from inanimate objects. This ability to cognitively see the living "essence" of things is imperfect and easily slides into assuming that there is a living essence in inanimate objects (Boyer, 2001). *Animism* is the sharpest example of this, but it is present in the more complex religious ideas that impute living substance to nonliving things and spaces.

8. Humans have what are called *theory of mind modules.* They are taken for granted, and people experience them as a seamless part of the conscious mind. But they are hardly simple. People know without being taught that other people have minds like ours, with wishes, beliefs, desires, and passions. We can read others' mental states with eye cues. In an intensely social species like ours, a theory of mind is crucial to working with other people, anticipating or reading their thoughts, their wishes, and their desires. Deficits in this capacity account for Asperger's syndrome and autism (Baron-Cohen, 1995).

Religious beliefs easily utilize this capacity. Gods have thoughts, wishes, desires, and memories. Gods usually have a human mind, with all the possibilities.

9. Human brains are equipped with *person-file systems.* We are born with them, and we store information about people in them. Person-file systems stay in our minds, even when the person is dead or long absent. It permits us to "talk", in the privacy of our own minds—*decoupled cognition*—with those close to us who have died. That is just one step away from formal ancestor worship.

10. Humans have a strong bias to interpret uncertain evidence as caused by an agent. The cognitive capacity for this detection of agency is hyperactive and hypersensitive. It has been called *HADD*, the *hypersensitive agent detection device* (Barrett, 2004). This agency contributes to religious beliefs. With the assistance of face detectors and other cognitive capacities sensitive to human forms, people can see human-like figures almost anywhere—the man in the moon, the cantankerous apple trees in Oz. The outcome can be a belief in a ghost or spirit. Another manifestation may occur when we ascribe agency to known non-agents, such as a storm cloud or the wind.

11. Our *natural kind capacities* include the assumption that death, a biological event, ends biological processes. However, our *theory of mind capacities* and our *agency detection devices* fail to register that death necessarily ends psychological processes. Biological death appears to be intuitive, whereas psychological death is counterintuitive. There is a pervasive *denial of death* despite the certain knowl-

edge of it. The result is massive conflict. When someone dies, our *natural kind capacities* say the person will never function biologically again. Our *theory of mind capacities*, however, continue to generate predictions about what the dead person thinks, believes, hears, and feels, most often when that someone was close to us. Ancestor worship and a belief in souls flow quite naturally from this conflict between these agencies of our mind when confronted with a death. And, who is closer to us than ourselves? This results in the pervasive human need to deny mortality. Religion fulfils this need by promising an afterlife for ourselves and those we love.

12. Gods personify, control, and appease the unpredictable. Gods also induce a fear of higher authority and insure subordination. People turn over the fruits of their labour to invisible gods, not just to the current king or tax collector. *Deference to authority* had survival and reproductive value in the EEA, but it creates a great vulnerability. Stanley Milgram's (1974) famous experiments, in which he induced subjects to give what would have been lethal electric shocks to others, showed us all how we are far more submissive to authority than any of us would care to believe. Religious belief, with its submission to religious authorities, can turn this capacity to murderous ends in times of severe conflict and war.

13. Religion exploits *childhood credulity*. Our survival is enhanced by the accumulated knowledge of prior generations. Natural selection designed child brains with a bias to trust and believe what adults say, especially when delivered in an earnest tone and cloaked with the mantle of authority. This is borne out by the Jesuits' famous claim that if you give them a child before the age of seven, they have him for life. This leads us to a question with enormous public policy implications. Do children have a right, a fundamental human right, to be protected from religious indoctrination (Humphrey, 2002)?

14. *Geography and ecology* also shape the religious ideas that our minds generate and accept. Religions of rainforest people tend to be polytheistic, with fewer interventionist gods, more equality for women, and less sexual repressiveness. Desert-derived religions feature monotheism with an interventionist god, women as inferiors, and greater sexual repressiveness (Sapolsky, 2005).

15. Central to understanding religion is its role in supporting our *"groupishness"*. We are an intensely groupish species, which is not surprising as a survival mechanism and is adaptive throughout our evolutionary history. Religion historically has served as one of the crucial death deserving tags that instantly distinguish a group, dividing the world into us and them (Boyer, 2001). Religious leaders exploit this *groupishness* to ensure loyalty to the faith and one's co-religionists.

Religions are also useful in acquiring resources and thwarting competition. The reality is that no religion has been successful by tolerating its competitors.

Religions must redirect loyalties and other identities to succeed. Various ethnic, racial, and diverse linguistic identities can fall under the umbrella of one religious identity. We tend to think of religions as promoting family values, but one of their main functions is to override those loyalties. The idea of subverting families may come as a surprise to those who think of a religious identity as oriented towards family values. But the family is a danger to religion. Families constitute rival coalitions. They have the unfair advantage of being bound together by kin emotions. The hostility towards family values is nicely illustrated by the following:

> "I came not to send peace, but a sword. For I am come to set a man at variance against his father, and the daughter against her mother, and the daughter-in-law against her mother-in-law. And a man's foes shall be they of his own household. He that loveth father or mother more than me is not worthy of me: and he that loveth son or daughter more than me is not worthy of me." [Jesus, quoted in Matthew 10:34–37]

In short, religion is a product of human minds, a by-product of cognitive capacities originally designed for other purposes. Once generated, religious ideas can act like viruses, infecting other evolved capacities of the human mind to promote the ends of religious leaders (Dawkins, 2006; Dennett, 2005).

Freud's personal religion

Sigmund Freud's militant atheism began in his youth. At 17, he told his friend Eduard Silverstein, "for God's dark ways, no one has yet invented a lantern" (Gay, 1988). Freud later called himself "a godless medical student", and that never changed (Gay, 1988). The year before he died, Freud noted, "Neither in my private life nor in my writings have I ever made a secret of being an out and out unbeliever" (Gay, 1988, p. 526). He took a stance we might all follow. All of his life Freud maintained that it was religious belief, not atheism, that needed to be explained (Gay, 1988).

In 1905 Freud noted religion's similarity with obsessive neurosis, forming the basis for his 1907 paper, "Obsessive Actions and Religious Practices", which put religion and neurosis under one roof. Both the rituals of an obsessive and the ceremonies of the believer serve to renounce impulses and act as self-protective defences. He made the succinct observation that "one might venture to regard obsessional neuroses as a pathological counterpart to religious formation, neurosis as an individual religion, religion as a universal obsessional neurosis" (Freud, 1907).

The Future of an Illusion reflected Freud's uncompromising stance. His view was that religion arose from man's need to protect against the crushing superiority of nature and was fundamentally an illusion of childhood, the fulfilment of the oldest, strongest, and most urgent wishes of mankind. Religion was as strong and tensile as those wishes. Where religions claim that a "god the father" made man in his own image, Freud postulated the opposite: men make gods in their father's image. All thinking may arise from wishful thinking, but scientific thinking is wishing disciplined and documented, requiring verification. Scientific thought remains open to examination, debate, demonstration, and disproof. Nothing is accepted on faith. Freud believed his obligation was to make religion, like all human conduct, accessible to scientific investigation.

In a sense *The Future of an Illusion* was the product of a promise Freud made to himself. On 20 August 1911, he wrote to Ferenczi that his mind was again turned to religion, that he might someday write about it in detail. Peter Gay (1988) makes it explicit.

> To demolish religion with psychoanalytic weapons, then, had been on Freud's agenda for many years. . . . Of all Freud's publications, *The Future of an Illusion* is perhaps the most inevitable and the most predictable. . . . His uncompromising secularism . . . denied matters of faith any privileged status, any claim to exemption from analysis. He respected no sacred spots; saw

> no temples that he, as a researcher, must not enter. [Gay, 1988, p. 527]

As it was for Freud, it is for today's secular scientists. There is no higher court than that of reason. This is the heart of Freud's argument:

> The very premises of science are incompatible with those of religion. He disdained all the bridges that modern historians have tried to build between the two, all the subtleties that modern theologians had spun. . . . As he said more than once, in more than one text, religion was, quite simply, the enemy. [Gay, 1988, p. 533]

The attempts of later psychoanalysts to reconcile psychoanalysis and religion would have been met with utter scorn by Freud and his early followers.

Freud knew that atheism also could become ideology, used as a defence, an adolescent rebellion against a father. Those who would quarrel with God could be reenacting in their ideology an oedipal battle they had lost at home. But for Freud himself, atheism was something better, a scientific investigation of religion. He was hardly a social reformer, but "concealed in Freud's psychoanalytic critique of belief lies a hope that to discover and disseminate the truth about religion may help to free mankind of it" (Gay, 1988, p. 534).

Freud was Jewish, a fact that some have used to argue against his atheism. Yet for him, it was a secular identification, ethnic rather than religious (Gay, 1988). He found the veneration bestowed on him by B'Nai B'rith awkward.

> "Altogether the Jews have celebrated me like a national hero, although my merit in the Jewish cause is confined to the single point that I have never denied my Judaism." His use of the term "the Jews" put him at a distance, a stranger among those who thought they were his brothers [Gay, 1988, p. 599]

Freud wanted to be clear. "I adhered to the Jewish religion as little as to any other." In his preface to the Hebrew version of *Totem and Taboo,* he said of himself that he was "wholly alienated from the religion of my fathers—as from every other" (Freud, 1912–13, p. xv). To a devout American physician he said that God had sent him no inner voices, and he would remain "an infidel Jew" (Gay, 1988, p. 599).

Freud the "infidel" forgot what Hebrew he knew and did not allow religious observances in his home life. The family ignored the Jewish family holidays, even though his parents had celebrated them. Freud shut down Martha's religious observance, to her pain and regret. His children were never taken to a synagogue. Freud's son, Martin, reported that the family's holidays were Christmas, which included presents under a candlelit tree, and Easter, with Easter eggs (Gay, 1988).

At the same time, Freud did maintain an indefinable element of identification with his Jewishness. It perhaps reflected his belief in a Lamarckian inheritance of acquired characteristics that his Jewishness had been part of his phylogenetic inheritance. Above all, he saw himself doubly alienated, a marginal man, and that outsider status gave him an advantage. He wrote to Oscar Pfister on 9 October 1918: "Quite by the way, why did none of the devout create psychoanalysis? Why did one have to wait for a completely Godless Jew?" (in Gay, 1988, p. 602). In his letter of 6 May 1926 to B'Nai B'rith he wrote,

> "That I owe only to my Jewish nature the two characteristics that had become indispensable on my difficult life's way. Because I was a Jew, I found myself free from any prejudices which limited others in the employment of their intellects, and as a Jew I was prepared to go into opposition." [in Gay, 1988, p. 603]

The Future of an Illusion

Within these contexts, Freud's seminal work on religion can be examined and compared with today's knowledge. By those standards, he was both prescient and wrong.

Sections I, II, and III

Some of Freud's premises are clearly in error. For instance, he believed that the human mind had thrust off its early programming. "It is not true", he wrote, "that the human mind has undergone no development since the earliest times and that, in contrast to the advances of science and technology, it is the same today as it was at the beginning of history" (p. 11)

There is now good evidence that our modern skulls do contain a Stone Age brain (Allman, 1994) and that the human mind, as it is currently constituted, was shaped by the Pleistocene and our long history of living in small kin-based groups as hunters and gathers. And while Freud believed that external factors gave way to a learned internal moral compass, new evidence also raises doubt about that. Freud's notion that "external coercion gradually becomes internalized; for a special mental agency, man's super-ego, takes it over and includes it among its commandments. Every child presents this process of transformation to us; only by that means does it become a moral and social being" (1927c, p. 11). We know now that we are born with a moral grammar that culture certainly influences, just as we are born with a native grammar that the particular language we learn takes advantage of (Hauser, 2006).

Freud makes a similar mistake in assuming that we are instinctively selfish and that civilization is required to suppress this selfishness. We now know that we are as instinctively cooperative as we are cruel. Natural selection at the level of the gene generates altruism as well as selfishness (Dawkins, 1976).

Freud was certainly partially right in his insight that we humanize nature, impersonal forces, and destinies and give them a human face. This is in line with recent discoveries about the origin of religious beliefs in our innate agency detection and theory of mind mechanisms.

Section IV

Freud then set up a straw man with whom he continued his arguments. Religious ideas, he posited, arose from the same needs that sparked all of civilization's other achievements. Man needed to defend against the superior force of nature, and then to rectify the suppression of instinct that was necessary to do that. These things, he said, were always painfully felt.

In Freud's view, primitive man addressed his perplexity and helplessness in the face of nature's forces by forming a relationship with those forces in an effort to influence them. It was natural, he said, even innate, for man to regard every event as the manifestation of beings who were like himself. It was the only way to comprehend his universe. So far, so good. But Freud believed that this was entirely driven by an infantile model, that man learned from infancy to establish an influential relationship with the forces of nature, personifying everything as a way of comprehending and thus controlling them. He called it "psychical mastering as a preparation for physical mastering" (1927c, p. 22). We now know that our cognitive vulnerabilities continue to personify and attribute agency to nature even into healthy adulthood.

In Freud's view, the mother satisfied the child's hunger, and because of that became the first object and protection against the world. The child's relation to the stronger father was complicated by ambivalence, because of his relation to the mother. Thus, Freud viewed religion as an outgrowth of the realization that, relative to the powers of nature, the individual would forever be a helpless child. The child would then project the presumed powers of the father onto the gods, whom he both created and dreaded, propitiating and entrusting them with his protection. This defence against the helplessness of childhood was Freud's lynchpin of religious formation. We now know that religious ideas arise from multiple natural capacities of our minds.

Section V

Freud notes here that the nature of religious ideas is that they are given without evidence. When evidence is sought, three objections arise: that the teachings deserve belief because our ancestors believed them; that proofs already exist as traditions handed down to us from those ancient times; and that, in any case, religions forbid questions about their authenticity. Such prohibition, he wrote, arose because people understand that religious claims by their very nature stand on shaky ground. The inherent irony of such prohibition—that the most important and fundamental questions whose answers could solve the riddles of life are forbidden—did not escape Freud. In any other context, we would not accept such flimsy answers to such fundamental questions. This presented him, and now presents us, with a remarkable psychological problem, perhaps the ultimate Catch–22.

Freud rightly criticized the *credo qui absurdum* of the early church, the notion that religious beliefs are outside the realm of reason and that their truths must be experienced inwardly and need not be understood. He thought the *credo* revealed a self-confession.

> Am I to be obliged to believe *every* absurdity? And if not, why this one in particular? There is no appeal to a court above that of reason. If the truth of religious doctrine is dependent on an inner experience which bears witness to that truth, what is one to do about the many people who do not have this rare experience? Can one demand that everyone believe something only open to a few? [1927c, p. 27]

Another attempt to defend religion's lack of evidence was the philosophy of "as if". For a variety of practical reasons we have to behave "'as if' we believed in these fictions. This is the case with religious doctrines because of their incomparable importance for the maintenance of human society" (pp. 28–29). Freud noted that one of his children always questioned the truth of a fairy tale, and showed distain when told it was fictional. Freud's hope was that "we may expect that people will soon behave in the same way towards the fairy tales of religion, in spite of the advocacy of 'As if'" (p. 29). This led him again to wonder why religious ideas, in spite of their lack of evidence, continue to exercise such influence on mankind, and he moves to answer that question in the next section.

Section VI

Religious beliefs are illusions, Freud notes, and gain their power from being the fulfilment of the "oldest, strongest, and most urgent wishes of mankind". In this context, he makes his strongest summary:

> As we already know, the terrifying impression of helplessness in childhood arouses the need for protection—for protection through love—which was provided by the father; and the recognition that this helplessness lasts throughout life made it necessary to cling to the existence of a father, but this time a

> more powerful one. Thus, the benevolent rule of a Divine Providence allays our fear of the dangers of life; the establishment of a moral world-order ensures the fulfilment of the demands of justice, which have so often remained unfulfilled in human civilization; and the prolongation of earthly existence in a future life provides the local and temporal framework in which these wish-fulfilments shall take place. Answers to the riddles that tempt the curiosity, such as how the universe began or what the relation is between body and mind, are developed in conformity with the underlying assumptions of this system. It is an enormous relief to the individual psyche if the conflicts of its childhood arising from the father-complex—conflicts which it has never wholly overcome—are removed from it and brought to the solution which is universally accepted. [p. 30]

Freud then made the distinction between an illusion, derived from human wishes, and delusion. While illusion and delusion are not far apart, he noted, illusions differed from delusions in that the latter essentially contradict reality. Illusions are not necessarily false, meaning unrealizable or contradicting reality. Delusions are.

Yet, Freud's distinctions remain unsatisfactory. How do we classify religious beliefs, beliefs that clearly contradict reality? Are they a form of delusion, a widespread cultural delusion? Are a religious analyst and his religious patient engaged in *folie à deux*?

Freud then responds to the age-old question: if religion cannot be refuted by reason, why not believe in it?

> If ever there was a case of a lame excuse we have it here. Ignorance is ignorance; no right to believe anything can be derived from it. In reality these are only attempts at pretending to oneself or to other people that one is still firmly attached to religion when one has long since cut oneself loose from it. Where questions of religion are concerned, people are guilty of every possible sort of dishonesty and intellectual misdemeanour. [p. 32]

Those individuals who make God the vaguest of abstractions receive Freud's sharpest contempt. He notes that those who admit to a sense of man's insignificance in the face of the universe are described as deeply religious. Yet what constitutes the essence of religion is not that feeling but the reaction to it, with religion as the remedy. For Freud,

> The man who goes no further, but humbly acquiesces in the small part which human beings play in the great world such a man is, on the contrary, irreligious in the truest sense of the word. [pp. 32–33]

Section VII

Freud questions the need for religion as a means to maintain morality. His imagined opponent asks,

> If men are taught that there is no almighty and all-just God, no divine world-order and no future life, they will feel exempt from all obligation to obey the precepts of civilization. Everyone will, without inhibition or fear, follow his asocial, egoistic instincts and seek to exercise his power; Chaos, which we have banished through many thousands of years of the work of civilization, will come again. . . . Countless people find their one consolation in religious doctrines, and can only bear life with their help. You would rob them of their support, without having anything better to give them in exchange. . . . Man has imperative needs of another sort, which can never be satisfied by cold science; and it is very strange—indeed it is the highest of consistency—that a psychologist who has always insisted on what a minor part is played in human affairs by the intelligence as compared with the life of the instincts, that such a psychologist should now try to rob mankind of a precious wish-fulfilment and should propose to compensate them for it with intellectual nourishment. [pp. 34–35]

Sadly, Freud responds,

> In former times it was different. Then utterances such as mine brought with them a sure curtailment of one's earthly existence and an effective speeding-up of the opportunity for gaining a personal experience of the after-life. [p. 36]

Of course, he had no way of knowing that the "former times" of death-deserving apostasy would rise again, becoming part of his future and our present.

Freud pointed out how unlikely it is that humans were happier when religion held sway,

> more moral they certainly were not. . . . The priest, whose duty it was to ensure obedience to religion, met them half way in this. God's kindness must lay a restraining hand on His justice. One sinned, and then one made a sacrifice or did penance, and then one was free to sin once more. Russian introspectiveness has reached the pitch of concluding that sin is indispensable for the enjoyment of all of the blessings of divine grace, so that, at bottom, sin is pleasing to God. . . . In every age, immorality has found no less support in religion than morality has. [pp. 37–38]

Asked whether mankind's need for religion is overrated, Freud turned to his then-current world. In his view, religion (and here he meant European Christian civilization) no longer held much sway, not because it promised less, but because people found the promises less credible, with one (but not the only) reason being an increase of "the scientific spirit" in the higher stratagem of human society. Freud stood up for the value of science and secular researchers.

> Civilization has little to fear from educated people and brain workers. In them the replacement of religious motives for civilized behaviour by other, secular motives would proceed unobtrusively; moreover, such people are to a large extent themselves vehicles of civilization. [p. 39]

Section VIII

Here Freud begins with murder. Civilization, he notes, has laid down rules against killing to prevent the cycle of revenge. This rational explanation often gives way to the assertion that God made the rule. Freud here points out that society could benefit more by leaving God out entirely and honestly admitting the human origin of the laws of civilized life. Unburdened by religion, laws "would lose their rigidity and unchangeableness as well. People could understand that they are made, not so much to rule them as, on the contrary, to serve their interests" (1927c, p. 41).

He follows this with his view of the cultural history of mankind, as outlined in the fourth essay of *Totem and Taboo* (Freud, 1912–13) about the primal murder.

> Even in present-day man purely reasonable motives can effect little passionate impulses and how much weaker they must have been in the human animal of primeval times! Perhaps his descendants would even now kill one another without inhibition, if it were not that among those murderous acts there was one—the killing of the primitive father—which evoked an irresistible emotional reaction with momentous consequences. From it arose the commandment: Thou shalt not kill. Under totemism this commandment was restricted to the father-substitute; but it was later extended to other people, though even to-day it is not universally obeyed. [Freud, 1927c, p. 42]

Here Freud was wrong. We now have reason to believe that killing was adaptive for most of our evolutionary history, and even became part of some early religions in the form of cannibalism and human sacrifice. The fossil evidence of murder for genetic survival is overwhelming. Violent death at the hands of other men speaks out through the nature of skeletal fractures, the frequency of cranial trauma, the presence of arrow wounds, the predominance of male skeletons, and the rate of left-sided wounds, a sign of being struck by a predominantly right-handed species. Across all cultures, the spontaneous play of boys centres around the techniques of primitive war: male-bonding, coalitions, and surprise attacks on their "enemies". Whether or not we like to admit it, the propensity resides in male brains, and all men start to practice it when they are just boys. The evolutionary benefit: the genes of the killers were the genes that survived (Buss, 2005; Buss & Duntley, 2000; Chagnon, 1988; Wrangham, 1999; Wrangham & Peterson, 1996).

To Freud, the primal father was the original image of God; here he snatches defeat from the jaws of victory. He thinks the religious explanation is right, that some sort of god actually played a part in the origin of the prohibition against killing. It was a god's influence, not any insight into social necessity, that constructed it.

> And the displacement of man's will onto God is fully justified. For men knew that they had disposed of their father by violence, and in their reaction to that impious deed, they determined to respect his will thence forward. [1927c, p. 42]

Freud believed that religious ideas include not only wish-fulfilment, but actual historical recollections. He poses the parallel that, to complete its development, a human child must pass through a phase of neurosis, because instinctual demands cannot be suppressed by the child's intellect but must be tamed by repression. The infantile neuroses—particularly the obsessional neuroses of childhood—are overcome in the course of development. In the same way, Freud posited, humanity in its development goes through stages analogous to neuroses and repression, something he returned to in *Civilization and Its Discontents* (1930a). For Freud, the instinctual renunciations crucial for our communal existence were achieved only by purely emotional forces. The percipients of a process resembling repression, which took place in prehistoric times, remains attached to civilization for long periods. "Religion would thus be the universal obsessional neurosis of humanity; like the obsessional neurosis of children, it arose out of the Oedipus complex, out of the relation to the father" (1927c, p. 43). Devout believers were guarded against the risk of neurotic illness because their acceptance of the universal neurosis of religion spared them the task of constructing a personal one.

Section IX

Here Freud again argues with his imagined opponent, saying that men cannot be guided by their intelligence but, instead, are ruled by instinct. How can he propose to replace emotional obedience to civilization by rationality? His imagined accuser notes the historical examples of the French Revolution and the then-current Marxist experiment in Russia at the time. Freud could have echoed one of today's notable critics of religion, Richard Dawkins (2006), and his conviction that religious education of children constitutes child abuse:

> Think of the depressing contrast between the radiant intelligence of a healthy child and the feeble intellectual powers of the average child. Can we be quite certain that it is not precisely religious education which bears a large share of the blame for this relative atrophy? I think it would be a very long time before a child who was not influenced began to trouble himself about God and things in another world. Perhaps his thoughts on

> these matters would then take the same path as they did with his forefathers. But we do not wait for such a development; we introduce him to the doctrines of religion at an age when he is neither interested in them nor capable of grasping their import. Is it not true that the two main points in the program for the education of children today are retardation of sexual development and premature religious influences? Thus by the time the child's intellect awakens, the doctrines of religion have already become unassailable. . . . How can we expect people who are under the dominance of prohibitions of thought to attain the psychological ideal, the primacy of the intelligence? [Freud, 1927c, pp. 47–48]

If religious instruction of children were prohibited until they reached the age of reason, might we be able to live in an entirely different world (Hitchens, 2007)? Do children have a fundamental human right to be protected from religious indoctrination (Humphrey, 2002)?

Freud ended the section with an uncharacteristic note of hopefulness: that men would use their scientific knowledge to increase their power further.

> By withdrawing their expectations from the other world and concentrating all their liberated energies into their life on earth, they will probably succeed in achieving a state of things in which life will become tolerable for everyone and civilization no longer oppressive to anyone. [1927c, p. 50]

Section X

Here Freud's imagined interlocutor chastises him for creating an illusion of his own: that generations spared the influence of religious doctrine in early childhood would easily attain the desired primacy of reason over instinct. Religion could be expelled from European civilization only if another system replaced it, his opponent points out, and that system would need to ultimately take over all the psychological characteristics of religion, including rigidity and tolerance, and prohibition of thought. Given the nature of human development, only through emotional forces could a child be induced to renounce instinct and master the task of life. His imagined opponent supports retaining the religious system as the basis of practicality, arguing that society wait until adulthood to influence an individual and pointing out the importance of imposing on a child some doctrinal system that shall operate in a way that admits no criticism. Of course, Freud's faux-opponent notes, the religious system is by far the most suitable for this purpose because of its wish fulfilling and power of consolation.

Freud acknowledges the difficulty of avoiding illusions and agrees that his hopes also may be illusory. But, he adds, there is no penalty for not sharing his illusions, which may be corrected by others. Unlike religion, his illusions are not also delusional. To his literary foe, he writes: "I think you are defending a lost cause. . . . The voice of the intellect is a soft one, but it does not rest until it has gained a hearing" (1927c, p. 53).

And then he delivers the final, fatal thrust.

> Observe the difference between your attitude to illusions and mine. You have to defend the religious illusion with all your might. If it becomes discredited—and indeed the threat to it is great enough—then your world collapses. There is nothing left for you but the despair of everything, of civilization and the future of mankind. From that bondage I am, we are, free. Since we are prepared to renounce a good part of our infantile wishes, we can bear it if a few of our expectations turn out to be illusions. [p. 54]

Conclusion

Religion's usefulness now lies in the past. Its foundational texts are obvious fables. Religion is a man-made burden that remains the enemy of reason, science, and free inquiry (Hitchens, 2007). It has been and continues to be an accessory to ignorance, guilt, murder, genocide, bigotry, racism, apartheid, slavery, misogyny, genital mutilation, persecution of homosexuals, the spread of AIDS, the re-emergence of polio, opposition to the vaccine against cervical cancer, impeding child immunization, obstructing basic medical research, tyranny, and suicide terrorism, to name only a few. It offers no useful explanation for anything. Religion resists the overwhelming evidence of the origins of our universe, our species, and our insignificant place in the natural world. The telescope and microscope destroyed any justification for its continued existence (Hitchens, 2007). Religion now only impedes political, social, and scientific advances. But because religion is man-made, an unfortunate by-product of parts of our mind designed to solve problems of evolutionary survival, we will remain vulnerable to its seductive tentacles.

The Future of an Illusion inspired the 13-year-old Christopher Hitchens, the author of *God Is Not Great.* Today Hitchens argues for the need for a renewed Enlightenment based on the proposition that the proper study of mankind is only man and woman. The fruits of unfettered scientific inquiry, with the availability of discoveries by electronic means to any willing citizen, will be harvested daily. Literature and poetry will be studied for their own sake and the eternal ethical questions they explore. Religion shall be banished from the discourse (Hitchens, 2007). The degree to which we can diminish religion's hold on our world is perhaps the greatest contribution we can make to the future of civilization (Weinberg, 2006).

Today we too can gain renewed inspiration from Freud's work in our fight for rationality over religion. He was ahead of his time in seeing that religion is a product of human minds and therefore open to scientific, psychological investigation. He may have erred in some of his conclusions, but on the fundamentals he was sound. Religion arises from unconscious processes, captures adaptive structures of our psychology, and derails rationality.

Freud asserts that what makes mankind truly different from all life on earth is not the specialness of being chosen by a supernatural power, but the specialness of self-reflective consciousness and the power of reason and science. There is no better response to religious critics of disbelief, reason, and science than Freud's closing statement:

> No, our science is no illusion. But an illusion it would be to suppose that what science cannot give us we can get elsewhere. [p. 56]

NOTES

I am deeply grateful to Salman Akhtar who invited a Darwinian fundamentalist to contribute to this volume and provided invaluable editorial assistance to the original draft. Clare Aukofer, as always, worked her skilled magic on my prose. Richard Dawkins, Daniel Dennett, Sam Harris, and Christopher Hitchens stood as my intellectual godfathers as I wrote this chapter. Their courage, clarity, and insights inspire.

4

Religious fundamentalism and violence

Vamık D. Volkan

This chapter describes what is meant by religious fundamentalism and the kinds of unconscious motivations that make some individuals cling to exaggerated religiosity. It also focuses on religious fundamentalism as a shared group process as it occurs in religious cults. An examination of the characteristics of an extreme religious cult provides a necessary platform from which we can take a closer look at global violent fundamentalist religious movements like al-Qaeda.

Definition

The English term *fundamentalism* as it relates to religious self-definition was coined in the late 1920s in the United States. Two Union Oil tycoons in California, Lyman and Milton Stewart, financed the publication of a series of pamphlets called *The Fundamentals*, which enumerated five points essential for Christian orthodoxy: biblical inerrancy, the virgin birth, Christ's atonement and resurrection, the authenticity of miracles, and dispensationalism. At that time "fundamentalists" were simply defenders of these five doctrines

(Balmer, 1989). Even though the term "fundamentalism" in relation to religion was first used in the 1920s, earlier in history and on countless occasions, individuals or groups from many parts of the world and from practically every faith turned to exaggerated religiosity.

The term fundamentalism in any religion is associated with the believers' list of unchangeable doctrines and is defined "in terms of its disciplined opposition to non-believers and 'lukewarm' believers alike" (Marty & Appleby, 1995, p. 1). Individuals and small or large groups who are involved in extreme religious fundamentalism believe they have a special relationship with divine power. Accordingly, they differentiate themselves from "others" in a strict fashion. The omnipotence associated with the belief in their special relationship with a divine power, combined with a determination to stand apart from non-believers or lukewarm believers, may lead to violence when "others" are perceived as threatening. However, religious fundamentalist movements, even the extreme ones, are not always violent. For example, "Old Believers" of Russian origin who are very strict fundamentalist religious individuals and who came to Estonia's Lake Peipsi region over 400 years ago are peaceful people. Violence belonged to their distant ancestors but not to them (Volkan, 1997).

There are fundamentalist religious groups within almost every faith tradition: Judaism, Christianity, Islam, Buddhism, Hinduism, Sikhism, and Confucianism. Since 11 September 2001, however, at least in the United States and the so-called Western world, the label "fundamentalism" has evolved as a pejorative word mainly associated with Islam. Meanwhile, Christian or Judaic fundamentalists are described by the terms "conservative" or "religious right".

Can psychoanalysis offer a theory to understand religious fundamentalism and its extreme forms? Prior to answering this question, a brief review of the psychoanalytic understanding of religion is warranted.

Psychoanalysis on religion

After noticing a close similarity between obsessive acts and religious practices, Freud viewed obsessional neurosis as a distorted private religion, and religion as a kind of universal obsessional neurosis. According to him, any individual's religious commitment is an expression of unresolved psychological issues from childhood. The terrifying impressions of helplessness in childhood arouse the need for protection, which can be provided through the love of a father. The duration of one's sense of helplessness—overt or covert—throughout life, Freud concluded, makes it necessary to seek an omnipotent father, an image of God, to assuage the feeling of vulnerability; thus, religion is related to shared illusion (Freud, 1901b, 1927c). Accordingly, there has been spoken—and sometimes unspoken—"animosity" between religion and psychoanalysis. Some psychoanalysts questioned Freud's assumptions. For example, Waelder (1960) concludes that Freud's ideas "may well be correct for the father religions, the latecomers in religious history, but [they] do not offer a complete elucidation of this psychogenesis" (p. 59). Nevertheless, as Loewald wrote in 1978, "under the weight of [Freud's] authority religion in psychoanalysis has been largely considered a sign of man's mental immaturity" (p. 57), an illusion "to be given up as we are able to overcome our childish needs for all-powerful parents" (p. 57). Loewald associated religion with the primary process. But he also stated that the secondary process is nourished by the former. Thus, Loewald opened a way for psychoanalysts to discuss the topic of religion, question Freud's assumptions, and add their own views (Sokolowski, 1990).

Winnicott's (1953) paper on transitional objects and transitional phenomena gave psychoanalysts a new way of understanding religion and its universality. During the first years of life, the transitional object becomes the first item that clearly represents "not-me" in the child's mind. Though this first "not-me" image corresponds to a thing that actually exists in the world, the transitional object is not entirely "not me" because it is also a substitute for the child's mother, whom the child's mind does not yet fully understand as a separate individual in her own right and whom the toddler perceives to be under his or her absolute control (an illusion, of course). Through a teddy-bear or a melody that is utilized as a transitional object or phenomenon, the child begins to know the surrounding world. It is not part of the child, so it signifies the reality "out there" beyond the child's internal world, the "not-me" that the child slowly discovers and "creates". What is "created" at first does not respond to reality as perceived by an adult through logical thinking. The child's "reality", while playing with a transitional object or phenomenon, is a combination of reality and illusion. Winnicott wrote:

> Transitional objects and transitional phenomena belong to the realm of illusion which is at the basis of initiation of experience. . . . This intermediate area of experience, unchallenged in respect of its belonging to inner or external (shared) reality, constitutes the greater part of the infant's experience, and throughout life is retained in the intense experiencing that belongs to the arts and to religion and to imaginative living, and to creative scientific work. [Winnicott, 1953, p. 242]

Long ago Freud, in a letter to Ludwig Binswanger, describes himself as dwelling in a basement while distinguished aristocratic guests such as art and religion visit an upper floor. He added, "If I had another working life ahead of me, I should undertake to find a place in my low hamlet for these aristocrats" (Binswanger, 1956, p. 115). It can be said that Winnicott brought these distinguished guests to Freud's basement.

Meissner (1984) reminds us that just as a transitional object can degenerate into a (pathological) fetish, "transitional religious experience can be distorted into less authentic, relatively fetishistic directions that tend to contaminate and distort the more profoundly meaningful aspects of the religious experience" (p. 107). Making peace between psychoanalysis and religion in the psychoanalytic literature continues; Blass (2004) provides a more recent example.

A metapsychology of religious fundamentalism

We can formulate a metapsychology of religious fundamentalism by accepting Winnicott's (1953) description of transitional object and transitional phenomenon, as well as Greenacre's (1970), Modell's (1970), and my (Volkan, 1976) expansion of these concepts as examined from an object-relations point of view. Elaborations on transitional objects and transitional phenomena allowed us to see more clearly the progressive, healing, and creative aspects of religious beliefs and feelings, as well as their regressive, destructive, and restrictive aspects. In order to focus on both aspects, I use the analogy of an imaginary lantern with one transparent side and one opaque side situated between infants or toddlers and their actual environment (Volkan, 2004; Volkan & Kayatekin, 2006). When toddlers feel comfortable, fed, well rested, and loved, they turn the transparent side towards the real things that surround them, illuminating these things, which they now begin to perceive as entities separate from themselves. When infants feel uncomfortable, hungry, or sleepy, they turn the opaque side of the lantern towards the frustrating outside world. At such times, we imagine that their minds experience a sense of cosmic omnipotence.

In "normal" development, toddlers play with their "lanterns" hundreds and hundreds of times, getting to know reality in one direction and succumbing, for all practical purposes, to a lonely, omnipotent, and narcissistic existence in the other direction, until their minds begin to retain unchangeable external realities, such as having a mother separate from themselves who is sometimes gratifying and at other times frustrating. During such repeated "play" toddlers' minds learn both to differentiate and to fuse illusion and reality, omnipotence and restricted ability, and suspension of disbelief and the impact of the real world. If their development is normal, they eventually develop an acceptance of the "not-me" world and adjust to logical thinking.

I suggest that humans have what I call "moments of rest" during which there is no need to differentiate between what is real and what is illusion, times when logical thinking need not be maintained. It is during these moments that the relation to the transitional object or phenomenon and playing with it echoes throughout a lifetime. During "moments of rest" a Christian might simultaneously know that it is biologically impossible for a woman to have a baby without the semen of a man but also believe in the virgin birth. Rationally, people might know that no one really sees angels, but they may behave as if angels exist. In other words, the *function* of the transitional object and phenomenon remains available to humans for the rest of their lives. The need for "moments of rest" varies from individual to individual and from social group to social group. Some people declare that they do not require such religious "moments of rest", but perhaps they refer to the same function by different names. For example, they may "play" the game of linking magical and real in astrology, or paint abstract paintings that represent a mixture of illusion and reality, or write poetry or become very good psychoanalysts who can easily travel between primary-process and secondary-process thinking with their associated affects and become models for their patients to do the same without much anxiety until they modify their psychic realities.

Metapsychologically we can say that religious fundamentalists are preoccupied with keeping the opaque side of the lantern turned against the real world that is perceived as threatening and frustrating. They refuse to travel between illusion and reality and attempt to keep illusion as their own special reality. Unlike infants who can probably block out the external world more thoroughly, adult fundamentalists are more aware of an environment that they perceive as threatening. This is a key reason why an extreme form of religious fundamentalism has the potential to strike out against threatening objects.

The imaginary lantern refers to the existence of a phase of life when illusions are "normal". It does not, however, offer ideas as to why children belonging to different large groups choose various religious beliefs and why some internalize fundamentalist religious ideas from childhood on and why some others, later in life, are attracted to exaggerated and sometimes violent specific religious doctrines.

When we are born we do not know what religion is, nor do we comprehend ethnicity or nationality. Erikson (1966) called children *generalists*: they do not belong to a large-group identity. As they grow up, children begin to possess a mixture of large-group identities, such as religion and ethnicity. They have no choice. Ownership in a large-group identity, such as a religious, ethnic, or national shared one, primarily depends on who children identify with in their early environment and what these people "deposit" in the children's developing self-representations. *Identification* is a well-known psychoanalytic concept that explains how children actively internalize and assimilate object images and functions associated with them. *Depositing* is a related concept in which an adult is more active than the child in putting certain self- and object images of their own into the child's developing self-representation (a form of *stable* projective identification) and then, mostly unconsciously and chronically, manipulating the child to perform certain tasks in order to maintain the deposited images within (Volkan, 1997). Parents and religious mentors such as priests or *imams* who are sanctioned by parents deposit images of prophets and other religious figures into the developing self-representations of children. The most organized and socially sanctioned "propaganda" for a better way of life comes from religious organizations (Volkan & Kayatekin, 2006). Due to experiences with environment, identifications, and elements that are "deposited" into them as children, some people grow up as fundamentalist religious individuals. Others, for personal reasons, will turn to an exaggerated religiosity later in life.

Two cases

Serpil

Serpil, a 25-year-old Turkish political science student, was barred from attending a prominent university in Turkey because she insisted on covering her head in the Muslim style. Women who cover their heads are not allowed to attend classes at Turkish universities, so instead of removing her headscarf while in the classroom in order to continue her education in Turkey, Serpil chose to emigrate to Austria, where there are no rules concerning female university students' head attire.

Serpil comes from a modern educated Turkish family. No one on either her father's or her mother's side of the family was religious, and no woman wore a headscarf. When Serpil was a prepubescent child, her father moved the family to a rather isolated location in Anatolia, the heartland of Turkey, for professional reasons. She had one younger sister and a happy home. While she was going through her adolescent passage (Blos, 1979) and searching for idealized objects, she idealized her father and felt very close to him. During a national holiday, youngsters from different schools participated in a parade and public dancing in a nearby city. Serpil prepared hard for this event and went to this city occasionally to rehearse for the parade and the dancing, wearing a costume with a rather short skirt. One day her father, who had accompanied her to this city, noted a young man's interest in his daughter, and when they returned home he gave her a stern lecture and asked her to be more careful about showing her legs to male teenagers. Serpil, who was at the peak of idealization of her father, was shocked. She thought that she had lost her father's unconditional love and her identity as her father's favourite "other", and she felt rage towards him. The following day Serpil's father was called for a work emergency in the countryside, and while driving there very fast he had an accident and died instantly. Serpil was filled with guilt feelings for having hated her father the day before. As years passed, she could not mourn her father's death. She became very religious and was convinced that she would meet her father again in heaven when she died. Eventually she covered her head, since she believed that that is what a good Muslim woman should do. For Serpil, external danger came from relatives and friends who, using logical thinking and references to science, tried to interfere with her belief that one day she would meet her father. Thus, she escaped to Austria, a Christian country that, paradoxically, was safer since most people there would not question her extreme religious beliefs.

Serpil spoke very fast. When she consulted me she was intellectually aware that she had not mourned her loss, so when I likened her peculiar speech pattern to a speeding car, she easily realized that her "symptom" was in the service of keeping her father alive: his mental representation that Serpil kept within her internal world was still speeding in his car, and the outcome of his reckless driving was not yet determined. In spite of her intellectual understanding of the link between her inability to mourn and her turning to religion, Serpil continued to declare: "My religion says that I will meet my father in heaven. Can anyone give me a guarantee that this is not so? Since there is no proof against my belief, I will follow all the fundamentals of my Muslim religion."

Serpil's case illustrates an individual's wish and illusion to fulfil a desire in another life through the utilization of a religion that exists within her society. One wonders if Serpil might have found another avenue for dealing with her guilt feelings and complicated mourning had not religious preoccupations in her cultural/societal environment already been stirred up.

At the time Serpil was going through the process of deciding to wear a headscarf, a religious political party had come to power in Turkey, and the various types of Muslim religious *tarikats* [cults], which would have been suppressed in the past, began to spread. The wives of prominent ruling political party figures such as the prime minister and the minister of foreign affairs, were—and still are—covering their heads. Thus, for a young woman looking for a magical solution to ease her guilt feelings for "killing" her father by her rage and to deal with a complicated mourning, there were "identification figures" to follow that eased her internal tension. The government was unsuccessfully fighting the legal and educational authorities to allow women who were covering their heads to attend classes at the Turkish universities, and Serpil took the government's side in this fight. The psychology of her behaviour is, of course, more complicated. A person in perennial mourning (Volkan, 1981) not only wishes to bring the dead person back—even in the next world, as the religion promises—but also to "kill" the dead person in order to complete the mourning process once and for all. Serpil's taking the side of the religious people and fighting her university—whose president once told me how the university was a bastion of modernity against religious assaults—was also Serpil's way of "killing" her "modern" father.

Paterson

I also analysed Paterson, who was in his mid-thirties when he became my analysand and who fit the description of a fundamentalist Christian very well. One day, when Paterson was at the oedipal age, his alcoholic father died while little Paterson was lying next to him. Paterson's mother moved to her parents' home with her son and began to share her bed with him, thereby encouraging his fantasy of oedipal triumph and his unconscious "belief" that he was his father's killer. One year later little Paterson's life turned upside down. One day, without any preparation, he was taken to a farm—the home of his new stepfather, whom he had not met until that day. His mother began to share her bed with this new husband, and Paterson was, in a sense, exiled to a lonely second-class place in the attic while his new stepsiblings had their own nice bedrooms. He felt that on the farm he was used like a slave. As could be expected, he turned his murderous rage towards his stepfather and his stepsiblings. One day during puberty he saw a dog delivering and then feeding her puppies. For Paterson, the newborn puppies unconsciously represented his stepsiblings, so he found a gun and shot the puppies to death. After this event, his vision of himself as a "murderer" crystallized in his mind. He had "sinned".

Besides his identifications with religious others in his community and besides the religious "propaganda" that he was exposed to while growing up, his "sinfulness" was Paterson's main motivation for turning to fundamentalist religion as an adult in order to be saved by Jesus. He developed extremely narcissistic social and sexual masochism and lived under a metaphorical "glass bubble" (Volkan, 1979), which covered his lonely but omnipotent kingdom. The rather large silver cross Paterson wore around his neck created a border between his glass bubble and the nonbelievers. As we worked together, Paterson induced a great deal of countertransference feelings in me. I was able, I believe, to handle them therapeutically and help Paterson escape his "glass bubble" and stop being so omnipotent yet masochistic.

Religiousness has been shown to be highly prevalent among psychiatric patients, especially among those with schizophrenia who exhibit religious delusions and hallucinations (Kirov, Kemp, Kirov, & David, 1998; Pieper, 2004). Paterson and Serpil were not psychotic; they used religion to cope with their internal mental conflicts. I am sure that neither will turn to violence, but others who are also not psychotic and who cling to fundamentalist religion may. I will mention two well-known cases: The first is Dr Benjamin Goldstein (later known as Baruch Goldstein). On 25 February 1994 Baruch Goldstein killed 29 and wounded over 100 Muslim worshipers in the Ibrahimi Mosque at the Cave of the Patriarchs in Israel. The second case is Mohammed Bouyeri, the Dutch-born son of Muslim Moroccan immigrants. In the name of religion he killed Theo Van Gogh, the great-great nephew of the renowned Dutch painter Vincent Van Gogh, as Van Gogh was riding his bicycle to work in Amsterdam on 2 November 2004 (Volkan & Kayatekin, 2006). I have no in-depth information about the personal psychological motivations that turned these two individuals into murderers.

When threats from the outside world become magnified, persons with religious fundamentalism may seek the company of others who also keep the opaque sides of their lanterns turned against the real world. Serpil received support from the growing religious fundamentalist movements in Turkey, and Paterson belonged to a fundamentalist church in Virginia that was actively using religion to influence social and political processes. Others seek comfort by joining cults or *tarikats* in the hope that the leaders of such religious organizations will make their uncomfortable "moments of rest" comfortable. Alas, such radical fundamentalist leaders also possess a lantern with an opaque side facing the outside world, magnifying the dangers that exist "out there". While there are peaceful cults and *tarikats*, others may carry out sociopolitical abuse that goes well beyond generating excessive propaganda or using religion to elect politicians or damage the reputation of others. They may also turn violent acts against themselves.

Encapsulated fundamentalism

In late 1995 I accepted an invitation to chair a Select Advisory Commission to the Federal Bureau of Investigation's (FBI) Critical Incident Response Group charged with examining insights gleaned from the behavioural sciences that might enhance the agency's ability to respond to crises such as the one in 1993 when the FBI attacked and burned the Waco cult compound in Texas. David Koresh was the compound's resident "prophet" who died in the attack. My chairmanship allowed me to study various Christian, Muslim, and Jewish religious cults in addition to those involved in the Waco tragedy (Volkan, 2004), but I have no in-depth information of similar movements in other religions.

In addition to David Koresh's Branch Davidians in Waco, some other cults and fundamentalist religious organizations can be considered *encapsulated* fundamentalist religious movements: Islamic *tarikats*, Jim Jones's Temple in Jonestown, Shoko Asahara's Japanese Aum Shinrikyo, Joseph's DiMambro's Order of Solar Temple, Gush Emunim in Israel, and even, in their initial stages, Hamas in Lebanon and Mullah Omar's Taliban in Afghanistan, to name just a few (Mayer, 1998; Moses-Hrushovski, 2000; Volkan, 2004; Volkan & Kayatekin, 2006; Weber, 1999; Wessinger, 1999). By the term "encapsulated" I am referring to movements that remain isolated within one large group and that often induce negative feelings and/or fear in those outside the movement within the same large group. Psychological processes that we see in individuals such as

Serpil and Paterson echo the psychology of religious cult leaders and, in turn, ten common characteristics of *extreme* religious cults or *tarikats*:

1. *A divine text.* Each encapsulated cult or *tarikat* has its own "divine text", whether it is written on paper or passed along verbally. For example, the text may be a specific version of the Bible, or an interpretation of certain verses of the Qu'ran. The "divine text" is irrefutable, non-negotiable.
2. *An absolute leader who is the interpreter of the divine text.* The leader of an encapsulated extreme religious fundamentalist movement is the sole interpreter of the group's divine text. No other interpretations are acceptable. The leader is usually a man: only rarely is the leader a woman.
3. *Total loyalty.* Membership in a cult or *tarikat* provides a sense of belonging for its followers. The members' total loyalty to the leader and to the divine text "removes" anxiety they might have due to intrapsychic and interpersonal conflicts, especially those that threaten individuals' identities.
4. *Tangible incentives.* Cults and *tarikats* create tangible incentives and economic dependence to ensure that members do not leave the group. The putative divine rule infiltrates members' everyday existence and intimate personal relationships, fundamentally changing them.
5. *Feeling omnipotent yet victimized.* Restricted extreme fundamentalist religious groups are pessimistic movements (Sivan, 1985). Pessimism arises because the members perceive their specific religious "fundamentals" to be continually under attack by nonbelievers or even lukewarm believers, Darwinists, Freudians, scientists, and rival religious fundamentalist groups that cite other texts as truly divine. Paradoxically, because they believe that their text is the true divine guide and their leader is the only true spiritual leader, a sense of omnipotence exists among the members of such groups.
6. *Extreme sadistic and/or masochistic acts.* The contamination of a shared sense of pessimism with a shared sense of omnipotence creates a special condition that allows extreme sadism or masochism to become tolerable. When a restricted extreme religious

fundamentalist group perceives a threat to the divine authority of the leader and to the survival of the group and its identity, the protection of the group and its identity becomes its primary preoccupation. The group feels entitled to destroy "others" who are seen as threatening to the group's survival. For example, in 1980, in Kano, Nigeria, sect leader Alhaji Mohammadu (Maitatsine) Marva, who had proclaimed a new era of anti-materialist reformed Islam, led his followers to the central mosque in Kano, where "non-believers" or "lukewarm believers" of his ideas were gathered. This event led to the killing of an estimated 8,000 people. The cult can also express its omnipotence with a grand masochistic gesture such as a massive suicide, like the one at Jim Jones's Temple in Jonestown. Those who kill themselves believe that through death they will merge with the divine leader and/or God, the omnipotent object, and thus crystallize their omnipotence and continue their existence in heaven.

7. *Alteration of the shared "morality".* What we observe in an extremely violent restricted religious fundamentalist group is the existence of an altered shared "morality" (altered shared superego) that accepts mass suicides or mass killings in the service of maintaining a tie to a divine power.

8. *Creation of borders.* Even during "safe times" when there is no imminent threat to the group's security, an encapsulated extreme religious fundamentalist organization builds physical borders like walls or barricades. But more importantly, they also build psychological borders around themselves, such as by wearing a specific colour or style of dress, a turban or a fur hat that separates them from others.

9. *Changing of family, gender, and sexual norms within the "borders".* As the leader of an extreme and restricted religious fundamentalist movement becomes more divine and omnipotent, he or she may become "the father", "the mother" and "the lover" for all the followers. Routine family systems become disturbed, and child-rearing practices change drastically. So-called "family values" are replaced by the leader's interpretation of the "divine text". The role of women is usually reduced to giving sex (pleasure) and food (milk) to the leader or other men belonging to the same group. Sometimes the cult leader "owns"

all the women and children in the group, just as David Koresh did at the Waco compound. In most *tarikats* women are forced to cover their faces or their bodies.

10. *Negative feelings and fear among outsiders.* Because an encapsulated extreme fundamentalist religious group feels special, divine, secretive, magical, omnipotent, masochistic or sadistic, and because they erect borders around themselves, they induce negative feelings and fear among people who live outside their borders. Outsiders perceive encapsulated extreme religious cults or similar organizations as a threat to their own religious or other belief systems.

Globalized fundamentalism

An encapsulated extreme fundamentalist religious movement starts to become generalized when the majority of "bystanders" within the large group, rather than having and maintaining negative feelings and fear about the movement, begin to support it, directly or indirectly. There are numerous causes that spread the influence of an encapsulated extreme fundamentalist religious organization. If the people in a society have gone through a massive trauma and have felt humiliated and helpless, the idea of a saviour becomes attractive to them. Such circumstances create an atmosphere that supports the emergence of a narcissistic political leader who believes in his or her own superior skills and who may, in the long run, either become very destructive or raise the followers' shared self-esteem (Volkan, 1980). Under similar societal circumstances, a cult or *tarikat* with extreme fundamentalist religious beliefs contaminated with its leader's omnipotence can also be attractive for the society as an answer to their existing misery. Traumatized societies, like traumatized children, tend to identify with feared objects (Šebek, 1994), and this leads members of such a society to gather under a shared superego that allows violence. Along with the appearance of shared psychological tendencies in traumatized societies, one should consider sociopolitical manipulations, coercions, propaganda, and economic incentives when examining the expansion of the influence of an extreme fundamentalist religious organization. The Taliban, whose name means "religious students", rose to power in

Afghanistan's post-Soviet wretchedness, its members originally recruited mostly from among young Pashtuns, Afghanistan's largest ethnic group. They first came to notice in late 1994, when they were hired to drive local bandit groups away from a 30-truck convoy that was trying to open a trade route between Pakistan and Central Asia. Eventually, the Taliban grew from that original core group of about 100 into a cohort of 35,000 men from 43 countries. The generalization and later globalization of the Taliban occurred after they presented themselves to bystanders as an antidote to corruption and after their leader, Mullah Omar, publicly put his arms into the sleeves of a cloak that was believed to have belonged to the Prophet Mohammed. In a sense, Mullah Omar illustrated a "concrete" connection to the prophet. The symbolism connected with this event significantly and psychologically motivated, I believe, the spread of Taliban's influence in Afghanistan (Volkan, 2004).

It goes without saying that today the best-known global fundamentalist religious movement is known as the al-Qaeda movement. Its leader Osama bin Laden is not the only recent figure to inflame what historian Bernard Lewis (1990) called "Muslim rage". Long before 11 September 2001 it was clear that Islamic religious fundamentalism, even its extreme forms, would find emotional support among large Islamic groups, especially in the Arab world, and that it could easily become globalized. Bernard Lewis noted:

> Islamic fundamentalism has given an aim and a form to the otherwise aimless and formless resentment and anger of the Muslim masses at the forces that have devalued their traditional values and loyalties and, in the final analysis, robbed them of their beliefs, their aspirations, their dignity, and to an increasing extent even their livelihood. [Lewis, 1990, p. 59]

Volkan and Kayatekin (2006) focused on the role played by modern Turkey's removal of the Caliphate in inducing a shared trauma in many parts of the so-called Islamic world.

On the surface, the characteristics of a global extreme fundamentalist religious movement seem different from those of encapsulated extreme religious groups. For example, al-Qaeda resembles a giant global commercial corporation, with secret funds and representatives in various countries and with a shared ideology contaminated with strict religious doctrines. It strives to become a world power by using any means, from engaging in effective political and religious propaganda to making financial deals. But it also performs horrendous acts of violence. Al-Qaeda complains about the Western commercial/technical/cultural/religious organizations that have infiltrated the Islamic world through "globalization" and are humiliating Muslims. While the technological and economic gains through globalization may be acceptable, a shared feeling of humiliation associated with globalization remains alive. In response to this, al-Qaeda has become, in a sense, a more drastic and more sadistic mirror image of Western globalization.

The characteristics that we can see more clearly in encapsulated extreme fundamentalist religious movements are present within the al-Qaeda movement as well. It contains a "divine" ideology (Salafism), and Osama bin Laden is its interpreter. (For an attempt to understand his internal motivations for turning to extreme religious fundamentalism, see Volkan, 2004; Volkan & Kayatekin, 2006.) Osama bin Laden has declared the United States and the West in general as the enemy and has "received permission" from Koranic passages such as Surah 8, verse 17, to strike at the "enemy". Followers blindly idealize Osama bin Laden—and the leaders of the local cells. They feel victimized but omnipotent and experience an altered "morality". They have built "borders" around themselves in order to maintain their large-group identity, and therefore we seldom know where they are and where they are hiding. "Divine" ideology replaces family values and many old traditional and religious beliefs.

Al-Qaeda induces extreme negative feelings and fear in "outsiders" in faraway locations, but many people in the locations populated by Muslims where al-Qaeda's influence is present, although not terrorist themselves, most probably have direct or hidden sentiments in support of the movement. This last characteristic basically differentiates this global extreme religious fundamentalist movement from an encapsulated one. What is most important is that when an extreme and violent religious fundamentalist movement such as al-Qaeda becomes globalized, it becomes intertwined with the psychology of large-group identity issues.

One can visualize Freud's (1921c) theory about large groups and their leaders as a gathering of people around a large Maypole, which represents the group's leader, joined as if in a May Day dance of identification with each other and of idealization and support of the leader. We can build upon this metaphor by imagining a large cloth over these people, a "tent canvas" of large-group identity. Following Erikson's (1956) description of individual identity, we can describe the large-group identity of tens of thousands, or even millions, of people—most of whom will never meet each other in their lifetimes—who share a persistent sense of sameness (we-ness). While people under a large-group tent are divided into subgroups (clans, occupations), they wear the tent canvas as a shared garment. At different times in history and at different locations in the world a child becomes the "reservoir" for deposited elements of one type of large-group identity more than elements of another kind of large-group identity, and so identifies with such elements. In some areas of the world large-group identity is primarily defined by religion and in other places the large-group identity is primarily defined by ethnicity. Usually various types of large-group identities are intertwined. In our routine lives, we are not necessarily aware of our connections with our large-group processes: we do not wake up each morning feeling intensely Catholic or Sunni Muslim or Italian or Uzbek. In our routine lives we are more concerned with subgroups under the tent—families or professional organizations, for example. In ordinary times, our relationship with our large-group identity is like breathing: while we breathe constantly, we do not usually notice that we are doing it unless our ability to breathe is threatened, such as if we are caught in a smoke-filled house on fire. When the large-group identity is threatened, people under the metaphorical tent become like the people who are caught in a smoke-filled room: they become constantly aware of their large-group identities and become preoccupied with its protection and maintenance, even if this preoccupation leads to destructive acts (Volkan, 1997, 2004, 2006).

When a global extreme fundamentalist religious movement weaves new religious symbols into the cloth of the metaphorical large group, that large group can be abused or manipulated in the name of one god or another. In conflicts between large groups where gods are present, gods cannot be questioned and gods do not negotiate: they give followers permission to kill nonbelievers and even "lukewarm" believers in order to protect and maintain the "new" shared identity and/or die in order to find omnipotence in eternity—an illusion.

Last remarks

Leaders' exploitation of people through religion has, I suspect, been occurring since the beginning of human history. I am reminded of cynical remarks made by Napoleon long ago:

> When one man is dying of hunger while his neighbour has too much to eat, he cannot accept this difference unless there is an authority which tells him: It is the will of God; there must be poor people and the rich people in the world; but later on, and throughout eternity, the distribution will be done in a different way. [Duverger, 1968, p. 174]

Some manipulations are mild, while others initiate most destructive acts. Psychoanalysts who are interested in contributing to the understanding of extreme fundamentalist religious movements, encapsulated or globalized, should not simply focus on affected individuals' personal perceptions of gods representing loving fathers and images of large groups representing nurturing mothers. Rather, they should focus on the psychology of large-group identity and how this identity can be manipulated to make people ready to do anything, including massive sadistic and masochistic deeds, in the illusory belief that they are protecting the large-group identity or bringing attention to it so that its continuing existence can be witnessed (Volkan, 1997, 2006). Those psychoanalysts who are willing to work in this area should, I believe, also be prepared to join in interdisciplinary work, since no scientific discipline alone can explain the horrific sociopolitical abuse of religion we have been watching lately on television and reading about in our newspapers.

5

The morality of an "oppressed group"

George A. Awad

In this chapter I focus on one aspect of Freud's *The Future of an Illusion*—namely, the morality of the group that he variously referred to as "underprivileged", "suppressed", "oppressed" and "uneducated:"

> These *underprivileged* classes will envy the favoured ones their privileged classes and will do all they can to free themselves from their own surplus of privation. . . . it is understandable that the *suppressed* people should develop an intense hostility towards a culture whose existence they make possible by their work, but in whose wealth they have too small a share. . . . It goes without saying that a civilization which leaves so large a number of its participants unsatisfied and drives them into revolt neither has nor deserves the prospect of a lasting existence. [Freud, 1927c, p. 12; italics added]

Subsequently:

> Civilization has little fear from educated people and brain-workers. In them the replacement of religious motives for civilized behaviour by other, secular motives would proceed unobtrusively; moreover, such people are to a large extent themselves

> vehicles of civilization. But it is another matter with the great masses of *the uneducated and the oppressed,* who have every reason for being enemies of civilization. [p. 39; italics added]

The group that I focus on is one of the Radical Islamists—followers of the ideology of Sayyid Qutb[1] and as expressed in action by the al-Qaeda.[2] They combine the sense of oppression with religion to justify their ideology, morality, and actions, even though they are not necessarily "underprivileged" or "uneducated". The following are my reasons for choosing them:

1. They are a large group, with a known ideology.
2. Qutb's book *Milestones* (1966) describes the formation and the teachings of this group.
3. In limiting my subject to one group and one book, I avoid unsubstantiated generalizations.[3]
4. Freud's essay is about religion; the morality of the radical Islamists is based *exclusively* on their interpretation of religion.

Undoubtedly, most of the Arabs and Muslims feel that they are oppressed. But who are their oppressors? In political propaganda the finger often points to external sources. However, Qutb focuses on the Arab and Muslim rulers, on imperialism and Zionism, as the sources of the oppression. *Milestones* was written in 1966, a time of personal despair, when the majority of his intended audience had turned their backs on Islamist ideology. These were the days of Nasser, Arab nationalism, socialism, and secularism. Furthermore, Qutb was ill and in jail, his compatriots were persecuted, and there was an incident involving opening fire and killing a number of Muslim Brothers in jail. Thus, at a time of despair and when his ideas seemed so far-fetched, the message of this book was an act of hope for the future.

Caveats

1. Radical Islamists constitute a unique minority group and should not be thought to be representative of Islam.[4]
2. Their use of religion to justify their morality is not unique.

There are Christian and Jewish groups who use their religion to justify their morality.

3. Freud focused on "European, Christian civilization" (Freud, 1927c, p. 38). I am focusing on a Middle Eastern Muslim group. Furthermore, the groups that Freud mentioned were part of a larger group. Thus, the "lower strata of society" can find satisfaction in the following brilliant observation by Freud:

   > This satisfaction can be shared in not only by the favoured classes, which enjoy the benefits of the culture, but also by the suppressed ones, since the right to despise the people outside it compensates them for the wrongs they suffer within their own unit. No doubt one is a wretched plebeian, harassed by debts and military service; but, to make up for it, one is a Roman citizen, one has one's share in the task of ruling other nations and dictating their laws. [Freud, 1927c, p. 13]

   Such satisfaction is not available to Radical Muslims, or to any Muslims, because they do not belong to the triumphant Western societies.

4. I do not share Freud's disdain and contempt for the "uneducated" "suppressed" or "oppressed" group. Nor do I share his valuation of the "educated people and brain-workers" (Freud, 1927c, p. 39). In fact, all the originators and many of the followers of Radical Islam are "educated people and brain workers".

The minds of the radical Islamists

The book starts with the following announcements: Communism has failed to provide for the economic needs of the communities[5]; Capitalism has succeeded greatly in providing for economic needs, but failed in providing life-giving values. There is no other way to provide for the spiritual needs of the world except for Islam (*clearly implying that all other religions have failed*). This division between modernity and tradition is characteristic of all post-colonial society. Even Qutb admits the superiority of Western modernity. However, in most groups, tradition was a defensive war against the loss of culture and identity and a means of preserving a sense of continuity. For his own purposes, Qutb changed a defensive war into an offensive war, giving a sense of superiority over the rest of world. For Qutb, the Muslim group whose manners, ideas and concepts, rules and regulations, values and criteria are derived from Islamic sources that vanished hundreds of years ago. Most of the world lives in *Jahilyyah* [ignorance of divine guidance].[6] A new group of Muslim vanguards needs to be constituted to lead the way (Qutb, 1966, p. 67). Qutb's book describes the signposts that this group needs to follow to reach a particular state of consciousness.

The formation of a new group: historical "truth" and isolation

The new group to be formed did not exist in 1966. However, their model is an earlier group: the generation of the companions of the prophet. The companions are described as being "without comparison in the history of Islam, even in the entire history of man" (Qutb, 1966, p. 21). There were three reasons for this:

1. The group lived according to the Qur'an, which was pure, and before Muslims got "mixed" up with other civilizations.
2. The group "turned to the Qur'an to find out what the Almighty Creator had prescribed for him [the prophet] and the group" (p. 27), and learned it slowly.
3. The group consisted of self-selected Muslims who cut themselves off from the *Jahiliyyah*—namely, the non-Muslim community. Thus the goal of the vanguard is to rise above the *Jahiliyyah* society and live only according to the Qur'an, without any "mixing or pollution" (p. 33).

Who were the companions? Most Muslims regard anyone who knew or saw Muhammad, believed in his teachings, and died as a Muslim to be a companion (Rahman, 1979). For example, Rahman stated that, "In Medina there were about thirty thousand, if not more, of the prophet's companions" (p. 61). Furthermore, many early Muslim historians believe this number to be between 100,000 and 124,000. While one may accept that a handful of companions, who were closest to the prophet, were an exceptional group, it is difficult to accept the exceptionality of over 100,000 people who simply saw the prophet.[7]

The issue is not only an idealization of the past, but the presentation of the past as historical "truth". No matter how much one agrees or disagrees with the extent of Spence's (1982) or Schafer's (1992) ideas about narration, no one with any knowledge of memory or reconstruction of the past (Freud, 1927c) would accept Qutb's statements as historical truth. Freud (1910c) warned us:

> It was inevitable that this early history should have been an expression of present beliefs and wishes rather than a true picture of the past; for many things had been dropped from the nation's memory, while others were distorted, and some remains of the past were given a wrong interpretation in order to fit with contemporary ideas. Moreover people's motive for writing history was not objective curiosity but a desire to influence their contemporaries, to encourage and inspire them, or to hold a mirror up before them. [Freud, 1910c, p. 83]

Qutb was writing not out of "objective curiosity" but "to encourage and inspire", as Freud said.

The social and intellectual isolation of the group

According to Qutb, the companions cut themselves off from the *Jahiliyyah*—namely, the non-Muslim community.[8] However, in today's Qutb parlance, *Jahiliyyah* refers to the whole world, including all existing societies. Thus the goal of the vanguards is to rise above the *Jahiliyyah* society and live only according to the Qur'an, without any "mixing or pollution" (Qutb, 1966, p. 33). There is a need to isolate the vanguards socially and intellectually.[9] The social isolation is complete: "A person who bears witness that there is no deity except God and that Muhammad is God's messenger should cut off his relationship of loyalty from the *Jahili* society" (Qutb, 1966, p. 85). "A Muslim has no country except that part of the earth where the *Shari'ah* is established . . . a Muslim has no nationality except his belief . . . a Muslim has no relatives except those who share the belief in God. . . . A Muslim has no relationship with his mother, father, wife and other family members except through their relationship with the Creator, and then they are joined through blood" (pp. 222–223).

Two ideas come together here: the creation of historical "truth" and the isolation of the group. This isolation is reminiscent of the isolation of cults or of an abusive relationship. Such isolation is necessary to induct a new recruit and to preserve the purity of the veterans.

The belief system of the group

God's sovereignty

"*La ilaha illa Allah*" means that "there is no deity except Allah". This refers to "*Uluhiyah*", which means sovereignty only to God (Qutb, 1966, p. 40), and he is clear that God's teachings apply to all times and all places. Thus, with one strike he removes not only "sovereignty" from the current Arab and Muslim leaders, civil or religious, but also their legitimacy. Such ideas did not sit well with the Arabs when they were written; those were the days of Nasser and Arab nationalism. However, when those regimes lost the 1967 War and failed to solve any of the problems facing the Arabs, Qutb's ideas became relevant to larger groups of people.

I think that Freud's ideas about the creation of God are relevant here: "Man not only makes the forces of nature not simply into persons with whom he can associate as he would with his equals . . . but gives them the character of a father. He turns them into gods" (1927c, p. 17). The Arabs were not dealing with the "forces of nature" but with military, economic, and social forces, and they turned to fathers to save them. When those fathers failed, they turned to the ultimate father, God, who is infallible and can never fail.

Specialness of the group

When men accepted God's sovereignty, "mankind was uplifted in its social order, its morals, in all of its life, to a zenith of perfection which has never been attained before and which cannot be attained afterwards except through Islam" (Qutb, 1966, p. 52). When they achieve that state, namely: "when their hearts became free of pride of lineage, of nationality, of country, of tribe, of household—when Allah Most High saw them to be morally *pure*—then he granted them the great trust, the conscious assumption of the *vice-regency* of the earth . . . they would be true guardians of the political authority, which would be entrusted to them so that they would establish the Divine law and the Divine justice" (p. 53; italics added).

The appeal is to the ego ideal, not to the punishing superego. There has once been such a prefect and pure state on earth, and it can be achieved again by following "true" Islam. Such perfection and purity are undoubtedly projections of wishes and fantasies: an illusion, to use Freud's term. There are no doubts in the mind of the radical Islamist: It is a belief or faith about the perfection of that past; you do not have to prove it, it is fact, an act of faith, an axiom. More importantly, it can be repeated. Such ideology appeals to the idealists who are disenchanted with the world and, most importantly, with the Arab and Muslim regimes. Thus "truth", "perfection", and "purity" raised them from hopelessness, helplessness, and humiliation to become God's representatives on earth.

Qutb increases the specialness of this group by focusing on their superiority: "the superiority of the Faith and its value above all values which are derived from a source other than the source of the Faith" (Qutb, 1966, pp. 265–266). Also, "a sense of superiority based on the permanent Truth centered in the very nature of existence" (p. 267).

A total system

Such belief system is all-encompassing. Proclaiming *La Illah ila Allah* and deeply understanding it require a belief in a religion whose "system extends into all aspects of life; it discusses all minor or major affairs of mankind; it orders man's life—not only in this world but also of the world to come; it gives information about the unseen as well as about the visible world; it not only deals with material things but also purifies intentions and ideas" (Qutb, 1966, p. 55).

The idealization of Islamic society

"Among the concrete and brilliant results of this attitude was that Islamic society became an open and all-inclusive community in which people of various races, nations, languages and colours were members, there remain no trace of these low animalistic traits" (Qutb, 1966, p. 88).

Even though Islam had always had a universal appeal, it started as an Arab religion, and the prophet's companions were overwhelmingly Arabs. Furthermore, Qutb here mixes fantasy and reality. The goal of human equality is the goal of most religions and many secular ideologies, yet none of them has achieved this goal, except for the exceptional few. "A community of belief" is a high ideal, but it doubtful that Islam has achieved that. Even Osama bin Laden is protected by Arab Islamists.

The rewriting of history goes on: "Their intermingling gave rise to a high level of civilization in a very short span of time, dazzling the whole world" (p. 88). Continuing with his veiled attack on Nasser, "This marvelous civilization was not 'Arabic civilization', even for a single day; it was purely an 'Islamic civilization'. It was never a 'nationality' but always 'a community of belief'" (p. 89). Here "truth" and fantasy come to be mixed with mystification. Qutb does not mention when the period that dazzled the whole world was. For most Arab and world historians, this was the early Abbaside period—from the eighth century onward. It was a predominantly Arab–Islamic society, and the reason for its dazzlement was that Muslims opened their minds and hearts to the world. They used Christian translators to translate Greek philosophy, which they incorporated and added to. The second period was in Andalusia. While the culture was primarily Arab–Islamic, there were strong Christian and Jewish influences. The Arab–Islamic culture "dazzled" the world when the "purity" of Islam was muddied by opening itself to other influences.[10]

The psychology of the group

Submission and loss of identity

A radical Islamic mind is not only different from other minds—it is primarily a revolution against the way Islam has grown for many centuries. While Islam means submission to God, for the radical Islamist submission takes on an extreme meaning. *You only follow what is in the Qur'an.* Nothing else matters. This means cancelling centuries of great Arab–Islamic contributions to civilization. The translation and incorporation of Greek, Persian, and Indian civilizations into Islam and transforming them became a dirtying of a "pure" and "prefect" belief system. The great debates between the philosophers and the theologians were cancelled. The purpose of the human mind is not to explore and create new knowledge, but to learn, find out *what is already there*, and submit to an all-inclusive and already known *total* system.

The primary goal is "pure submission" to Allah. "Indeed the spirit of submission is the first requirement of the faith" (p. 56). The question is, submission to what? The Qur'an? There are several interpretations of the Qur'an, including one by Qutb himself. Furthermore, there are four schools of Jurisprudence in Sunni Islam and a separate Shia one.

Everything else follows from this submission. Thus, "The love of the divine Law *al-shari'ah* should be a consequence of pure submission to Allah and of freedom from servitude to anyone else, and not because it is superior to other systems in such and such details" (p. 63). The *Shari'ah* is superior to other "man-made" laws, but it is not up to us to evaluate it or compare it to other laws. Thus, "One should accept the *Shari'ah* without any question and reject all other laws in any shape or form" (p. 63). It is difficult to argue or question God. If something does not make sense to us, the problem lies in us and in our inability to understand the deeper meaning that God intended.

Such submission resonates with Eric Fromm's (1942) explanation for the changes in Christianity that set the mental conditions for the rise of Nazism. Luther needed to find certainty by eliminating the isolated individual self and becoming an instrument in the hands of an overwhelming strong power outside the individual. For Luther and Qutb, this power was God, and in unqualified submission they sought certainty.

Luther did more than bring out the feeling of insignificance that already pervaded the social classes to whom he preached: he offered them a solution. Not only by accepting his own insignificance but by humiliating himself to the utmost, by giving up every vestige of individual will, by renouncing and denouncing his individual strength, the individual could hope to be acceptable to God. Luther's "faith" was the conviction of being loved on condition of surrender, a solution that had much in common with the principle of complete submission of the individual to the state and the "leader"—the tendency to give up the independence of one's own individual self and to fuse one's self with someone or something outside oneself in order to acquire the strength that the individual self is lacking. The more distinct forms of this mechanism are to be found in the striving for submission and domination, or in the masochistic and sadistic strivings as they exist to varying degrees in normal and neurotic persons, respectively. The isolated individual becomes an automaton, loses his self, and yet at the same time consciously conceives of himself as free and subject only to himself.[11]

An equivalent loss of self and identity is illustrated by Qutb: "*Al-din lil-waq'i* ['religion is for living']. This life is completely harmonious with human nature and satisfies all needs, needs that are only determined only by the One Who creates and Who knows His creatures. . . . It is not the function of religion to provide justification for whatever kind of life someone is leading and bring an authority, which he can use to justify his actions" (Qutb, 1966, pp. 158–159). Also: "They [the Companions] lost their personalities and identities in this matter, acting as workers for the One in authority, and were pleased with God in every decision and in every condition" (p. 296).[12]

Closing the mind in the name of purity

The isolation of the vanguards is not only social, but also intellectual.

Such relationship with God can be compared to the "contracts" between masters and slaves[13]: "he has to live according to the laws of God and he has no choice in the matter. In this respect there is no difference between him and other inanimate or animate objects of the universe. All unconditionally submit to the Will of god and to the laws of His creation" (Qutb, 1966, p. 164).

The system is total and complete. "this *Shari'ah* is also part of that universal law which governs the entire universe, including the physical and biological aspects of man" (p. 164). We submit and close our minds. Thus, knowledge that is associated with science will also come under the influence of religion: "Thus, blessings fall on all mankind, as this way leads in an easy manner to the knowledge of the secrets of nature, its hidden forces, and the treasures concealed in the expanses of the universe" (p. 167).

Radical Islamists closed their minds to all the social changes in the world, particularly feminism. The women's role is clear: "if woman is freed from her basic responsibility of bringing up children . . . then such a civilization is 'backward' from the human point of view or *'jahili'* in Islamic terminology" (p. 183). Like all religions, Islam is a "masculine" religion, where men rule over women. However, the Radical Islamists go further, and the control of men over women is absolute. Women have only one job, which is to raise children. The primacy of men over women reflects their own emasculation and loss of control over their own lives and their regression into control over women.

To ensure the closure of the mind, there are restrictions as to where a Muslim can seek knowledge from: ". . . in matters of faith, in the concept of life, acts of worship, morals and human affairs, values and standards, principles of economics and political affairs and its interpretation of historical processes . . . he should learn all these from a Muslim whose piety and character, belief and action, are beyond reproach" (pp. 202–203). Beyond whose reproach? There is no method for selecting this person in Islam. Should this man (and it will be a man) be Sunni or Shia? Or, even within the Sunnis, which interpretation of the Qur'an and *Shari'ah* should this man belong to? While a Muslim is "allowed" to learn certain sciences from a non-Muslim, this does not include "the origin of the universe, the origin of the life of man" (p. 204) or "Darwinist biology" (p. 206).

Jihad in the name of God

Qutb's concepts about Jihad were translated into action by several Muslim groups, guided by Qutb's conception of morality. The word *moral* refers to, "Of or concerned with the principle of right and wrong in conduct and character." Thus morality refers both to beliefs and to behaviours. What is the morality of this group?

Qutb starts with his disdain for "defensive Jihad". Then he divides the world into "Us" and "Them". "Us" are only those who accept his version of Islam. "They" are the *Jahili* societies: ". . . we may say that any society is a *Jahili* society which does not dedicate itself to submission to god alone, in its belief and ideas, in its observances of worship, and in its legal regulation. According to the definition, all the societies existing in the world today are *Jahili*" (Qutb, 1966, p. 148). Then the Others, the non-believers, were divided into three categories: those with whom there was peace, those with whom the Muslims were at war, and the "*Dhimmies*". The *Dhimmies* are "the non-Muslim peoples residing in a Muslim state for whose protection and rights, the Muslim government was responsible" (p. 95). I would call this splitting—a general term with multiple meanings. Freud used splitting in three different ways: splitting of consciousness or psychic groupings, which was developed early in his writings, splitting of representations, which was developed in the middle stage of his writings, and splitting of the ego, which appeared later in his work (Brook (1992). A fourth meaning is splitting of the ego into an experiencing and an observing ego (Freud, 1940b [1938]; Sterba, 1934). There is a fifth type of splitting: "Us" (good) vs. "Them" (bad).

The antagonism to the rest of the world becomes evident: "He called them to the submission to the one god and rejection of the lordship of men. On this principle there is no compromise nor any flexibility. . . . Thus there is no compromise or flexibility with most of the world, including the Islamic world." Then Qutb's message becomes grandiose: "Islam provides a legal basis for the relationship of the Muslim community with other groups. . . . This legal formula is based on the principle that Islam—that is submission to God—is the universal Message which the whole of mankind should accept or make peace with" (p. 101).

These teachings stimulate the grandiosity of disenfranchised and oppressed groups and make their Islam the centre of the world. The world has to adjust to them, to make peace with them. They do not need to adjust to the rest of the world.

In the following paragraph, Qutb advocates offensive and violent Jihad—not what most Muslims believe the greater Jihad is, which, to my mind, is similar to psychoanalysis: the greater Jihad focuses on the self and achieving understanding and change. In contrast, "*Jihaad bis saif* [striving through the sword], which is to clear the way for striving through preaching in the application of the Islamic movement" (p. 110). The advocacy of removing anything in the face of Islam by force is repeated again and again. However, this permission to fight is given to the "oppressed" by the Qur'an: "permission to fight is given to those against whom war is made because they are oppressed, and God is able to help them. These are the people who were expelled from their homes without cause, except that they said that our Lord is God." This is a curious verse to quote, because it goes against Qutb's reasons for Jihad:

- to establish God's authority on the earth;
- to arrange human affairs according to the true guidance provided by God;
- to abolish all the satanic systems of life;
- to end the lordship of one man over others, since all men are creatures of God and no one has the authority to make them his servants or to make arbitrary laws for them. These reasons are sufficient for proclaiming *Jihaad* (p. 127).

This is aggressive Jihad, and does not include the Jihad of those who were "expelled and oppressed.

After listing all societies in the world as *jahili*, Qutb attacks the "ultimate aims of the Jews and Christians against Muslims" (p. 211). Then he goes on with his splitting of the world into "Good and bad".[14] "[T]here is only one place on earth which can be called the home of Islam [*Dar-ul-Islam*], and it is that place where the Islamic state is established and the *Shari'ah* is the authority. . . . The rest of the world is the home of hostility [*Dar-ul-Harb*].[15] A Muslim can have only two possible relations with *Dar-ul-Harb*: peace with a contractual agreement or war" (p. 221). The idea of live and let live, or peaceful coexistence according to international law, is not a option.

"The foremost duty of Islam in this world is to depose *Jahiliyyah* from the leadership of man, and to take the leadership into its own hands and enforce the particular way of life which is its permanent feature" (p. 245). Some of them took the position of defence and justification. Qutb took the position of attacking the Western *Jahiliyyah*, its shaky religious beliefs, its social and economic modes, and its immorality: "look at these concepts of the Trinity, Original sin, Sacrifice and Redemption, which are agreeable neither to reason nor to conscience" (p. 260). I think that these teachings are the consequences of such beliefs. As a result of the "superiority" and "correctness" of his group, and the "inferiority" and "wrongness" of the others, they are dehumanized and can be attacked.

Methodology

The style of writing is like a sermon, addressed to people going through existential crises and looking for definite answers to anchor them.

- Things are repeated again and again.
- History is presented as a final, total, and undisputed truth.
- Appeals to the idealism of religious youth, who believe that they are doing the work of God.
- Appeals to their narcissism and grandiosity, by placing them at the centre of the world that the world has to adjust to.
- Mystification and double-binding of the followers.

Qutb mixes submission with idealistic principles: ". . . the principles and values [of the Islamic civilization are] . . . the worship of God alone, the foundation of human relationships on the belief in the unity of god, the supremacy of the humanity of man over material things, the development of human values and the control of animalistic desires, respect for the family, the assumption of the vicegerency [sic] of God on earth according to His guidance and instruction, and in all affairs of his vicegerency, the rules of God's law (*al-shariah*) and the way of life prescribed by Him" (p. 196).

Then, with a combination of exaggerations and misrepresentation of history, Qutb takes credit for what was he had discredited in his scheme, namely, "mixing" the purity of Islam: "the experimental method . . . originated in the Islamic universities of Andalusia and of the East" (p. 208). The contributions of the Islamic world to science, mathematics, medicine, and so on cannot be underestimated. However, the experimental method did not *originate* in the Islamic world. Furthermore, the culture and civilization of Andalusia was a combination of Islamic, Christian, and Jewish influences and was not the "pure" system postulated by Qutb.

Mystification occurs when two opposite ideas are juxtaposed together: "There is no compulsion in religion" (*Holy Qur'an* 2: 256). However, this sentence is immediately followed by the following: "while on the other hand it tries to annihilate all those political and material powers which stand between people and Islam". *Jihad's* goal is to remove any systems that stand between people and Islam. Thus the only choice people have is to choose or not choose Islam. It seems to me that other religions are not an equal option.

What Qutb and his followers do not realize is that these conditions that allow for the preaching of Islam already exist in the Western democracies. People can and do choose Islam without any powers standing between them and Islam. In Qutb's system Muslims who choose not to be Muslims, or who choose another religion, will be killed for apostasy. However, again and again Qutb returns to mystifying and contradictory ideas. Here is the ultimate: "Islam is a declaration of the freedom of man from the servitude to other men. Thus it strives from the beginning to abolish all those systems and governments which are based on the rule of man over men and the servitude of one human being to another. When Islam releases people from this political pressure and presents them its spiritual message, appealing to their reason, it gives them freedom to accept or not to accept its beliefs" (p. 109). Idealism is mixed with limitations: freedom of man from man, but the only freedom is to accept or not accept Islam. Thus, this struggle is to expose the world to what they already know is the only superior religion. What happens if one is not to accept Islam? "However, this freedom does not mean that they can make their desires their gods, or that they can choose to remain in the servitude of other human beings, making some men lords over others. Whatever system is to be established in the world ought to be on the authority of God deriving its laws from Him alone" (pp. 109–110).

The goal of this method of presentation is to create a fantasied utopia, but at a price: *losing the ability to reflect or mentalize.* This is no different from many other groups. One has to believe in one unshakable truth, and everything else is wrong and evil. New information has to be negated, defended against, and trivialized. New information is never to be used to gain new information that may alter one's perspective.[16]

Concluding remarks

I think that choosing this or any other ideology is an active decision. Many young Muslim men drift to religion to find meaning in a life where their insignificance is acute. At the Mosque they meet other young people, and as a small group they drift to such ideology. They choose what to study and what to learn, and they actively choose what they learn.[17] The totality, perfection, and truthfulness of the system appeals to and allays their existential anxieties. Those teachings appeal to their idealism, grandiosity, and narcissism and make them the centre of the world. By dividing the world into "good" and "bad" and demonizing and dehumanizing the other, the boundaries between universal goodness and badness become lost. In that respect, they lost humanistic morality, which has resulted in their justification of the killing of innocent people.

NOTES

1. Qutb, an Egyptian, was born in 1906 in the village of Mouche, in a region known as Al-Saed. He received his elementary education there, moved to Cairo in 1920 and received a Bachelor's degree in art in 1933. He worked for the ministry of education, while writing from an Egyptian nationalistic perspective. His shift towards Islamism started before, continued during, and crystallized after living in the United States for about two years, between 3 November 1948 and 20 August 1950, during which time he received a Master's degree in Education. After his return to Egypt he joined the Moslem Brotherhood Party. In 1952, the Egyptian revolution led Nasser to power, and within a couple of years Nasser and the Brotherhood clashed. When, in 1954, members of the brotherhood tried to assassinate Nasser, he charged the whole Party and jailed them. Qutb spent most of the next 12 years in jail, until his execution on 29 August 1966.

2. Al Qaeda was formed by the union of the followers of Osama bin Laden (Saudi Arabia) and Ayman al-Zawahiri (Egypt). Bin Laden was the

product of Wahabism, the Wahabi version of Islam, with its strict interpretation of Islam. Al-Zawahiri is the product of an off-shoot of the Muslim Brothers Movement, which is related to the teachings of Qutb.

3. Qutb was a prolific writer of poetry, novels, literary criticism, interpretation of the Qur'an, and studies on various aspects of Islam. A number of publications describe and discuss his oeuvre. e.g. Haddad, 1983; Abu-Rabi, 1996. I focus only on his last book, *Milestones* (1966).

4. It is reassuring that senior FBI agents recognize this. Thus Randy Parsons, who ran the FBI's counterterrorism division in Los Angeles from 2002 to 2006, asked: "How did he [Adam Gadahn, an American member of al-Qaeda] convert, not to Islam, because obviously what he is into is not mainstream Islam, but to a particularly virulent, violent, radical view of Islam? How does somebody get to that?" (Khachadourian, 2007).

5. This was written in 1966, when communism was a major power.

6. This is the translation used in this book. However, the translation of *Jahiliyyah* has come to mean ignorance.

7. Author's note: It is unclear as to which group Qutb is referring to: the close companions, or the over 100,000 people. Such lack of clarity, as I show, is typical of Qutb's writing.

8. It is debatable that this group cut themselves off from their surroundings. They met with the prophet and prayed with him; however, they wanted to convert the rest of their tribe. Their community boycotted and persecuted them. The escape to Maddinah was due to safety, rather than to isolate themselves.

9. I deal only with the social isolation in this section. Further on I deal with the intellectual isolation of the group

10. If that was the period of the companions, then the achievements were the conquests of Syria, Iraq, North Africa, Europe, and Central Asia. The intellectual contribution of the Arabs during that period was writing history. Furthermore, while faith played an important role in these conquests, economic and social factors played equally important roles.

11. Again, I want to stress that Qutb's teachings are not representative of Islam. No one would consider Lutheranism and Calvinism as the only Christianity. Radical Islam is equivalent to Lutheranism and Calvinism.

12. Fromm's interpretation of Luther is eerily similar to my interpretation of Qutb, at least in the area of submission and loss of self and identity.

13. I became aware of contracts between "Masters" and "Slaves" when a lawyer asked me to evaluate a contract that a mother signed with her new "master". I became aware of several websites advertising "Master" and their philosophy, which focused on the elimination of the self and "the ego".

14. Such a Manichean view of the world is illustrated by Ayman al-Zawahiri; the Al Qaeda's main theoretician refers to an American convert to al Qaeda as "a perceptive person who wants to lead his people out of darkness into light" (Khachadourian, 2007).

15. The exact translation is "House of War".

16. After finishing writing this chapter, I read Chris Hedges book (2006) about the American Christian Fundamentalists. The book gives the same description that I postulated about Radical Islamists. This shows that such dynamics are not particular to Islam, but to fundamentalism in any religion. Hedges is aware of the similarities: "But then the Christian Right and the radical Islamists, although locked in a holy war, increasingly mirror each other. They share the same obsessions. They do not tolerate other forms of belief or disbelief. They are at war with artistic and cultural expression. They seek to silence the media. They call for the subjugation of women. They promote severe sexual repression and they seek to express themselves through violence" (p. 24).

17. This goes against the common wisdom in the West, that such ideologies are inculcated into the minds of the young by the surrounding society and its propaganda. These young people choose to learn from Jihadist websites. There are thousands of other websites that they could choose to watch and read.

6

Illusion, disillusion, and delusion: war and faith in the Andes

Moisés Lemlij

> The society of the "great harmony", the radical and definitive new society towards which 15 billion years of matter in movement, of that part which we know of the eternal matter, makes its way necessarily and inexorably. It is the only and irreplaceable new society, with neither exploited nor exploiters, neither oppressed nor oppressors, with no classes, no State, no parties, no democracy, no arms, no wars.
>
> The Communist Party of Peru (PCP), the Shining Path, in 1986

Freud thought that the origin of religion was to be found in the terror of nature, disease, death, conflict with fellow humans, which led our first ancestors to seek an all-powerful father and protector. Religious beliefs would then be the product of these phylogenetic residues, which are reproduced ontogenetically during infancy. We could then say that religion is the result of the denial of death. In general, the Freudian theory of culture "is a deeply critical theory about how human beings fall short of who they can be by refusing to be the mortal beings they are" (Drassinower, 2003, p. 1).

It has often been said that Freud was a clinical optimist and a social pessimist, but in *The Future of an Illusion* (1927c) his hope for the advance of reason and of civilization is clear. He sees in the decline of religion in the Europe of his day an opportunity to start a great cultural transformation that would move beyond one stage of the evolution of the human race, a task in which psychoanalysis would play a central part. "[T]he time has probably come, as it does in analytical treatment, for replacing the effects of repression by the results of the rational operation of the intellect" (p. 44). Certainly, Freud felt that psychoanalysis could guide an "irreligious education" that would help in the process of mourning in the face of death instead of stopping it.

> "The grandeur of the plan and its importance for the future of human civilization cannot be disputed. It is securely based on the psychological discovery that man is equipped with the most varied instinctual dispositions, whose ultimate course is determined by the experiences of early childhood experiences. [1927c, p. 9]

The Future of an Illusion reveals the link that exists in all cultures between the denial of death and authority, illusion and domination. Indeed, when Freud wonders about the relationship between religion and culture, he "does so in a context designed to articulate the helplessness of the human infant to the dynamics of political power" (Drassinower, 2003, p. 109). From this perspective, religious ideas rest on the desire for protection men feel in order to mystify authority, so that they "fulfil the political function of investing cultural prohibitions with solemnity" (p. 123). Freud proposes the transformation of the nature of authority—the substitution of the "affective" foundation of obedience with a "rational" foundation. He was confident that religious irrationality could be replaced by reason, by a sensible social contract. For Freud, the pedagogical application of psychoanalysis would be a concrete historical chance of transforming a culture rooted in illusion. In my opinion, however, Freud was the victim of the same illusion of which he accused religious believers.

To develop this idea, I will start with Freud's statement that there are lay religions that have the same characteristics as any theistic religion. Like the latter, they are perverse illusions, delusions. As on other occasions, I will take an example that is based entirely in one particular space and time: the place is Ayacucho, a region in the Peruvian Andean highlands; the date is 1960–2000. It was there and at that time that the main development and activities of a terrorist political group—the Shining Path—whose structure and ideology had markedly religious features although they claimed an absolutely rational and material basis, were concentrated.

Obviously, my choice is not by chance. After a number of years in England, where I did my psychoanalytic training, I returned to Peru in 1981, precisely at the time of the Shining Path's conflict with the Peruvian state. I panicked when I heard a bomb explode near my house, I wept for a close friend murdered by the subversives, I had to negotiate with a terrorist group that kidnapped a member of my family, I supervised the cases of victims and perpetrators of violence, and, together with other colleagues, I tried to understand what was happening. From this position, I tried to understand what had happened then, to shed some light on the relationship between religion, violence, and civilization.

The Shining Path's people's war against the Peruvian state

> The dream of reason produces monsters.
>
> Francisco Goya

17 May 1980

On the eve of the first general elections in which Peruvians were to elect the President and Congress after 12 years of military dictatorship, two hooded men—later known to be students of San Cristóbal de Huamanga University—stole and burned 11 ballot boxes from a polling station in Chuschi, a small village of Ayacucho.

December 26, 1980

In Lima, hanged dogs appear strung from lampposts, with placards on them with the words "Teng Hsiao Ping, son of a bitch".

Thus did the Shining Path commence its people's war against the Peruvian state. It was to last over 12 years and would leave a toll of 70,000 dead and US$ 30 billion lost. What did the Chinese leader "hanged" in Lima have to do with the burning of the ballot boxes? One of the bloodiest episodes in the Shining Path's history and the justification made for it five years later by the party leader, Abimael Guzmán, still in the midst of the war, may give us some clues to untangle the path of the dream of reason which turned into religious fanaticism.

3 April 1983

Members of the Shining Path burst into the village of Lucanamarca, Ayacucho, and killed 69 villagers.

> The villagers were outraged by the crimes committed by the Shining Path, and had allied themselves with the military. As a reprisal, members of the Shining Path rounded up all the people in the village square and then tortured them, massacred them, murdered them. [Clara: *Ideele*, 1996, p. 24]

> They killed anyone they met. They came into the village and killed my husband, my nephew and my nieces. They picked out over sixty villagers and took them to the square, they made them lie face down in a line at the church door and they began killing them. The children were crying and screaming with fear. They shut all the children in the church. They forced the rest of us to watch. First they hacked my nephew Sucra Ebanans to death with an axe and then they killed the others with axes and machetes: men, women and children. But before they killed them the women terrorists stabbed them in the neck and in the spine so they would suffer more. Three villagers tried to defend them, but they were tied up and murdered cruelly with boiling water. About seventy people were killed that day. [Elsa: *Ideele*, 1996, p. 25]

> Seeing the use of armed retinues and reactionary military action, we responded categorically with one action: Lucanamarca. Neither they nor we have forgotten this because there they saw a response they had never imagined, there over eighty people were annihilated, that is the truth, and we acknowledge it: we went too far there. The main thing however is that we hit them (the military) hard, we pulled them up short and they understood that they were facing a different kind of combatant in the people's war. The bad thing is the excess. Excesses can occur, the thing is to reach a point and not go beyond it, because if you do, you put it off course [Abimael Guzmán: *El Diario*, 1986, p. 3]

Background

Ayacucho in the 1960s and 1970s

Ayacucho has long been the centre of important events in Peru's history. Its capital, of the same name, was a major city under the Viceroyalty, home to distinguished Creole families until the troubled times of Peru's independence. It was the site, in 1824, of the decisive battle that sealed Peru's political destiny, with the defeat of the Spanish under the command of the Viceroy La Serna by the patriotic forces commanded by Antonio de Sucre.

However, by the middle of the twentieth century the city—and the region of Ayacucho in general—had, like many other Creole urban centres in Peru, lost a large amount of its economic and social importance in national life, and it became one of the country's poorest and most backward regions. The natural difficulties of communication between the regions owing to the mountainous geography could not be tackled effectively in the nineteenth and twentieth centuries. The near-permanent political and economic instability of Peru from its earliest days as a republic served to deepen the disintegration within its borders and hence strengthened the regionalist trend in each area of the country.

Regionalism also led to the appearance of local power structures that eclipsed the power of central government. The peasant farmers and the small urban populations were subjugated by an elite mainly composed of land-owners, merchants, bureaucrats, and clergy, who were closely inter-related. This situation was common to all Peru's regions, and in Ayacucho it had two special characteristics.

In the city of Huamanga, a small elite who claimed to be heir to ancient Spanish escutcheons co-existed with a small *mestizo* middle class that provided the bureaucrats, merchants, and teachers. The Roman Catholic Church still retained the position of the first moral power for the citizens (Millones, 2005). The vast rural area surrounding the city was populated by several indigenous ethnic groups that remained true to their roots, but who had a growing interest in becoming part of capitalist economic activity in order to break out of the poverty and deprivation in which they lived.

Rather than resign itself to this isolation, the *mestizo* intellectual elite, which made up Ayacucho's middle class, was for decades asking for the San Cristóbal de Huamanga University to be re-opened.

Its only centre of higher education, it had been founded in the seventeenth century but was closed since the nineteenth century. It was only in 1959 that President Manuel Prado responded to the clamour of the people of Ayacucho, re-opened the old university, and provided it with sufficient resources for it to uphold for several years the academic excellence the population so wanted.

Formation: 1960–1980

Abimael Guzmán Reynoso was born in Arequipa in 1934. The illegitimate child of an Arequipean merchant, he lived with his mother until he was an adolescent, when he moved to his father's house. Later, he became known as a good student of philosophy at San Agustín University in the city where he was born. He graduated and presented a dissertation on Kant's theory of space (Gorritti, 1994). In 1962 he was recruited as a lecturer by Efraín Morote, Chancellor of San Cristóbal de Huamanga University. At the time, the university received funds from abroad and aspired to become an efficient centre of regional development, through providing an education geared to the needs of industry and technology. When Guzmán arrived there, the university had relatively few students—some 400 undergraduates—and 40 teachers (Scott Palmer, 2005). The future leader of the Shining Path swiftly got in touch with the city's inactive Communist Party and worked with a group of young militants in a series of activities aimed to increase the Party's numbers. Already under the sway of the Left, the university became the Communist Party's battleground and recruitment centre. This drastically undermined its academic quality. According to Guzmán, this was a price worth paying for the growth of the Party (Scott Palmer, 2005).

Guzmán sent students to register the poorest communities and to carry out other kinds of community work, which enabled him to reach those who were not at the university. His objective was clear: to use the university to recruit, educate, organize, and subsidize growth in the communist cadres of Ayacucho (Scott Palmer, 2005). He took care to hire, as lecturers, party leaders, many of whom did not have the required academic qualifications. One of these was Luis Kawata Makabe, a young man who stood out among Guzmán's followers because of his great intelligence and his ability to draw new members, owing to his remarkable personal charm and his captivating speech. However, his lack of discipline and the importance he had acquired in the Party soon sparked a falling-out with Guzmán, who had him expelled from the Party and destroyed him psychologically (Scott Palmer, 2005). This is a good example of the degree of psychological manipulation Guzmán gained over his militants.

In 1963 the rupture between China and the Soviet Union divided Peru's communists. Guzmán had for some time maintained a position closer to the Chinese version of the Communist Revolution. Thus, when the PCP divided into two factions, he took the position of Peking. However, he was having difficulties dealing with the growing restlessness among the young people who wanted an armed uprising like the Cuban Revolution. Guzmán considered the latter, and the Soviet version of the Revolution, to be revisionist versions of the true Marxist revolution. The Maoist model required the organization and discipline that suited his aspirations.

At the time, Peru's political atmosphere was hotting up. As Guzmán was one of the Party leaders, his arrest seemed imminent. He was therefore sent to China on a learning visit. There he saw Mao and the Cultural Revolution at their apogee and learned the techniques of underground struggle and armed violence. On his return from China, Guzmán enjoyed great prestige as one well-versed in dialectical materialism; he was now called "Comrade *Puka Inti*" (Red Sun). However, he found a weaker party with a stronger pro-Cuba faction. In 1967, the Maoist faction, led by Saturnino Paredes and closely shadowed by Abimael Guzmán, left the Party.

In June 1969, Guzmán was arrested and sent to Lima, accused of sabotaging the Land Reform. The pro-Soviet Communist Party newspaper accused him of being a CIA agent. He was freed in a month, but he was temporarily detained a number of times between 1972 and 1979 (Scott Palmer, 2005). Shortly afterwards, the tensions within the Party between Paredes and Guzmán worsened. Guzmán was expelled, and with him went the whole group of followers, to form another Party. Each leader named his party the "only" Communist Party of Peru. To distinguish between them, they were called by the names they used in their newspapers. Paredes' party was called "Red Flag" and Guzmán's "Shining Path", taking the name from the publication: "*For the 'Shining Path' of Mariátegui*".

In 1976 Guzmán decided to leave the university, go out to the countryside, and prepare his armed struggle from there. The death of Mao and the accession of Teng Hsiao Ping in 1978 produced confusion in the Peruvian Maoist faction. Their revolutionary idols were no longer alive, and under Teng Hsiao Ping's leadership China had adopted the revisionist measures Guzmán so criticized. It was then that he decided, following Marx, Lenin, and Mao, to make himself the "fourth sword of Marxism". The new centre of the left-wing revolution in the world would be Ayacucho and "Gonzalo Thought" its essential guide. President Gonzalo was the pseudonym Abimael Guzmán had taken for the armed struggle. He thus defined his radical position and opposed all those who differed from it at all. His thoughts were unique and true.

The beginning of the armed struggle and the initial response of the Peruvian State (1980–1989)

The left-wing reforms of the Revolutionary Government of the armed forces under President General Velasco Alvarado did not fulfil the expectations of the military or the Left. In the highlands certainly, the cooperatives and new administrators not only clashed with traditional systems of production but also in many ways became the new vertical form of control over the indigenous communities. The SINAMOS (Social Mobilization Support System), created to help community organizations with their development projects, soon became an agency for controlling the peasant farmers. It gave little or no real power to the peasant farmers to take decisions on their destiny, and hence they quickly rejected it. The Shining Path used this and other cases to object to government reforms, arguing that Peru's socioeconomic structure had not changed. Guzmán was never interested in being involved in Peru's democratic growth, and from the start of his armed struggle he avoided any kind of communication with other left-wing groups.

The second phase of the military government, led by General Francisco Morales Bermúdez, saw the transition to democracy. The military realized that their reforms had been ineffectual and chose to pass the problem to the civilians. The villages in the Andes, for better or worse, had begun to have more interaction with the capitalist world of Peru's coast. In this context, when many left-wing groups were getting ready to take part in political life within the law, the Shining Path decided to start a people's war.

From the burning of ballot boxes in Chuschi in May 1980, which marked the start of the armed struggle, to 1992, when he was captured, Abimael Guzmán was hidden in Lima or somewhere protected. He had brought about the greatest armed uprising in Peru's history, but then, as before, he remained the Marxist theorist accompanied by books, not a guerrilla who put his life at risk.

Prior to its incursion into in the highlands, the Shining Path carried out careful intelligence work to get to know the topography and the organizational structure of the Ayacucho villages. They knew what the immediate problems facing the people were—the constant clashes with bureaucrats and government authorities, for example, and the scourge of the cattle rustlers. They also knew which authorities they would have to eliminate to take political control of the area (Isbell, 1994). In the beginning they would appear suddenly and hold quick trials of thieves, corrupt authorities, and even adulterers, which initially obviously won them the support of the population.

In the second half of 1981 and early in 1982, the Shining Path established organizational structures, such as the MOCT (the Working Class Movement) and the People's Committees. They forced authorities to resign publicly from their posts and replaced them with young people with blind faith in the Party. Other changes, however, were less successful or were outright failures, showing the weaknesses and incongruencies of the Shining Path plan. The Party intended to regroup the peasant farmers according to where they lived, completely ignoring the complex structural systems of Andean societies. They also wanted to ban local festivals and get rid of the traditional authorities, the *varayoqs* (Isbell, 1994).

All of this was happening without Lima or even the city of Ayacucho taking it particularly seriously. By October 1981, the Shining Path had taken control over nine villages in the province of Cangallo, which was declared to be under a state of emergency by the government and placed under the command of the police force. By then the initial acceptance by peasant farmers had turned into distrust and fear, but also resistance. The peasants had quickly recognized the authoritarian nature of the Shining Path, and of course many of its postulates were incomprehensible to them. The Shining Path pressed them to invade land or to stop going to the weekly market, so that they would be restricted to subsistence farming. The peasant farmers had their own agenda, and the Shining Path made it clear how little they cared about this and how they would impose their own plan. When they started to kill people in authority simply because they resisted Shining Path orders, the peasant farmers began to ask the state for help. The people of Chuschi saw clearly how much their lives meant to the Shining Path when the latter left them at the mercy of the police repression it had itself provoked. In spite of this, they asked for a police station, because they feared the Shining Path more than the police.

In mid-1982 seven policemen died in a Shining Path attack on a police station in Vilcashuamán, in Ayacucho. This, plus the escape of 304 prisoners from Huamanga jail, drew the attention of the government and the general public. It was obvious that the Shining Path had become a terrorist group, and police action was unable to contain it. In view of this brutality, President Belaunde turned to the armed forces. At the end of that year "political-military commands" were established and took over the internal control of the state of Ayacucho, with the mission of dealing swiftly with the problem of subversion.

The spiral of violence between the two groups caught the defenceless peasant farmers of Ayacucho's highlands in the cross-fire. The terrorists' decision to blend in with the local population overwhelmed the forces of order with distrust and desperation, and they saw enemies everywhere. Under President Alan García, who took power in 1985, the APRA (Alianza Popular Revolucionaria Americana) Party government tried to alter the direction of events by changing the counter-terrorist strategy. Taking the view that political subversion was the product of extreme poverty and the state of neglect of most of Peru's highlands, the government promoted an active programme for injecting money into the region and helping those who had migrated, fleeing the violence, to return home. Although in the beginning this policy seemed to work, after a brief interval, during which subversion seemed to be under control, the economic debacle in the rest of the country brought the changes sought to a sudden halt. The situation was to worsen soon, and the Shining Path was to feel strong enough to move beyond Ayacucho.

It entered the neighbouring states in the central Andes—Junín, Pasco, Puno, and Huancavelica—and it expanded gradually from the River Huallaga to the regions in Peru's jungle, San Martín, Ucayali, and part of Loreto.

By the end of the 1980s, the country's economic, social, and political situation could not have been worse. The sense of insecurity was enormous, highland populations migrated en masse, fleeing the violence, and much of the urban population fled abroad. There was no proper coordination between the police and military forces. The situation exploded in March 1989, when the army was unable to go to the aid of a police station in Uchiza, in San Martín, and the besieged policemen were massacred by the terrorists. The year ended with the murder, by the Shining Path, of 39 people from the village of Canayre in Ayacucho.

Defeat (1990–2000)

There had been nearly a decade of armed struggle between the State and the Shining Path's terrorist subversive guerrilla war. The group's original approach had initially made it difficult to foresee the nature of its intentions and immediate actions. Indeed, those early months served to teach the Shining Path the techniques of armed struggle. Without this interval of freedom of action provided by the government, its plans would not have developed to the point where they became uncontrollable. But the armed forces and the Peruvian state also had to learn to tackle this new phenomenon, although they took nearly a decade to do so. Serious intelligence work was needed to capture the leaders and quash the guerrilla war.

Between 1988 and 1989, the armed forces redesigned their counter-subversive strategy, with the aim of regaining the people's trust and forming a common front against the terrorists. The new 1989 manual on fighting subversion, plus more careful intelligence work, also involved the army approaching the poorest villages most likely to be targeted by the Shining Path. In 1990, shortly before the change of government, the APRA government's Minister of the Interior, Agustín Mantilla, created the GEIN (Special Intelligence Unit). Its mission was to capture the Shining Path command circle and leave it leaderless. At the same time the military supported this and promoted the peasant farmer patrols as "self-defence committees" against the Shining Path—perhaps their most shrewd counter-terrorist strategy. In other words, civilians and the state on the same side.

The Maoist strategy was the alliance with the poorest peasant farmers, but in the River Apurímac valley it was the peasants who led the resistance against the Shining Path and, together with the armed forces, won the hegemony of the area. Some villages, such as Chungui, where Evangelical church fundamentalism predominated, organized themselves in the manner of *montoneros*, such as those in the war against Chile or in rebellions against the old local landowners. The Shining Path raided a number of churches and machine-gunned the congregation, which increased anger against them. Both groups strove to win the minds and souls of the dispossessed and helpless. The Shining Path offered revolution, the evangelical churches offered Paradise. The evangelicals considered the members of the Shining Path devils and the Anti-Christ. The Shining Path considered the evangelicals traitors of the people. The sacred texts were the Gospel and "Gonzalo Thought".

> For the Shining Path it was very hard to win over these communities, so it began to fight them. The evangelical churches developed an ideological answer which it was to put into practical action: for the Last Judgement, the Earth had to be free of "demoniacs". It was therefore necessary, with God's protection, to fight against the forces of evil. Thus the bloody repression of the Shining Path met in response the armed action of the evangelicals and the political war became to some extent a religious war, since the evangelicals did not see themselves to be fighting an ordinary enemy, but the Anti-Christ himself. [Del Pino, 1996, p. 118]

The Shining Path had come up against a series of important institutions: "the extended family, the peasant community, the rules of reciprocity, the age hierarchy, rituals, festivals and the religious dimension in general" (Degregori, 1996). It is not by chance that the uprisings against the Shining Path took place precisely during the religious festivals it wanted to eliminate as a remnant of the feudal system.

The government of Alberto Fujimori, which came to power in July 1990, continued to support the new anti-subversive strategy.

However, the results were slow to come, and the Shining Path began to commit bloody acts to show their strength in Lima. In February 1992, María Elena Moyano, a left-wing leader of the Women's Movement in the densely populated district of Villa El Salvador who spoke out against the Shining Path, was cruelly murdered, and her body was blown up. In July, a car-bomb exploded in Tarata Street in Miraflores, an upper-middle-class area, leaving 25 dead and 155 wounded. These attacks had a profound effect on the population of the capital, which had until then not suffered much from the terrorist attacks.

It was in September 1992 that the new counter-subversive strategy won its most important victory, capturing Abimael Guzmán. Clearly, this was the beginning of the end of subversion, given the enormous power concentrated in the person of Guzmán. From that time on the state counter-offensive covered several fronts with the support of the public, which led to the rapid disintegration of the Shining Path.

One of the factors that contributed to bringing about the capture of Guzmán and the subsequent decline of the movement was the Shining Path's decision to take Lima. Guzmán believed that at the end of the previous decade he had achieved "strategic equilibrium" in the peasant armed struggle. According to his evaluation, the state forces were so destabilized that the fall of the capital was imminent. This perception was shared by many terrified Peruvians, but an analysis of the Shining Path's internal condition during those years gives us a different picture. In fact, its progress on the coast had weakened its essential characteristics of centralism and cohesion. The growth in the number of militants made it increasingly difficult to avoid infiltration and facilitated surveillance by the state intelligence apparatus. Another important measure was the Repentance Act, which gave legal benefits to former terrorists who provided the authorities with information to break down the movement. When he fell, Guzmán had been out of touch with his power bases in the Andes for months. While his presence in Lima was gaining ground, he had lost ground outside the capital. He was, in fact, far from taking control of the country.

Captured and put on public display, Guzmán called on his followers to "continue the struggle". Taking up this cry, Comrades Feliciano and Artemio continued the resistance in the Peruvian

Andes. In August 1993 the Shining Path murdered 65 people in the Tsiari Valley, in the region of Junín. Of these, 21 were indigenous Normatsiguengas, and the rest were settlers.

The time spent behind bars was to weaken Guzmán's will. He had never himself personally taken part in the actions of the armed struggle. In 1999 Feliciano was captured, and the movement was practically destroyed. Nevertheless in the new Millennium the Inter-American Court of Human Rights reviewed the summary trials by anonymous judges held under Fujimori's government, in response to complaints made by the imprisoned terrorists.

The Shining Path no longer represents a threat to the Peruvian state. But the psychological, social, and economic scars the conflict left on the population still produce continual controversy. The Truth and Reconciliation Commission created by the Transition government of Valentín Paniagua estimated that between 1980 and 2000, 69,280 people had been killed, 85% of them in Junín, Huánuco, Huancavelica, Apurímac and San Martín. The responsibility of the armed forces and the various governments who tackled the problem of subversion are still the cause of constant friction in public opinion.

The ideology of the Shining Path

"Gonzalo Thought" was understood by his followers to be a further stage of Marxism—that is, the road that would lead to the proletarian revolution on a world-wide scale.

> It is the application of Marxism–Leninism–Maoism to the Peruvian revolution which has generated "Gonzalo Thought" . . . applying the universal truth as faithfully as possible to the concrete conditions of our country, manifested in "Gonzalo Thought". [*El Diario*, p. 5]

Guzmán claimed to have made a contribution to Marxism at the same level as Marx, Lenin, and Mao. Hence in his early writing he refers to Marxism–Leninism–Maoism, and subsequently he adds "Gonzalo Thought" to the trilogy. The basic contentions of the Shining Path's armed struggle are based on Maoist thought and its strategy for taking power through the "people's war". A special place was reserved, however, for the ideas of the founder of the Peruvian Communist Party, José Carlos Mariátegui.

> The way of the revolution is from the country to the city. Mariátegui showed us this way when he passed the following judgement: "Once the feudal system of the land owners is overthrown, urban capitalism will lack the strength to resist the growing working class". . . . This way of the revolution in the backward countries has been systematised by Mao Tse Tung [Guzmán, 1976]

This incongruous combination was the result of crudely superimposing Mariátegui's view of early-twentieth-century Peru and Mao's view of 1930s China onto the complexities of Peru in the second half of the twentieth century. The Shining Path certainly avoided seeing both the profound changes that had occurred since Mariátegui had made his analysis and the differences between Peru and China.

Guzmán's basic contentions can be summarized in half a page: Peru continued to be an essentially rural country, in which the great majority of the population were peasant farmers, and theirs was the major economic activity. Hence, following Mariátegui, the problem of Peru is the problem of the peasant farmers—that is, the problem of the land. This is in the hands of a small number of land-owners who keep the working population in servitude. This gives rise to a key assessment: Peru is a semi-feudal country. The land-owners are not, however, really a leader class, but just a dominant class, which is, in turn, subjected to the orders of another higher class, the foreign capitalist–imperialist class. This gives rise to another key assessment: Peru is a semi-colonial country. In this system, there are few workers because of the meagre industrial development of the Peruvian economy. Peru's basic driving force is the peasant farmers, the subjugated great majority. It is they who are destined to carry out the Marxist revolution in Peru, to change the unjust social order for a communist system. To achieve this, there is only one way: the People's War. This concept, developed and put into practice by Mao Tse Tung, stresses the peasant farmers' capacity to rise up against the state, destroy it, and then build another one. But the peasants are not aware of this "truth", or of the reasons for their poverty, or of the way to solve it, and therefore the Party is so important. The Party must direct the People's Army and try to establish a united front from the various social classes in the country, to bring the prevailing order to an end. Hence the struggle against the capitalist system and the semi-feudal society would start in the countryside and move on to the cities, where it would have to win over the working class and the petit bourgeoisie and, at times, the grand bourgeoisie. For Guzmán, the conditions worldwide for the revolution to triumph are a given. According to a "scientific" analysis of the circumstances, the destabilization of the capitalist system and the awakening of the peasants' class consciousness were a fact.

This was a simple and concrete view, easy for his militants to understand, since they only knew of Marxism what Guzmán told them. It represents a kind of sacred truth, which transforms Guzmán's rational argument into a religion rather than an ideology, and its mentor into a kind of spiritual leader who has all the answers. The followers become a "crusading" army with the historical mission of transforming the world, regardless of the human cost.

> The idea that revolutionary violence will build a new, just and mutually supportive society is more deeply internalized by those who are saturated in aggressive feelings. [Portocarrero, 1998, p. 21]

The fertility of violence is justified as a scientific truth. The important point is that impulses be channelled by an ethical and rational authority. Much of the efficacy of the Shining Path's arguments is due to the fact that they hide the root of their success—the dependence on the irrational—and bring to the fore the appeal to reason and intelligence. Violence is not just the grave-digger of history but also the midwife of the new society, and it involves punishing traitors and putting pressure on the weak, raising their awareness. Raising awareness through terror is an indispensable necessity. President Gonzalo, "the fourth sword of Marxism", presents himself here as a Messianic hero and the highest authority over all others. His identification with the figure of the Messiah coincides with expectations of the appearance of a redeemer. In him merge the image of the chosen son and redeemer father. Guzmán acts as a cosmocrat: he sees himself as the director of the new re-ordering of the world or the cosmos.

> His vision of the world is similar to certain cosmogonic tales in which the forces of chaos constantly threaten the cosmos. Salvation then may be in the hands of a hero not born of woman, a pre-destined figure, who at first is unaware of his mission but then, thanks to ever more visible signs, will understand his duty, and thanks to his strength and extraordinary courage, will be able to ward off the threats and re-order the world. [Portocarrero, 1998, p. 45]

Class hatred is postulated as a noble and lofty sentiment, which will be productive in the form of revolutionary violence. Hatred guarantees the belief that the only solution is destroying your enemies. This legitimates cruelty as a means of destroying the established order. The fallen are likened to martyrs and become models. Hence the glorification and honouring of their dead. According to Eloy Neira, "once there are absolute ends, cases, concrete situations, flesh and blood individuals no longer matter, they disappear" (quoted by Portocarrero, 1998, p. 29).

As an endogenous group, the Party kept itself apart from the rest of the Peruvian Left, which led to a total focus on one single point of view. Guzmán found a way of transforming his political ideology into a kind of "faith", above all reason, which made his party a sectarian and self-sufficient group.

> The Shining Path member is very similar to the clergy of a sect. Both describe a situation of emergency and crisis and propose a road to salvation, with the corresponding way of life. But these arguments do not compete for the same public. The Shining Path appeals chiefly to young people from the poor in the Andean highlands, with a relatively high educational level, brought up in the Roman Catholic tradition and in left-wing political socialization. [Portocarrero, 1998, p. 61]

The process for young militants to join the Shining Path shared the characteristics of a rite of passage or initiation into a religious sect. To reach this degree of conviction required seeing the armed struggle as a personal rupture that would enable them to see the light.

Shining Path ideology went beyond the classic Maoist People's War and proposed getting rid of evil at its root, a purifying violence. It aimed to build not only a new state but also a new society, controlled by the Party down to the last detail.

> On the basis of a conception of the individual as something sinful, putrid and with no solution, Guzmán invited his listeners to eliminate their privacy, to join a collective which would absorb all their energy. This renunciation was put forward as the foundation of a life style which leads to a state of grace. [Portocarrero, 1998, p. 49]

Many of the Shining Path's documents were imbued with Biblical language. To understand its argument, it is necessary, therefore, to take into account the Christian religious tradition (Degregori, 1993, p. 111), since it aims to create in its militants the need to be "born again".

Illusion, disillusion, and delusion

The violence produced by the religious ideology of the Shining Path is one more example of a phenomenon that has been repeated again and again throughout human history. Technological change has altered weapons, but there have been few changes in the motives and conduct of men. In the beginning, as Freud states in *Totem and Taboo* (1912–13), terror and wonder awoken by natural phenomena—sometimes destructive, sometimes beneficent—created the need to pay them homage and plead for their protection. As time went by, this cult of higher forces, to which were attributed power over people's destiny, developed in a number of ways and was transformed into various systems of belief in one or several gods, which involved a set of complicated rituals, moral codes, and practices, administered by institutions and by people who performed the highly privileged role of obtaining their favour, interpreting their wishes, or conveying a "revealed" truth.

Clearly, scientific knowledge can replace some religious concepts, but not religion itself. At times of change in paradigms—before the French Revolution, for example, or at the end of the nineteenth century—traditional religions have been replaced by political ideologies that have all the characteristics of a religion: in other words, by systems of belief and values that, like religious dogmas, provide a single explanation for the existence of human beings and predict a Utopian future for a "chosen" few", who are required to be devoted activists and militants.

"We will reach an irreplaceable society, with no classes, no state, no democracy, no weapons, no wars, there will be nothing except the Party" (Guzmán, 1976, p. 4). The "chosen" group coheres through the consolidation of dependence, the identification of a foreign enemy, the search for a scapegoat, resentment, envy, and hatred of strangers, cliché sentimentalism, and the banality of aggression (the narcissistic banality and paranoid fundamentalism described by Otto Kernberg). Like the theistic religions, these political ideologies/lay religions need large ritualized spectacles and the demonization and denigration of others. According to John, Lord Alderdice, in the twentieth century alone, the search for Utopia and the disregard and denigration of the Other has left a death toll of 170 million people.

When a traditional society suffers from a chronic malaise due to the perception of social and economic exploitation, which generates profound despair, this can lead to a crisis that becomes an explosion. There follows a tendency to atavistic regression towards an identification with the primitive father, put forward in *Group Psychology and the Analysis of the Ego* (1921c), combined with the search for dependence put forward by Bion—a situation it is extremely difficult to leave. In other words, the conditions for the search and appearance of a "Saviour" are created. If we take the example of Abimael Guzmán and examine it from the perspective of Rank and Bion, it will be a charismatic, educated person, from another community or one who has returned from a mysterious and secret place (China), with more power or knowledge (military, religious or philosophical), who has been anointed and is beyond ordinary and daily events. He will surround himself with disciples and an almost holy family—and a close circle of women—and will maintain that he is the reincarnation of an ancestor (Mao) confirming prophecies (Marx, Engels, Lenin, Mariátegui). He will promise security, stability and justice and will call on the dispossessed (the peasants of Ayacucho)—communities that have lost their right to speak and their prestige—and will offer to transform them into a new elite after the total change. The price is total submission to dogma. He will affirm that the proof that this will definitively happen is in ancient prophecy and will seek to merge with cultural heroes. The over-simplified Marxism, digests of the texts of Politzer, and Chinese leaflets that inspired the Shining Path have more than a chance similarity with, for example, the Catholic Catechism. It is the group universe ruled by dependence and the submission of the basic assumption of dependence of which Bion speaks. And this gives rise to the absolute polarization between good and evil.

In the struggle without quarter or mercy, the Messianic leader will punish sinners and ask his followers to be willing to make the final sacrifice. Guzmán, like bin Laden, believes that he possesses the revealed truth and hence the right and the duty to lead his followers towards Utopia along a road wet with the blood of a million dead—not only enemies but also the faithful—which is not accidental but necessary.

> The glorification of violence is the beginning of his argument, its founding moment. Indeed, in the eulogy and idealization of violence moral and "scientific" observations are interlinked with powerful feelings of aggression. This confluence produces a call to violence, an urging to action. The argument runs that it is good to experience hatred, because that way a better society will be achieved. The Shining Path leader makes a call to violence, alleging that it is motivated by moral feelings and directed by intelligence well aware of the ends it seeks. [Portocarrero, 1998, pp. 19–20]

Rabid violence becomes ritualized violence, transgression receives no forgiveness, and the loyal person who dies will be the "heroic martyr". This is the basic premise of attack and flight. At times it is difficult to distinguish beneficiaries from victims, since the punishment is more evident than the reward, but we observe pleasure being taken in seeing the person punished and the sacrifice in the midst of a terrible spectacle. The crusader–missionary, heir to prophets and representative of the Messiah, is free of all guilt through his struggle against pagan–infidel–bourgeois. There is no excessive violence. There is sacrifice to a cause, relating it to its peers in the people's war or Jihad, which will use the bloodshed to make fertile the way of the new redeemer (Bion's "pairing"). In Guzmán's words: "The revolution is a purge to obtain absolute purity, perfection and truth, polarity ends with the elimination of one of the poles"; "there is no place for half-way positions . . . whoever opposes the revolution will be crushed like an insect". The Great Flood, Sodom and Gomorra: for there to be a renaissance, there must be a total purge.

The great regression that necessarily occurs in the form of the libidinization of violence, in which feelings of absolute omnipotence—concealing the omnipotent will to control—is mixed with delivering the Utopia of the Garden of Eden: in the words of Bertolt Brecht, "the shark telling the sardines that Paradise is down his throat".

> I have tried to understand political violence on the principle that it is not instinctive behaviour or a reflex, but that it arises when people's aggressive impulses, potentiated by the frustrations of poverty and injustice, are brought together and moulded by ideologies and organizations which argue that violence is the only possible way of effective change. It appears when the idea is circulated that acting in hatred is the only way to transcend what is undesirable. Thus the absolute conviction of the fertility of violence can be incarnated by those called. In other words, what could be called the argument of blood—a persuasive idea engages, burns and mobilises. [Portocarrero, 1998, p. 11]

In my opinion, religion is a disguised illusion of salvation that provokes catastrophes. It could also be postulated that the belief in a higher being is the product of an evolutionary mistake in the genes, an irreducible genetic malformation, as suggested by Dawkins, the author of *The God Delusion* (2006). But as we have seen, political ideologies that are the product of an idealization of reason are as perversely illusory as religions.

> In the end, all fanatics are the same. They use the religious creed or the political one (Stalinism, Maoism) as an excuse: a tragic mixture of the literal reading of the religious or political texts; a rejection of all innovation or adaptation to social and cultural change; the sacrilization of their actions carried out, supposedly, in the name of the watchwords written in those texts or spoken by their leaders, the only ones capable of interpreting the true sense of the sacred words; and a feeling of being the ones chosen by a god worthy of the most intense of paranoias. With this cocktail we can fabricate Basque or Serbian ethnic nationalists to Al-Qaeda terrorists, moving through some wondrous Khmer Rouge, Likud members and skinheads. Out of sight, in the wings, we can find seated at the same table, a member of ultramontane Catholic sects with Orthodox Jews or

> Wahhabies, applying the corresponding *sharia* as a formula of social control. They do not dare to come out onto the stage, they are even appalled at the barbarous nature of those who call themselves their followers, but deep down they share the same concept of a combative and vengeful God who chooses some to fight others in exchange for the promised land or eternal Paradise. Fundamentalism, nationalism, terrorism, Judaism, Christianism, Islamism, Integrism, dogmatism. . . . Who will spare us from so many isms? [Elorza, 2004, p. 1]

Individuals facing impotence, being devoured and dominated by implacable forces that strip them of autonomy of action, can defend themselves by turning this into a sensation of omnipotence through a fantasy of domination. In other words, they exchange the feeling of being a puppet for one of being the puppeteer. Earl Hopper (2003) has described some of the psychic processes that occur during times of social disintegration, inconsistencies in traditional structures and disillusionment with religion and other institutions. These faults produce the group phenomena defined by Bion.

The psychic processes of those who have known terror of annihilation fluctuate between the fission and fragmentation and between fusion and confusion with damaged and lost objects. They show a tendency to form loosely connected groups through a process of aggregation in response to fission and fragmentation, and a tendency to form a crowd in response to fusion and confusion.

In the case of the Shining Path we can see a process of unification of fragments (aggregation) that expand to neutralize the feeling of impotence that previously dominated the members of his hordes. In this way his militants managed to affirm their—previously threatened—personal identity and entertain the fantasy of sharing standard rules of solidarity, beliefs, and values—a fantasy that turned them into a single unit within a different universe. We might say that through a traditional process of identification with their leader, President Gonzalo became the archaic father. But we should also mention the contentions of Janine Chasseguet-Smirgel with regard to the "perfect group", linked more to the primitive mother, which favours an imitative identification of the individuals to fuse with the group, from which all impurity and variants are eradicated to subdue its members absolutely to law, order, and group rules—namely, a kind of primitive justice.

If these perfect groups formed by aggregation are to maintain their cohesion, the organization must become bureaucratic, which entails the idealization of the leader who is identified with this. Hence diversity is considered to be delinquent disobedience and cultural standardization to be a collective achievement. The members of the Shining Path identified with an idealized image of Guzmán, but unlike identification with the crowd, which involved a process of fusion with it, in this case they came to the fore as representatives of their organization, reproducing in their own context the ideal and fantasized ideal of Guzmán. This allowed them to apply an implacable "justice": murders characterized by surprise attacks on their victims. Through murders, seen as a political act that served the function of conveying a message aimed to provoke the re-ordering of society, the Shining Path members were fused and transubstantiated with their leader and obtained a pleasant feeling of triumph over victims who had got their just deserts.

In the Shining Path, we can see not only the transference of the basic assumption to a crowd, but also an aggregation in the terms of a crowd greater than that which they wished to expand omnipotently, and at the same time keep a distance from, in order to be able to control and dominate it. While the members of the Shining Path identified with the chosen leader, at the same time they offered themselves as an object for identification to those whom they wanted to control and those whom they did not allow to disobey or disagree. Not only did they identify with the leader, but they took his position in the group around them.

Traditional group theory establishes a difference between "task groups" and "basic assumption groups". In my opinion, the fourth basic assumption of aggregation-crowd proposed by Hopper is particularly relevant for understanding the Shining Path, whose organization combined both aggregation and the crowd and took on the task of realizing the basic assumptions: the violent aspects of the shared feeling of omnipotence became the conscious task of the group.

Abimael built his argument on the three swords of his predecessors in the revolution: Marx, Lenin, and Mao. He was a prophet who heralded his own Messianic arrival. But if he was the fourth sword, each of the students of Huamanga University who joined the Shining Path believed that they had become the fifth sword of the revolution.

However advanced the world is, there will always be an Abimael, a bin Laden, a Torquemada, a Hitler, or a Stalin, who will appear at unexpected moments when there is a feeling that a final catastrophe is approaching and that we need to cling to a hope of a new renaissance. Hence Freud's idea of substituting religious beliefs with scientific knowledge, of transforming a culture rooted in illusion for another based on a social contract inspired by reason, involves a constant and renewable struggle against the malevolent violence of narcissism. As Joel Kovel says, perhaps we can exonerate Freud for not knowing better, in 1927, that

> civilization has little to fear from educated people and brain workers—although one would have thought that World War I would have given him more pause than it seems it did. Sixty years later, with the visible systematic ruination of the globe visible all about us as the fruit of these brains, we are obliged to reject Freud's uncritical adulation of science. This is, it must be emphasized, not the same thing as rejecting science, but it does mean reintegrating science with those spiritual elements that were split off at the beginning of the modern era, when the soul became the isolated and driven ego. [Kovel, quoted by Drassinower, 2003, p. 129]

7

Freud's omission of the maternal in God: was he disillusioned with mothers?

Jennifer Bonovitz

> the primal father was the original image of God, the model on which later generations have shaped the figure of God. . . . Religion would thus be the universal obsessional neurosis of humanity; like the obsessional neurosis of children, it arose out of the Oedipus complex, out of the relation to the father.
>
> Sigmund Freud, *The Future of an Illusion* (1927c), p. 43

Freud's impassioned criticism of the infantile derivatives of religion is well known. Less recognized is the striking omission of the maternal and feminine in this formulation. Freud allowed no possibility for the life-giving, growth-promoting, maternal, sustaining functions of God, nor does he consider even a destructive derivative of the mother–child relationship in his construct of God. Religion is sought as a necessary defence against "the crushing superiority of nature" and the "painfully felt imperfections of culture".

He describes a God born of the child's fear of the father, as well as of his need for protection by the powerful parents, primarily the father. "Now that God was a single person, *man*'s relation to *him* could recover the intimacy and intensity of the child's relation to *his father*" (1927c, p. 19). This is a *son* in relationship with a *masculine deity* who punishes transgression and strongly defends against internal and external attackers of all persuasions. He inspires fear in the service of controlling the destructive instincts and assuages fear by promising to protect against the destructive vagaries of everyday life. The protection provided by the first love object, the mother, "is soon replaced by the stronger father, who retains that position for the rest of childhood" (p. 24).

The one positive aspect of Freud's God is to protect civilization from the great mass of the uneducated and oppressed, who have every reason for being enemies of civilization. "So long as they do not discover that people no longer believe in God, all is well" (p. 39). For the educated, on the other hand, there is hope: "science has given us the evidence by its numerous and important successes that it is no illusion" (p. 53). The passionate love, worship, awe, or any mention of goddesses, women, mothers, daughters, and the maternal functions of a deity are strangely absent throughout Freud's *Illusion*. The possibility that, for some, God is not masculine but feminine is not considered.

Let me turn now to an exploration of some of the feminine attributes and maternal forms and functions of God, the mysterious being that humanity has searched for, created, destroyed, and used since the beginning of time. I begin with the Earth Mother Goddess, the one whose creative presence in the human psyche has been recorded in rock carvings, sacred paintings, oral history, written scriptures, and music down through the ages. This is followed by sections on the comforting function of the mother God who provides soothing and solace in times of great pain; the feared mother God who seeks to inhibit and control; the transfigurational God associated with the transformational mother of infancy. Vignettes from clinical work with children and adults from a variety of cultures are interspersed to show just a few of the many forms and functions that the maternal aspects of God may take in the course of an analytic journey.

The primordial Earth Mother Goddess

According to ancient Egyptian scriptures, "In the beginning there was Isis, Oldest of the Old. She was the Goddess from whom all becoming arose. As the Creatress, she gave birth to the Sun when he arose upon this earth for the first time" (Walker, 1983, p. 453). There have been countless forms and transformations of the Earth Goddess, the eternal mother, the giver of life. In the Judeo–Christian tradition it is written "Then Adam called his wife Chava (Eve) for she was the mother of all life" (Genesis 3:20). The mystic kabbalist Moses Cordovero (1588) writes of the Schenina as a feminine element representing the omnipresent, nurturing, inner aspects of God, whereas the transcendent and infinite are qualities of the masculine in God. A contemporary Rabbi, Tzvi Freeman, elaborates:

> She was the other side of the image of G-d. For G-d is not just a boundless light, beyond all things. G-d is something in the here and now, within all things, giving them life, being what they are being. In her source above, she is "the Schenina"—the Divine Presence That Dwells Within. [Freeman, 2004, p. 21]

In Hinduism elements of the Divine Mother are worshiped in many forms and by many names, including Shakti, Kali Ma, Durga, Lakshrini, Saraswati, Ganga, and Uma (Kurtz, 1992). "Just as child believes its mother to be all-powerful, and capable of doing anything for the child, a devotee believes the Divine Mother to be all merciful, all-powerful and eternally guiding and protecting him with her invisible arms" (Hindunet.org). As Rao (2005) points out, there is a recurring motif of physical power and energy in a goddess who in the end joins with the male. Thus Minakshi, born with three breasts, sets out to conquer the universe. Her third breast disappears when she meets Shiva, and she then accepts him as her lord. Kali often appears as a frightening manifestation of the destructive power of the divine. She is sometimes depicted with garlands of human skulls around her neck. Her followers see this image as capturing the suffering in the world and the eventual return of all things to the Goddess at the time of death (Rao, 2005 p. 290).

Islam has at least 99 names for Allah, many of which are associated with feminine attributes. Two of the most common of these are ar-Rahman, the Most Merciful, and ar-Rahim, the Compassionate;

Siassi and Siassi (2008) note that the etymological roots of both these words go back to *Rahm*, the Arabic word for the womb. Other names associated with maternal aspects of God are al-Ghafur, the All Forgiving; al-Halim, the Forbearing, the Indulgent; al-Wadud, the Loving, the Kind One; and as-Sabur, the Patient, the Timeless. PeNkaLai Katalikkiren (2008) writes: "'Masculine' and 'feminine' are not simply equivalents of the human male and female, since all men and women have elements of both masculinity and femininity within them. That Allah is Absolute is the principle of masculinity, that Allah is Infinite is the principle of femininity." While Mary, the mother of Jesus, is not elevated to the status of the divine in the Qur'an, she is given a privileged destiny as the mother of the holy Prophet, Jesus Christ (*Holy Qur'an,* 1946, p. 771).

Many Christians turn to Mary to provide a representation of the universal mother. Thus Goethe wrote of her as "Supreme and sovereign Mistress of the World. . . . Oh Virgin, in the highest sense most pure, oh Mother, worthy of all our worship, our chosen Queen, equal with the gods" (quoted in Walker, 1983, p. 611). Ochs (1977) traces the gradual ascendance of Mary in Christian art from a position lower than Jesus in the first five centuries to a haloed, central figure by the sixth century and then to the Queen of Heaven in the cathedral art of the ninth century. Walker notes that the early Christian church opposed the worship of Mary, fearing that she was

> only a composite of Marianne, the Semitic God–Mother and Queen of Heaven, Aphrodite–Mari, the Syrian version of Ishtar; Isis as Stella Maris, Star of the Sea; Maya the Oriental Virgin Mother of the Redeemer the Moerae or trinity of the fates; and many other versions of the Great Goddess. [Walker, 1983, pp. 602–603]

From time immemorial humankind has sought for an understanding of creation, from the birth of a child, to the creation of the universe. Despite valiant attempts by their scientifically minded parents, little children in particular may cling to their own variations of a maternal God to create meaning in times of great perplexity about the mystery of creation. The following vignette describes how a Hindu child aged 8 years, 7 months constructed a story about the mystery of new life in her mother's belly.

First clinical vignette

Veena was seen four times for help with acute separation anxiety, which began during a family visit from her home in India to relatives in the United States. She refused to leave her mother's side and screamed when put to bed at night. Given that her mother was six months pregnant, it was not surprising that Veena had become fascinated with a mother duck and her six babies, requesting that mother, but never father, take her daily to the college campus where the duck family lived on a pond. She told the following birth story in both words (mother translated a mixed Hindi and English rendition) and pictures.

"It was the mummy duck, she was named Saras and she had lots of wings waving in the sky. First she kissed the earth and prayed. It was beside the pond. There was lots of pouring water and red fire to cook the rice. She ate some of it. That made her fat and then they just sprouted right out of her."

Veena's mother provided me with understanding of many of the elements of the story. The name "Saras" given to mother duck came from a story, recently told to Veena by her aunt, a musician, concerning Saraswati, the Goddess who is depicted riding a swan with one set of arms playing a veena (stringed instrument) and another pair carrying a scroll and a *mala* (set of beads)—hence the wings waving in the air. The little girl had been fascinated by the fact that a goddess played a musical instrument bearing her name and inquired, hoping to meet her, if she lived by the duck pond. Since coming to the United States, she had insisted on hearing the story nightly.

The kissing of the earth seemed to come from observation of mother duck's pecking the earth for food. The praying connected with a recent *puja* held at her home in India to ask for blessings on the household and to ask for protection of the mother's pregnancy. The child had picked up on the fact that some of the prayers related to "the big bump" in her mother's belly. During the ceremony there had been ritual hand-washing (lots of water) and a red lighted lamp (red fire) had been waved back and forth. Some of the food prepared included cooked rice, which everyone in attendance subsequently ate.

It was fascinating to see how this child's construction of the pregnancy/birth story was so richly informed by the interplay of her cultural/religious heritage and her age-appropriate developmental challenges and conflicts. The story she wove told much about her inner world. Her use of elements of the *puja* served to provide a tether to her sorely missed home and extended family (Akhtar, 1992). Significantly, despite her mother's educative attempts, Veena's creative fantasy excluded father, or indeed any male imagery. In part this had to do with her wish to deny father's special relationship with mother in their bedroom, and she was especially disturbed by the product of this relationship, the "big bump" in mother's belly.

Veena's phase-specific ambivalence towards her mother was further fuelled by her mother's emotional withdrawal, due to severe morning sickness, in the first trimester, and extreme fatigue at the end of her day's work as a nurse in a public clinic. In addition, father had shown intense excitement about the pregnancy once it became known that a much-wanted son was on the way—another narcissistic wound and source of anxiety for the little girl. Sensing his diminished investment, Veena defensively and creatively retreated to the world of mother and the intriguing goddess, Saraswati. Her previously intense curiosity about the source of babies was satisfied for a time by the stories she herself created about Saras, the mother duck, and her family by the pond. She angrily resisted any efforts on the part of her parents to talk about the baby in her mother's belly. For a time she was able to avoid knowing the unpleasant truth of her betrayal at the hands of both father and mother.

My intervention took the form of providing a safe, neutral space for Veena to construct a narrative in both images and words that not only assuaged her intense curiosity but supported much-needed defences against knowing the "truth". At the same time I encouraged the parents to support their little girl's imaginative turning to the powerful Goddess Saraswati for help during a very perplexing and stressful time in her young life. When I offered an explanation of how the Goddess served many useful functions in terms of providing a palatable explanation for the mystery of mother's pregnancy as well as a connection with home in India and a way to cope with the complexities of family life, both parents responded with relief and with empathy for Veena, whose acute separation anxiety quickly attenuated. They were able to postpone her disillusionment until the return home provided her with the support of familiar surroundings and extended family.

Mother God as a source of solace in times of unmentalized pain

The feminine in God is frequently seen as more compassionate than God the Father. Thus the Roman writer Lucius of Patrae begins his hymn to Isis with

> O Thou holy and eternal Savior of the human race. . . . Thou bestowest a mother's tender affections on the misfortunes of unhappy mortals. . . . Thou unravellest even the inextricably tangled web of Fate. [Walker, 1983, p. 453]

Down through the centuries beleaguered humanity has sought the comfort, wise counsel, protection, and powerful intervention of a primordial mother. Jesus, as portrayed in the New Testament, may be viewed as a softer, more maternal transformation of the stern Father God of the Old Testament. He is frequently depicted with long hair, flowing robes, and a gentle, tender expression. This is captured in a prayer taught to Christian children: "Gentle Jesus, meek and mild, listen to a little child."

Nowhere is the female image of compassion and solace for human suffering more manifest than in Mary, the Mother of Jesus. Among her many appellations are: Virgin most merciful; Health of the sick; Refuge of sinners; Comforter of the afflicted; Mother of good counsel; Mother of consolation. Devotees pray the Rosary in troubled times to seek peace and hope. Praying the Rosary begins with contemplation of the joyful mystery of Christ's birth and continues on to the final five glorious mysteries having to do with Mary's Assumption into heaven, where she intercedes with her Son as a powerful Queen and merciful and loving Mother. The following clinical vignette illustrates a child's use of Mary as a source of solace after the sudden death of her mother.

Second clinical vignette

Lucy, a 5 year old child, lost her mother in a tragic accident. Her mother had been a devout Catholic, and Lucy accompanied her almost daily to church. This little girl was brought for help by her grieving father, who felt unable to bear the pain of her distress.

At first the child could not talk but sat with me, frozen, silently fingering her mother's Rosary beads. I sat with her quietly in this "dead" space for several sessions, at times rocking, at other times making soft moaning sounds. Eventually I commented that it seemed to help to have mother's beautiful Rosary beads to hold and to carry with her everywhere. Lucy nodded, and some minutes of silence she asked if I knew how to pray the Rosary. I knew that she had heard her mother do this almost daily, probably from the beginning of her life *in utero*. I said that I would learn the Rosary and offered that we could perhaps do this together. In time we did chant the prayer of the Rosary together over and over, always at the beginning of each session and sometimes as a way of ending.

Horton and Sharp (1984) write about language as a form of transitional relatedness with potentially soothing functions. They cite research on co-actional vocalization, which begins in infancy and is the forerunner of "choral speaking, prayer in recitative form, work songs, group singing or chanting, and other soothing joint vocalizations" (p. 172). Smith describes a haunting, holy sound he heard in a Tibetan monastery:

> In the first stage of his mantric meditation, the lama sounds the chords himself, but as his meditation deepens it appears as if the god invoked in doing the sounding and he, the lama, is resonating. And when his meditation reaches its climax, distinctions between lama, god, and sound collapse entirely, and all that remains is one holy chord. [Smith, 1973, p. vii]

So it was with Lucy. Her voice and mine blended together, resonating with the lost voice of the mother she sought to bring back. Our praying aloud in one voice brought her great solace. We had constructed a ritual in the analytic space, which had a privileged meaning, embedded, as it was, in the child's early sensory—auditory, visual, and tactile—relationship with her mother (Brinich, 1982). After a time Lucy told me that she wanted to learn how to do this by herself, as a way of feeling closer to her mother at bedtime. Winnicott (1953) views the repetition of sounds, songs, and tunes as a child falls asleep as falling within the domain of transitional phenomena.

Lighting candles in the church she used to attend with her mother also provided solace. Lucy asked her father to take her there daily so she could pray before a statue of Mary, Our Mother of Consolation, holding the infant Jesus. "Now she is my mother." Indeed, Lucy's greatest consolation came from an image of Mary, which she saw in the trees outside her bedroom window every night as she lay in her bed longing for her dead mother. She asked if Mary came to tell her that her mother was in heaven, watching over her. I assured Lucy that I did indeed believe that the vision of Mary came to reassure her that her mother was now watching over her and always would.

The tangible rosary beads and the vision of Our Lady provided Lucy with a transitional relatedness to her mother. The sacred string of beads helped her to manage the dreadful separation, to stay connected, in a sense to deny the unbearable (Winnicott, 1960). From an analytic perspective, Lucy's vision may be seen as an illusion, delusion, visual hallucination, transitional phenomenon, or divine visitation, depending on the analyst's personal cultural/religious belief system. Freud writes that an illusion of God is "the product of human wishes" (1927c, p. 31). Certainly Mary's visitation fulfilled Lucy's fervent wish to be in some sort of union with her beloved dead mother. Contrary to Freud's vision of our illusions, this one was derived from the strength of the child's passionate attachment to her mother, not her father, and took a feminine form.

Fear of the woman in God: a threat to the self

> "Rise, O Lord, in Your anger:
> assert Yourself against the fury of my foes"
>
> Psalm 7:7

Representations of the maternal/feminine in God are not always comforting. At times they may be experienced as confining, smothering, emasculating, even murderous. They may impede rather than facilitate or affirm a self that desires both autonomy and intimate attachment. For boys, in particular, there may be a pressing need in the service of separation/individuation from their mothers to denigrate and distance themselves from a maternal God.

Third clinical vignette

Jason, a 12-year-old African American child who lived with his mother and sister, was brought for treatment because of problems at school and church. He was defiant with teachers and his mother and had begun to hang out on the streets with his friends on Sundays, refusing to go to church. Prior to this he had been a star in the church choir and a drummer in the praise band. Moloney (1954) writes of the paralysis that occurs to the ego when the infant's rhythms are rejected in favour of the mother's need to dominate. In early childhood Jason had been outwardly compliant, but as he entered adolescence, the need to rebel became an imperative requiring that he refuse to accept even the most reasonable requests. With his mother, in particular, he announced a "no-give-in" policy. To use Moloney's words, he was constantly "battling within himself, his self-strivings perpetually entrenched, and yet always seeking to gain an inch against the 'enemy'" (p. 121).

After a rocky beginning during which Jason mostly rolled his eyes, looked out the window, strummed his fingers on the couch, and whistled, I had the thought to invite him to bring in one of his smaller drums. To the rhythm of the beat he began to tell me his plight in a sort of singsong rap. Unfortunately I do not have the lyrics, but the essence was that he was surrounded by women who were always telling him what to do or not to do. Now he was being forced to see me three times a week. "I can't take it no more. I can't get no air to breathe. I can't take it no more. There's nowhere left to hide." When we eventually came to the subject of God and church attendance, he told me, "I don't want no God that's just a pussy, for my Mom and for you too Dr B. Ain't goin' to get me to go to church no more and put on those sissy choir robes!"

This reminded me of Person's (2001) description of three strategies often used to assuage conflicts between obedience and rebellion. These are seizing the godhead, submission to God, and the godfather fantasy "whereby an attempt is made to clothe a mere mortal in the cloak of godly power" (p. 1133). I commented, "Maybe you need a different God—one that can kick butt and isn't afraid to stand up for Himself with women."

"Damned right! Hey, I want that old God that turned the woman into salt because she didn't pay him no mind. Where can I find him, anyway? All our pastor gives us is that sissy Jesus stuff about turnin' the other cheek. Ain't no good to me on the street. Not unless you want me to go down. Sometimes I think she [his mother] want me to be her girl."

Jason had a desperate need to identify with strong male figures, to reject attempts by women to control him, and to preserve his manhood against both internal "sissy" fears and external threats on the street. His rejection of the God his mother used to frighten him into submission was in the service of establishing a masculine identity and conquering his fear of being engulfed by the omnipresent woman. He wanted the strong father God who could help him rebel against the submissive obedience demanded by his mother.

The maternal in God as transformation object

> Thus, in adult life, the quest is not to possess the object; it is sought in order to surrender to it as a process that alters the self.
>
> Christopher Bollas (1979), p. 97

The concept of a metamorphosis of the self through a relationship with God is a prominent aspect in many religious experiences and beliefs. Long after the end of the interactive process in which the mother transforms her infant's internal state by rocking, stroking, kissing, feeding, bathing, changing, traces persist, in the older child and in the adult, of what Bollas (1979) terms the "transformational object". He describes a "recurrent experience of being—a kind of existential, as opposed to representational knowing" (p. 97). It is a type of knowing that is tied to a wordless form of object seeking that brings a deep, "unthought" fusion with the other and inspires a sense of the reverential, sacred, and transcendent. In his *Confessions,* St Augustine writes: "I will soar, then, beyond this power of my nature also, ascending by degrees unto Him who made me. And

I enter into the fields and roomy chambers of memory, where are the treasures of countless images, imported into it from all manner of things by the senses" (Fuller, 1947, p. 109). The intensity of the tie stems, not from desire, but from the possibility of a profound change in the self-state, part of an inchoate, unknowable, way of being that Winnicott attributes to the "female element" (Abram, 1997 p. 81). These transformations are perhaps best captured in the rhymes and rhythms of poetry using imagery of rebirth, enlivening, vitality, elation, or illumination from within.

Wordsworth (as quoted in Goldman, 1993, p. 106) describes the preverbal traces of adult immortal experience as follows:

> But for those first affections,
> Those shadowy recollections,
> Which be they what they may,
> Are yet the fountain-light of all our day,
> Are yet a master-light of all our seeing.
>
> William Wordsworth, from "Intimations of Immortality from Recollections of Early Childhood"

The following snippet of a brief analysis describes the transformational experience of a man grieving for his mother.

Fourth clinical vignette

A 54 year old Hindu man, Dr P, came for analysis because of a deep depression after the death of his mother. He felt "dead within", alienated from his wife and children, and cut off from his religious practices, which had hitherto been very important to him. He described a close relationship with his parents, who lived in India. The decision to emigrate to the United States had been difficult, and he continued to feel guilty about leaving his ageing parents in the care of a younger sister. There was a nagging feeling that if he had been there to supervise her medical care, his mother would not have died. Every elderly woman he saw in his general medical practice reminded him of her, and he was stricken with remorse for not visiting her before she died.

After a couple of months with the analytic focus primarily on the complex origins of his deep sense of guilt, Dr P was able to meditate again and to read the holy scriptures of the Bhagavad-Gita.

Zaehner (1966) describes it as "the sacred fount from which rapt devotion to God naturally flows" (p. 11). Rao (2001) refers to the healing dimensions of the *Gita* and to its potential for unearthing "psychoanalytic truths in unexpected places" (p. 194).

About six months into the analysis, and in the midst of a strongly positive maternal transference, Dr P came to his session is a state of elation, even ecstasy. As he lay down on the couch, he declared, "*Never was there a time when I did not exist, nor you, nor in the future shall any of us cease to be.*" I was startled, not realizing at that moment that he was quoting from the *Gita.* He went on to tell me that after the previous day's session he had been playing the *tabla,* and this verse came bursting into his head. He heard it as a sonorous sound, blending with the base of the *tabla,* and he believed that the words came from the Lord Krishna himself. He felt a warmth suffuse his body and a great sense of peace swept over him. In that moment the heavy weight of grief and guilt lifted, and he knew that he and his mother were one. Soon after this transforming revelation, Dr P ended his analysis, telling me that he felt an inner glow that he had never before experienced in his life. He feared that further analysis might destroy it. As I understood it, meditating on the *Gita* had come to serve an analytic function (Reddy, 2001) "not primarily interpretative but more as an object" (p. 156), which facilitated Dr P's healing of the dreadful rupture in his psyche caused by his mother's death. His ecstatic experience was reminiscent of the psychic transformation and the healing techniques of the mystical guru described by Kakar (2007).

Why was Freud's illusion so resolutely masculine? A look at his early mothers

> it [psychoanalysis] believes there is no one so great that it would be a disgrace for him to be subject to the laws which govern normal and pathological activity with equal cogency.
>
> Sigmund Freud (1910c), p. 63

I now turn back to Freud's illusory God. The question here is not why Freud put his faith in science and not in God: it is about his exclusion of goddesses, and the many maternal functions attributed to deities in most cultures from "the beginning" to the present time. Was Freud's illusory, masculine God a manifestation of an absence, a void, a painful loss, encoded in a place that he could not reach with his brilliant intellect?

The child Freud suffered multiple traumatic losses of maternal figures (described below), along with their sustaining, containing, self affirming functions (Clark, 1980; Gay, 1988; Hardin, 1987). These catastrophic early disruptions in primary attachments may help explain a certain psychic blindness and perplexity that pervaded much of his attempt to understand the "dark continent" of the woman's psyche. Internal representations of a reliable and powerfully protective mother may have been poorly formed and shrouded in unsymbolized, painful, split-off affective experiences in the first three years of his life.

Freud's introduction to God came from neither mother nor father but from his devout Roman Catholic nursemaid, one of the "uneducated masses" he later came to fear. In a series of letters to Fliess written in 1897, Freud reported memories of his nurse that had surfaced in his self analysis. He credited her with providing him with the "means for living and surviving" and related that she told him a great deal about God and hell, as well as sex. His mother answered a letter asking about the nursemaid as follows: "Of course, an elderly woman, very shrewd indeed. She was always taking you to church. When you came home you used to preach, and tell us all about how God conducted his affairs" (quoted in Hardin, 1987, p. 628).

This intense surrogate mother attachment, and, with it, Freud's encounters with God and the Catholic church in Freiberg, ended abruptly when the nursemaid was arrested and incarcerated for stealing from the family. These events occurred right about the time that Freud's mother was confined to bed before giving birth to his sister Anna. He described a conscious memory of "crying my heart out because my mother was nowhere to be found". Knowing that his older half-brother Philipp was implicated in the disappearance and locking-up of his nursemaid, Freud urged him to open a cupboard door so he could search for his mother. As an adult, he realized that his anguished insistence was fuelled by fear that his mother "must have vanished just like my nurse not long before" (quoted in Hardin, 1987, p. 629).

We can only speculate about the reasons that Freud's care was given over to "another mother". We know that his baby brother Julius, born when Freud was 15 months old, died about seven months later, and only a month prior to this, his maternal uncle Julius had died. Baby Sigmund's first few years were marred by multiple losses and by poverty and were most likely permeated by maternal depression and depletion. To add to all of this, soon after the disappearance of the nursemaid, the family moved from Freiberg first to Leipzig and a year later to Vienna.

Freud at age 43 years writes of the deeply mourned loss and traumatic dislocation (Akhtar, 2007):

> I now think that I have never got over the longing for the beautiful woods of my home . . .". During the next six years four more sisters and a brother were born, depleting even further the maternal supplies available to the little boy. Another catastrophe afflicted the family when Freud was 9 or 10. His paternal uncle Josef was indicted and imprisoned for trading in counterfeit rubles. The calamity turned his father's hair grey in a matter of days from grief and from worry that more of the family might be implicated. [Gay, 1988, p. 8]

Of the multiple traumas in Freud's early years, paramount were the abrupt disappearance of his nursemaid and the many disruptions in the relationship with his mother. Grief over the death of her brother Julius and then her infant son Julius no doubt intruded into the mothering of her firstborn. Added to Freud's childhood afflictions were the dilution of maternal availability subsequent to the birth of seven younger siblings, interspersed with two relocations and the loss of his father to grief and shame over the imprisonment of Uncle Josef.

Freud's resilience is remarkable, but it is not surprising that throughout his life Freud was plagued by a deep narcissistic vulnerability, a certain object hunger, and a propensity to end passionate attachments in painful disillusionment. Letters to his wife Martha were tender, but in the flesh there was an absence of intimacy, and there is a strong likelihood that he found a second wife/mother in an affair with his sister-in-law, Minna. Freud's inability to understand the inner life of women may in part be illuminated by his fear of them, which led to a defensive devaluation. For example, in a reply to Jung's confession of his sexual involvement with his analysand Sabina Spielrein, Freud noted: "The way these women manage to charm us with every conceivable psychic perfection until they have obtained their purpose is one of nature's greatest spectacles" (quoted in Lotto, 2001, p. 1302). Was this an unconscious commentary on the early seductions and then betrayals by both his mother and the nursemaid? Did the painful experiences with his "primordial" women lead him to overlook the contribution of the infant–mother relationship to all future relationships, including that with an "illusory "God?

Freud's reaction to his mother's death is relevant here. He himself was puzzled by it. In a letter to Ernst Jones three days after her death, he described feeling free of the "terrifying thought that she might come to hear of my death" (quoted in Lehmann, 1983, p. 237) but "no grief otherwise, such as my ten years younger brother is painfully experiencing." A day later he wrote to Ferenczi: "It has affected me in a peculiar way, this great event. No pain, no grief . . ." (E. L. Freud, 1960). Lehmann (1983) suggests some link between Freud's reaction to his mother's death and the complexity of his reactions as a child observing her grief after the death of his baby brother.

Noting the aversion to dealing with deeper pre-oedipal issues, Lehmann (1983) draws our attention to Freud's self revelation in his discussion of the oceanic feeling: "Let me admit once more that it is very difficult for me to work with these almost intangible quantities" (quoted in Lehmann, p. 244). In light of this, it is noteworthy that when Romain Rolland (cited in Freud, 1930a) first presented his concept of the "oceanic feeling", Freud readily traced its origins to early infantile states of being. The boundaries between infant and mother ebb and flow, and all experience of time is co-extensive with the subject's ego. In contrast to Rolland's profoundly religious interpretation of this state, Freud was sceptical about such "prehistory" of mental development. He reaffirmed his own view that religious needs derive from childish helplessness and a need for the father's protection (Lehmann, 1983). This contributed to his followers' view of the "oceanic feeling" as a regressive and potentially pathological phenomenon (Moore & Fine, 1990).

> Less comfortable to the Western mind is the possibility that re-capturing the infantile bliss of oneness with the universe might be a positive and transcendental occurrence. In the

> context of such "Eastern" perspective on the oceanic feeling, it should be remembered that Rolland was deeply involved with the study of Hindu scriptures and was the author of the biographies of Bengali mystics Sri Ramakrishna Paramhansa and Swami Vivekananda. [Salman Akhtar, personal communication, 3 June 2007]

Freud's inability to take this perspective may have emanated from his personal dread of recalling early mother–infant symbiotic states that were, for him, laden with procedural memories of breech, separation, and trauma. Winnicott (1946) makes reference to such a fear of women as being rooted in the infant's absolute dependence on his mother for care. "Fear of the mother who had absolute power at the beginning of the infant's existence to provide, or to fail to provide, the essentials for the early establishment of the self as an individual" (p. 164). From what we know of his early life, it seems that both of Freud's mothers failed him, leading to his lifelong search for, and fear of, dependence on a sustaining, affirming other. According to Fitzpatrick-Hanly (1992), Van Buren (1989) suggests that Freud's choice of the Oedipus myth, and his interpretations of his dreams of the Botanical Monograph and Irma's Injection, were determined by his need to deny experiences of dependency and vulnerability. Did he also need to deny his early communion with both his nursemaid and God in the church in Freiberg?

Not all of Freud's followers eschewed religion. Jung viewed religious experience as a compelling reality rooted in the universal unconscious and as "the only road to authenticity" (Laor, 1989, p. 218). He used the term *anima*—from the roots *an*, heavenly and *ma*, mother—to describe a part of the mind that is often symbolically connected with both earth and water. He believed that each man's first and formative experience of the anima is with his mother (Jung, 1937).

Erikson (1959) also included the important role of ethnic and religious affiliation in his concept of identity, even though he did not address the issue of religious belief *per se*. Loewald was more specific about this and suggested a developmental pathway for religious belief:

> The mature individual being able to reach back into his deep origins and roots of being finds in himself the oneness from which he stems, and understands this in his freedom is his bond

> of love with God. The concept of God itself seems to change from that of a blindly omnipotent power to that of the transformation and incarnation of such power in individual freedom and love" [Loewald, 1953, p. 13].

Balint (1968) includes religious ecstasy as one of the experiences of adult life when a state of complete harmony is experienced. "This *unio mystica*, the re-establishment of the harmonious inter-penetrating mix-up, between the individual and the most important parts of his environment, his love objects, is the desire of all humanity" (p. 74). Bion's concept of O is perhaps the most "religious" psychoanalytic concept to date. He used it "to denote ultimate reality (namely, absolute truth, the godhead, the infinite, the thing-in-itself)" (Eigen, 1981, p. 422). "O" falls into the domain of faith "that there is an ultimate reality and truth—the unknown, 'formless infinite'" (quoted in Eigen, p. 424).

On the contemporary psychoanalytic scene, Kakar (2003, 2007), Meissner (1984, 1986, 2001), Ostow (1995, 2001), Rao (2001, 2005), Reddy (2001), Rizzuto (1979, 2001), Thomson (2001) and Neri (2005), among others, continue to make significant contributions to psychoanalytic understanding of the manifestations of religious belief and disbelief in psychic development and functioning.

Rizzuto's (1979) empirical research, though limited in scope, suggests that all children form a mental representation of God in the course of their development. Pointing both to the utterances of the Psalmists and to her subjects' responses in her study, she identifies the essential human need "for connection to a worthwhile, lovable, and loving object who hears us, understands us, and responds to our need not to be alone in the world in helpless pain or empty opulence" (p. 27). On the matter of technique, Rizzuto cautions against reducing the analysand's religious experience to its genetic sources and recommends exploring it tactfully in a present-day relational context (2001, p. 32).

Meissner (1986), a Jesuit priest and a psychoanalyst, attempts a rapprochement between religion and psychoanalysis. He uses a developmental perspective and draws upon the concept of transitional phenomena to close the gap between theological and psychoanalytic understandings of religious experience. While accepting that the *mental representation* of God is the product of dynamic, conflictual, defensive, and structural influences, Meissner asserts unapologetically that, to the believer, "God is not just a representation, not even a transitional phenomenon; . . . he is an active and creative force acting and causing effects in the hearts and minds of his people" (2001, p. 82).

Ostow, a scholar of the Talmud, a committed Jew, a neuroscientist and psychoanalyst, rejects the view that religion and mental health are incompatible. In his exploration of spirit, mind, and brain (2006), he pinpoints the origins of awe, spirituality, and mysticism in infancy but goes on to trace their role in shaping a mature identity. In his view primary religious experience is rooted in psychobiology and is universal. He identifies a "religious instinct", which comprises a readiness and need to come together with others in a submissive attitude towards a commonly recognized deity (Ostow, 2001, p. 217). Thomson, on the other hand, draws upon psychoanalysis, cognitive neuroscience, and anthropology to explain why all religious ideas "are basically human concepts with alterations" (Thomson, 2001, p. 130) and are essentially the by-products of mechanisms that evolved for other adaptive reasons (p. 131).

The concepts of faith and trust are strongly associated with religion, but their place in psychoanalytic theory remains ill-defined. Neri's exploration of the overlap between faith and trust as well as his description of the "igniting and driving force" of faith in the analytic endeavour (2005, p. 79) make a significant contribution. He identifies the "F-factor" as an important psychic function that the analyst may have to employ to help patients who are trapped in chronic depression. He notes that Bion regarded the Act of Faith as representing the gap between theory and the psychic phenomena, or reality, experienced by the analyst in any given session.

Perhaps here the F-factor protects the analyst from joining the patient's sense of futility and deadness. Neri identifies a group of patients for whom one of the main tasks of psychoanalytic work is "the recovery of a certain amount of faith in the goodness of life" (2005, p. 81).

Many of these patients suffered early maternal deprivation or were the repository of their mothers' trauma-derived persecutory internal objects. The experience of the containing functions of a maternal, faithful God helps them to discover or recover a sense of their internal goodness. In Winnicott's words, "man continues to create and re-create God as a place to put that which is good in himself, and which he might spoil if he kept in himself along with all the hate and destructiveness which is also to be found there" (1963, p. 94).

An interesting perspective on the defensive functions of idolization of men, masculinity, and male deities is advanced by Sayers (1991). She suggests that the idealizing fantasy, often reinforced by male-dominated religions and religious images, enables us to escape from the painful conflicts of love, hate, envy, and gratitude, all of which remain unresolved in our inner representations of the maternal figure.

Concluding remarks

Religious beliefs and rituals, traces of the maternal in God, may be conceived as occupying an intermediary space, first created between mother and infant ((Winnicott, 1967, 1971). It is intensely personal, in part culturally determined, but always preserves important traces of the early mother, or mothers. Akin to the transitional object, it is to some extent uninterpretable, impenetrable, mysterious and sacred. "I am therefore studying the substance of *illusion,* that which is allowed to the infant, and which in adult life is inherent in art and religion. We can share a respect for *illusory experience,* and if we wish we may collect together and form a group on the basis of the similarity of our illusory experiences" (Winnicott, 1953, p. 231).

Freud was not unsympathetic to the difficulty of living life bereft of our illusions (1927c, p. 53). It was his hope that the voice of intellect would in time promote love between men (here again he excludes women), conquer the instinctual life, and bring about a decrease in suffering in a way that religion has not. Eight decades later, this hope has not been realized, but some would say optimistically that we are well on our way to dispensing with the need for religious belief. Bion, Lacan, and Winnicott would argue for a different perspective. Each one gives *being* a privileged place that is distinct from *knowing,* and in so doing they make room for a creative experiencing of the ideal as an important dimension of emotional life (Eigen, 1981). "By emphasizing the positive aspect of ideal experiencing as an irreducible term of human experience, these authors make it difficult to permit any facile "mother" or "father" reductionism . . . in the tendency to equate God with father (Freud) or mother (Klein)" (p. 430).

Scientific knowledge has contributed much to our understanding of the mind and its unfathomable functions and malfunctions. There are some domains it may not be able to explain. We may have to allow for that intermediate space wherein dwell elements of secret desire, passion, the totally irrational, the mystical, the divine and the demonic—some of them bearing the handprint of the early mother, who is both real and imaginatively created.

8

Three archaic contributions to the religious instinct: awe, mysticism, and apocalypse

Mortimer Ostow

Of course there is no religious instinct. I use the term as a metaphor for the almost universal readiness of individuals to cohere into social units in which all participate in cultic practices and shared beliefs in a supernatural entity with parent-like functions. Religious behaviour and thought seem to possess both primary, universal components and secondary, diverse components. The primary components should be sought in the psychobiology of the human organism. The secondary components can be understood in terms of local cultural, environmental, and historical influences.

This chapter discusses three of the many primary universals, perhaps determinants of the religious "instinct", and describes their psychodynamics, their neuroscience background, and how they develop. I address these determinants from within the Jewish religious tradition, since that is the only one in which I have any competence, but I believe that with respect to these archaic mechanisms, the various religions resemble each other. I place awe, mysticism, and apocalypse in a specific sequence—the sequence in which they appear at the inception of the prophecies of the three major prophets of Israel. Arlow (1951) spoke of the experience as the consecration of the prophet and pointed out that in each case the procedure involved is identification with the superego by incorporation of the divinity through one of the body orifices. The most complete statement is contained in the Book of Ezekiel.

Awe

Awe is a subjective emotion, usually intense, characterized by elements of dread and reverential wonder, or submission in the presence of something sublime. It is implicitly associated with religious feeling. Awe is not frequently encountered in clinical practice, although almost everyone can recall experiences of awe. These are favoured by exposure to structures whose size is almost incommensurate with human dimensions. Natural formations, such as mountains or bodies of water, inspire awe; great buildings, like the cathedrals, seem to have been designed to inspire awe. Sometimes one experiences awe in the presence of enormous masses of people or a person of prodigious accomplishment. Presumably it is the extreme dimensional variance, the discrepancy in size or intensity or loudness between a percept and normal human dimensions, that creates the affect state that we call awe.

Since awe is generally associated with preternaturally strong perceptual experiences, we may wonder whether its evocation involves the mechanisms of perceptual regulation. Clinical experience permits us to make some guesses about the correlation between some observed phenomena and neuroanatomy. Temporal lobe seizures may include experiences of illusion. Illusions of size, distance, and loudness are common. Penfield and Jasper (1954) recorded the mental productions of epileptic patients whose brains were stimulated during surgery. One patient, during stimulation of the right temporal region, stated that he was dead, that he was in the House of the Lord, and that he saw saints who were both violet and blue. He repeated a prayer over and over. Subsequently he described the experience as a dream that he was in heaven. Another patient would, during her seizures, dream that she was in church or in a convent and hearing a song.

Gloor, Olivier, Quesney, Andermann, and Horowitz (1982) report responses to stimulation of several points of the right temporal lobe of a patient with temporal lobe epilepsy. Among the responses were expressions of fear associated with water—mostly a fear of being pushed or falling into water. One could wonder whether this alludes to what has been called the "oceanic feeling".

Analysing reports of number of investigators, Bear and Fedio (1977) have put together a list of personality traits said to be characteristic of patients with temporal lobe epilepsy. Among these are: "*religiosity, philosophical interests* and *dependence*" (p. 458). Associating awe with religious feeling in general, these reports suggest that awe might be related to temporal lobe function.

Let me add another neuroscientific consideration, actually a hypothesis. It does seem to be true that memories are laid down categorically. That means that memory images that fall into the same category are stored in close proximity to each other, and distant from memories that fall into other categories. For example, Squire and Kandel (1999) cite work to the effect that images of living creatures are stored in locations other than those that hold the images of inanimate instruments. George, Dolan, Fink, Russell, and Driver (1999) have established that images of faces that are familiar are recognized as such at a point in the fusiform gyrus, while faces that are unfamiliar are recognized in locations that are slightly posterior.

I suggest that when categorical boundaries are crossed, the crossing is regularly accompanied by the appearance of a specific affect. Recently, someone gave me a gift—a slim volume, for which he had had a special slipcase prepared. He had known of my interest in Freud's thoughts about religion, and so I was not surprised when it turned out that the book was *Moses and Monotheism* (1939a). Since I already had several copies, I was grateful for the gift, but not impressed. However, as I removed the book from its case, I came upon a flyer advertising this particular edition of *Moses and Monotheism* as the first published in any language. I realized for the first time that the book had initially been published in English rather than German, because Freud was living in London at the time. That was a little more impressive. When I opened the cover and looked at the flyleaf, before I was able to appreciate cognitively what I found there, I felt a sudden brief thrill. Only a fraction of a second later did I realize the reason for the thrill—namely, that I saw an inscription to Wilfred Trotter penned by Sigmund Freud himself. Here was a direct personal experience of something that had hitherto remained in my mind as historical, almost legendary. I propose that it was the crossing of the boundary between the immediate and the historical that created the momentary thrill.

Squire and Kandel (1999) further report that memories are categorized by size. If this is so, then we may imagine that when the individual confronts structures of an entirely different scale, such as huge mountains, endless spaces, or deep chasms, another such boundary may be crossed, generating a special affect, namely the sense of awe. The association of awe with religion is almost implicit. In both the Jewish and the Christian Bibles, references to awe appear on almost every page. Our paradigm, the Book of Ezekiel, begins with a description of Ezekiel's chariot. There are numerous and repeated awesome images: storm, fire, radiance and preternatural creatures, lightning, penetrating flashes, wheels, "tall and frightening" and "covered all over with eyes", the "awe-inspiring gleam as of a crystal", loud sounds suggesting "mighty waters", and the "din of an army", the sapphire throne, the radiant genital, the rainbow.

Allusions to awe, both verbally and experientially, constitute a large part of formal prayer. Conditions and practices of worship seem designed to inspire awe. I include here magnificent temples and cathedrals, compelling music, unison singing, pageantry, and the assembly of large numbers of worshipers in one place. It is of further interest that the historic mythology of many religions includes giants as predecessors of the group or community.

In the light of these several considerations, I propose some hypothetical inferences. Since awe seems to be a response to major discrepancies of scale, it would seem reasonable to attribute its origin to the earliest experiences of the infant who must be impressed by the large sizes, loud sounds, and bright lights that he first encounters at the hands of his parents and the world in which they live. Though it would seem impossible to retrieve them, it is inconceivable that there is no affective response to the enormous scale of these perceptions. Addressing this issue of non-retrievable but influential memories, neuroscientists have created the category of non-declarative or "implicit" memory. Squire and Kandel (1999) describe one variety that attaches affective labels to current perceptions relating instinctual imperatives to previous experience. I suggest that the affect of awe in response to the major discrepancies of scale that we have mentioned represents activation of the non-declarative residues of early experience.

Though awe is mostly associated with fear or at least reverence, some awesome experiences arouse feelings of comfort and even active pleasure. To understand the relation between these two aspects of awe, we must recall that most types of affect arise in the context of instinctual function. Ethologists have taught us to distinguish between appetitive and consumatory behaviour (Ostow, 1957, 1958). And Panksepp (1998) reminds us that each of these phases is associated with its own characteristic affect. Considering the tiny infant in the hands of the gigantic parent, when circumstances are not propitious, the infant will scream in terror. With cuddling and feeding, this will subside. Distress will give way to a pleasant sense of satiety. The giant can threaten and can also protect and give pleasure. I propose that fearful awe corresponds to the fear in the presence of danger, and comforting awe to the sense of relief from danger and the pleasure that follows.

Although my argument is more suggestive than compelling, I interpret the foregoing observations to imply the following propositions. The original awe-generating experience creates a complex of feelings. For the infant, the gigantic, parent-like figure will sometimes seem dangerous, at other times comforting. The behaviour of this figure cannot always be anticipated or controlled, but it can be propitiated or it can be provoked. The influence of this constructed universe persists into adult life as a readiness to experience awe under off-scale and unusual circumstances.

Mysticism

Students of mysticism define it generally as the personal experience of contact with a deity or with a universal secular entity. There are many varieties of mystical experience, but to avoid getting too far afield, we shall confine ourselves here to unitive experience, such as that described by Ezekiel. Following the description of the awesome spectacle, the *merkavah* or chariot, we read that Ezekiel recognizes the presence of the Lord and flings himself on his face. He experiences the entrance of a spirit into his body and hears God's message. God feeds him a scroll in which are written "lamentations, dirges, and woes". He is then carried away by a spirit.

I quote here excerpts from a letter that describes a mystical experience. It was written by a patient who had suffered a long course of bipolar illness, which had created great difficulties in his object relations and business judgement. The episode described occurred during a period of depression associated with frightening visual impairment, during the course of which he wrestled with the problem of how to provide material security for his wife if he should predecease her, without significantly depleting his valuable collection of antiquities:

> *My worries increased regarding the financial situation, and I began to look for even more drastic ways to solve it. This was undoubtedly due to the blow of the virtual loss of my sight, to the increasing pessimism about my health in the near term, and therefore, the need for procuring additional security for my wife. I was lost in juggling all of the possibilities of how to keep the essence of my collection, the integrity of my commitments, and the security of my wife.*
>
> *For several days of intense thinking, I struggled with these conflicting needs until I happened to see an old story that I knew well, of David and Bathsheba, which was rather well done with Gregory Peck as David. . . . Far be it from me to compare myself to David. . . . He was a young shepherd who beat Goliath, and for the early part of his life, fought sincerely for the Lord of Israel. As he grew in power, and prestige, and adoration of the people, his life turned to materialism, greed, lust, and he committed, for that period, one of the most heinous crimes in Jewish history.*
>
> *. . . when David realized or was told by a prophet what a dreadful sinner he had been, he went to the altar of the temple still existing, and made one of the most noble repentance speeches I have ever heard, and pled not for himself, but for his wife Bathsheba, who was about to be stoned as an adulteress. . . . What amazed me about this story was how God was able to look into his heart and to know that not only was his repentance true, but he was a man of such genius, in spite of his crime, that he made him his choice as the elected antecedent of the Messiah.*
>
> *What all this has to do with me, I still can't figure out, except that suddenly—and never before have I had such an experience—some power*

> *told me how to solve my present problem and not knowing exactly what to do, I went to the synagogue on the following Friday and made an anonymous offering of $1,000 with a note saying, "I thank the Lord of Israel who showed me what my tasks and solutions should be." The solution, of course, was that I could not have my cake and eat it too, and that while I did not regret the collection I had amassed, it was time now to give it up, even with pain, for the sake of assuring a greater security to my wife, which would permit me to sleep and die in a much happier frame of mind. And furthermore, if I did not die, it would relieve some financial strains in order to have a more joyful ending.*
>
> *As God had predicted for David, for me it was not only painful, but also very difficult, more than I expected, and remember I insisted on protecting my reputation and the integrity of my commitments. I was really not surprised that for whatever reasons and especially as my sight goes down, my spirits go up and down day by day, but on the whole, I am happy with the route I have taken, though I do not really know why I took it. All I know is that hard as it may be, it is the right thing to do.*

Mystical experiences reported to me have invariably been associated with longing for reunion with a lost object, usually an object of childhood, the mother or the father. The earliest post-biblical recorded Jewish mysticism, *merkavah* mysticism, focuses on the image of Ezekiel's chariot with its divine passenger. The mystic visualizes and hopes to encounter God there. A later variant, *hekhaloth* mysticism, based Chapter 6 of Isaiah, imagines God presiding from a large throne in a huge temple.

Mysticism encompasses more than unity with God: it includes the notion that the entire universe is integrally related, one part to the other. The "oceanic feeling", the term for such unity that Freud (1930a) attributes to Romain Rolland, signifies the feeling that the individual is materially immersed in and part of a universe, limitless and unbounded in space or time. This feeling is subjective, not an article of faith; it brings with it no assurance of personal immortality, but it is a source of religious energy that is seized upon by the various churches and religious systems and directed by them into particular channels.

In a state of mystical union [*unio mystica*] the individual regresses to the pre-separation–individuation state. The object with whom the mystic unites is symbolic: sometimes mother, sometimes father, and often an undifferentiated parental object, not gender-specific. Do we know enough about neuropsychoanalysis to suggest an anatomic locus for these mystical operations? The mystical process is driven by a hypertrophied attachment drive, the expression of the tie attaching the infant and child to its mother; and subsequently attaching all of us to those we love. Panksepp (1998) demonstrates that the anterior cingulate cortex must be intact if attachment forces are to prevail. Visual images such as occur in mystical speculations, hallucinations, and trances probably require the activity of the occipito–parieto–temporal regions (Solms, 1997). Penfield was able to elicit visual hallucinations by stimulating the lateral aspect of the diseased temporal lobe (Penfield & Jasper, 1954; Penfield & Kristiansen, 1951).

Another clue comes from the patient whose mystical illumination I described above. Soon after this experience, he developed, for the first time, *déjà-vu* experiences, initially frequent, then virtually continual. These acquired delusional intensity. He came to believe that he could anticipate the future because he had already experienced everything that he had encountered. He knew what was going to happen next.

Déjà-vu phenomena almost always result from disorder of the temporal lobe (Penfield & Kristiansen, 1951). Though neurologic evaluation of this man yielded no definitive diagnosis, Sjögren's syndrome was suspected because he had complained of painfully dry eyes. This diffuse systemic disease involves tissues of many organs, including, at times, the brain. We can speculate that the patient's *déjà-vu* phenomena and his newly acquired susceptibility to mystical experience are attributable to the same brain lesion or to a disorder at a different but closely approximated location. Indeed, thereafter both the *déjà-vu* and the mystical tendency continued concurrently.

Since the mystical reunion is meant to provide surcease from stress, anxiety, and depression, the opioid-endorphin mechanism might be involved. In addition, there is reason to suspect that it is related to the oxytocin attachment mechanism.

The developmental antecedents of the mystical experience can be recognized in the process of separation–individuation. The alternating affects of excitement and anxiety that accompany this transition need not be inferred: they are immediate and obvious to anyone within the ambit of the baby or young toddler. When anxiety supervenes, it elicits a tendency to reverse the process of separation. I propose that the attempt to restore unity with the parent gives rise to the mystical experience. In adults the experience may consist of a sense of being united with the image of the parent figure—now displaced onto a deity—or, in a trance, conviction of the literal experience of visual, auditory, or tactile contact, or in a dream the imagined transport to the deity in a vehicle or encountering him in a chamber. As is the case with dreams, the mystical experience probably affords gratification by elaborating appropriate neurochemicals.

The following vignette should perhaps be classified under the rubric of ecstatic mysticism. The speaker is a middle-aged Jewish woman.

> The first time that I was in Israel was in September 1961. The last time was last year [1998] on Yom Ha'atzmaut (Israel Independence Day), except I was here in Riverdale. I generally do not consider myself a "mystical" person. I was taught from an early age to analyse and weigh in an intellectual fashion. . . . But last year something happened that was very different from anything that I had experienced before.
>
> The Riverdale Jewish community had organized a parade and celebration. I went partly because I wanted to and partly because I figured I should. Well, am I glad! The parade, about a mile long, started from our shul and wound through the streets of the neighbourhood, passed Riverdale Temple, ending up at the Hebrew Institute. The parade was okay, led by the Cathedral High School Marching Band (yes, from a Catholic school), and at the end there was the Manhattan College [a Catholic college] bagpipe band. (Only in New York!) At the final location there was a bandstand and an orchestra. They played a medley of music, people started to dance, and after a short time the program started.
>
> First was a moment of silence with a siren blaring in memory of all of the fallen of Tzahal [Israel army]. The cantor sang a special *"El maley rachamim"* for the army dead. And then was one

> of the most unusual moments of my life. It is hard to describe. The cantor from Riverdale Temple sang *Hatikvah* [the Israeli national anthem]. She has an incredible operatic voice. But while she was singing, I was someplace else and not standing on a street corner of Riverdale. Suddenly I really was in Israel, seeing again some special places. It was as if I were in the taxi in 1961, when I first visited Israel, going up the old road to Jerusalem just as the sun was coming up, and in the Emek looking out over the fields, and in Haifa somewhere and visiting the Kotel [Western Wall] for the first time. I was in one place and in all of the places seemingly at the same time. It was absolutely unbelievable. I don't think that I have ever had an experience just like this before. Even now, an hour or so later, if I close my eyes, I can continue to see places where I have been, and some not for many, many years, so vividly. It is as if I were there right now. . . . Hard to believe that when I began this evening I was feeling discouraged, and not excited about the holiday at all.

The last sentence of the account seems like a postscript, but it illustrates an important aspect of mysticism: the mystical experience may be encouraged by a feeling of discontent or depressive unhappiness. This induces the wish to reunite with the parents. This woman's mystical experience was encouraged by the several acts of union that she witnessed within the community and, in general, the assembly of large numbers of people. She was affected also by the music, the prayer for the fallen soldiers, and the singing of the Israeli national anthem. The physical, sensory, and emotional intensity of the day contributed to the mystical experience. The Israeli taxi, like Ezekiel's chariot, transports her to the place of mystical encounter.

Dictionary definitions of religion speak of belief, worship, adoration, reverence, and rites; *religious*, as an adjective, expresses commitment to such beliefs or forms of worship. But such a definition fails to convey the essence of what I have called the "religious instinct"—that is, the psychological readiness and need to engage with others in common submission to a divine entity. Nor do I propose this latter as a sufficient definition: religion is a multifaceted enterprise. But I believe it captures that aspect which relates to the three issues under discussion.

How are awe and mysticism related to religion? I doubt that anything that is called a religious experience can fail to include elements of awe or mysticism or both. Awe and mysticism can occur outside a religious context, but they seldom do.

The example below illustrates religious feeling that is evoked by experiences of awe and mystical union. A woman had travelled to a resort for a professional meeting:

> That summer's meeting was at the South Seas Plantation on Captiva Island. I had never been on the Gulf Coast and was totally swept away. I was used to the Atlantic Ocean—cold water and waves. The Gulf was unexpected—the water was warm and "bouncy". I could stand for an hour, with my sunglasses on, up to my neck in water, and never get pulled off my feet. It was totally relaxing.
>
> In the evening, people would go down to the beach and go swimming. It was hot outside, and going in the water cooled us off, and it never got so cold that you couldn't stay in the water. The third evening we were there, we learned that there is a kind of plankton that is phosphorescent and that there was a large area of the water around the resort where these creatures were swimming. You couldn't see them, but they made the water glow. None of us really knew what that meant, but it was an interesting fact.
>
> That night, when we went down to the water, I was blown away. The effect of these creatures' being in the water is phenomenal. When I would bring my hands out of the water over my head, the water dripping off my hands and arms looked like it had silver glitter in it. People were jumping up and down, making splashes of glitter. Each night more and more people came down to swim, and that night there must have been about fifty people in the water. The moon was full, beautiful, and really bright. When I looked out over the water, I saw all of these jumping, bouncing people, silhouetted against the horizon, throwing up splashes of glittery water.
>
> I had never experienced such a combination of things. I stood in the water, up to my neck, and felt like I stepped back and

> saw it all spread before me—the people (all of whom were having a blast), the glittery water, the moon, the temperature. It came to me so clearly that such a combination of wonder and beauty could only happen because of the existence of a God, of a higher being. Never had I so surely felt that presence as I did at that moment.

Apocalypse

Apocalypse is a literary, religious type of prophecy that appeared in Israel about two centuries before the Common Era, and perhaps earlier in Persia. It purports to foretell the future on the basis of revelation (the word apocalypse means revelation) to a divinely inspired sage or prophet. The prophecy usually consists of a series of dire implications directed at a specific population—sometimes the prophet's own people, sometimes their enemies—warning of punishment of the utmost severity. However, in the end there is reconciliation and rebirth. All of this will happen at the "end of days"—the eschaton. The genre includes certain other stylistic characteristics and often a messianic deliverer. Apocalypse is ordinarily thought of in connection with religion. The secular apocalypses are few and far between. The destruction foretold is seen as punishment for immoral and irreligious cultic behaviour. The complex of fantasies and associated affects that characterizes apocalypse seems to grasp the imagination of the people and is used to enforce religious discipline and conformity

From the name given to the phenomenon—apocalypse—it is evident that theologians consider revelation to be at its essence. As a psychoanalyst, however, I find the sequence of anticipated of death and destruction followed by rebirth to be central.

Why is the apocalyptic mode of thought so congenial? I believe that it gives expression to a basic psychophysiologic function, the regulation of mood. Patients with borderline or cyclothymic personality often exhibit obvious and sometimes intense mood swings in daily life. These manifest during a psychotherapeutic sessions and certainly in their dreams. The shifts are less obvious in depressed or manic patients, but we can still easily detect them in dreams. Among patients without affect disease, close attention will detect much more subtle yet definite mood swings during the session, but not always in their dreams. I infer that mood swings occur constantly among all of us, subtle, controlled, and limited in range among most, and frequent and striking in the presence of affect disease. I believe we possess a normal mechanism for mood regulation that strives towards but does not achieve homeostasis. When mood rises towards euphoria, sooner or later a corrective downward swing begins. As mood declines to depression, the corrective tendency reverses it towards euphoria. I believe that normally mood oscillates within a period of about 45 to 90 minutes, corresponding to the REM cycle. Panksepp (1998) speaks of a 90-minute basic rest-activation cycle. Most of us are not aware of these subtle oscillations, but if sufficiently intense, we may become aware of the resultant moods. Though we usually see them as internally derived, those so disposed will attribute them to an external source.

Strong moods will violate ego boundaries and colour perceptions of the world about us. It is not that we are depressed: the sky is falling. When an individual recovers from depression, the world seems new and fresh and promising. Thus, fantasies of impending apocalyptic catastrophe can be seen to reflect the anticipation of a depressive crash, while dreams of rebirth and salvation project our psychic recovery—the internal homeostatic correction. The alternation of destruction and rebirth played out in each apocalyptic episode reflects the internal mood oscillation that I have described.

One must include in the category of apocalypse those persecutory campaigns attacking a designated enemy perceived as a source of danger (e.g., representing the anti-Christ) and thereby inviting messianic redemption. Persecuting sects from the Middle Ages are described in Norman Cohn's work, *The Pursuit of the Millennium* (1970). These apocalyptic persecutions mirror the acute rages of the borderline and of the affectively psychotic patient who believes that his violent, apocalyptic attacks on others will achieve his own personal redemption from persecution.

In both the personal and community apocalypses, guilt is owned by the victim: that is, he feels guilty (see Lamentations). But guilt is also applied to the persecutor. This subjective guilt and the divine inspiration attributed to the prophet establish the link to religion. This is the guilt that is ordinarily found in most cases of depression and that usually invokes moral condemnation to explain it.

We know something more about the brain's participation in apocalypse than we do in the case of awe and mysticism. Mood can be influenced by the activation or deactivation of a number of loci in the brain. One system that I find especially interesting is that which Panksepp (1998) calls the *seeking system.* It serves to sustain the activity of the principal instincts, holding them in a state of readiness to be triggered. It consists of a neural tract that arises in the periaqueductal grey of the brainstem, courses through the medial forebrain bundle of the lateral hypothalamus, and reaches the orbital medial region of the frontal lobe; it operates by means of the dopamine neurotransmitter system. These circuits, Panksepp says, contribute to feelings of engagement and excitement. Under the influence of electrical stimulation of the system, subjects report "invigorated feelings that are difficult to describe. They commonly report a feeling that something very interesting and exciting is going on" (p. 149). The system is activated by dopamine stimulants which create "an energized psychic state", while a "sluggish depressive state" (p. 149) accompanies blockade of the system with antipsychosis drugs. If the system is damaged, a generalized behavioural inertia results.

We know of several different sources of depressive sentiment. Arresting the activity of the seeking system causes not only inertia but also depression. Corticotropin-releasing factor secretion is elicited by stress but also creates negative moods. Panksepp (1998) describes a fear system, which originates in the central and lateral areas of the amygdala and projects downward into the brainstem. Stimulation of this system creates subjective feelings of foreboding such as one experiences in apocalyptic dreams. Imaging studies suggest that the right brain exerts a generally depressive affect so that gross lesions affecting the right cerebral hemisphere leave the patient not appropriately depressed by his disability, whereas lesions on the left, which seems to exert an antidepression tonus, leave the patient depressed. Which of these several depression mechanisms participate in the spontaneous depressive process and whether others may be involved as well is not evident at the present time. I suspect that those structures of the right brain that exert a depressive influence oppose the seeking system in effecting mood alternation and regulation.

Psychopharmacologic agents exert their influence at different points in the mood-regulating system. Unfortunately, the mechanisms involved remain as yet obscure. Dopamine and norepinephrine seem to be associated with primary antidepression activity. It is not clear whether serotonin has a direct antidepression effect or merely alleviates psychic pain or facilitates norepinephrine release. Since serotonin exerts an essentially inhibiting influence in the brain, I would guess that the serotonin-sparing antidepression drugs act to suppress the activity of the right-brain depressive mechanism, whereas the dopamine agents reinforce the energizing activity of the seeking system.

The interplay of apocalyptic mood and dreams with psychopharmacology is nicely demonstrated in a patient's dream (Ostow, 1995):

> "*My wife and I were somewhere in the mountains in some small village. There were four people coming on horseback. They were knights like the Four Horsemen of the Apocalypse. They had stopped to tell us that there was going to be an earthquake and some of the area will be flooded. We were on a small island. They told us to move to a larger island, which we did. While we were there, the earth began to quake, fire began to flow, and the small island where we had been was inundated with water. We were clinging close to the ground while the earth was shaking.*" [p. 54]

The four knights in the dream were identified by the patient with the Four Horsemen of the Apocalypse. He could not remember their names or exactly what they stood for, but he knew that they represented portents of great danger and ultimate destruction. In the dream, however, he was struck by the fact that the four horsemen were actually saviours and helpers.

The dream's apocalyptic theme suggests the prospect of destruction as punishment for sin. However, the patient escapes. The explanation for the failure of the apocalyptic threat can be found in the patient's history: in view of his lifelong masochism and depressive character, he had begun a programme of anti-depression drug therapy a year earlier. His response to all medication had been positive but only temporary. However, 17 days prior to the dream, 20 milligrams of fluoxetine (Prozac) had been added to his regimen. He responded with pronounced remission of his symptoms. The dream reflects the remedial effects of the added Prozac in the patient's seeing himself as one of the saved rather than one of the doomed, and the Horsemen as friends rather than demons.

This case illustrates the influence of mood on the outcome of the mythic drama as it is played out. We see here not only the congruence between the affect correction homeostatic mechanism and the prototypical apocalypse, but also how antidepression medication modifies the outcome of the dream apocalypse.

From the point of view of the practicing psychiatrist and psychoanalyst, it is important to observe that just as prevailing mood determines the content of dreams, so it determines also the content of waking thought. Conversely, careful studies of session transcripts will reveal that shifts of mood often arise internally. Reality is not the only determinant of our moods. Moods are generated internally, in a regular and often predictable succession, and affect our perceptions of reality.

Perhaps to an even greater extent, the social organism, the group, adopts common moods and attitudes and interprets current experience in this light. Group moods can be belligerent, pacific, generous, or defensive. We see alternating group enthusiasm and group despair in market behaviour. Group apocalyptic thinking and behaviour, persecutions, pogroms, and religious enthusiasms are usually entrained by the prophets of apocalypse.

The examples of mystical experience that I have given above have each been followed by a strong alteration of mood, all positive. Here is a dream of a man who had been depressed for years, but was in partial remission.

> "*I was in Brooklyn on Eastern Parkway, driving past the headquarters of the Lubavitch Rebbe. I was sitting in a room with Hasidim. They said, 'This time it really happened.' 'No, it couldn't.' What were they talking about? I walked out. They were all talking. It turned out that the Rebbe had died, and these people believed that he was directly related to God. A number of times he'd been sick, but hadn't died. Now he had died. If he had had divine protection, he should not have died. They paraded him around on a chair. He would ascend to heaven in a fire.*

> *They put me in a chair, which I thought was strange. They were rocking me back and forth. I fell off the chair. There was a fire. I fell into it.*"

There is a room in a headquarters. The Lubavitch Rebbe is presented as a charismatic, religious figure. We find a *merkavah*, the chair in which the Rebbe would be translated into heaven. The patient associates to the Jewish wedding custom of elevating bride and groom on chairs carried by the more vigorous guests. Occupying the chair represents an oedipal (or perhaps Promethean) violation of the father's privilege. The dreamer specifies a host of ministering subordinates, the Hasidim, who—like the hostile angels of Isaiah 6—throw the dreamer down to his fiery death. Fire accompanies the ascent to heaven and also awaits the traveller who is ejected. Clearly, the intent of the dream is Promethean, to ascend to divine heights and to displace the father god. For that, the dreamer is punished.

The mystic's attempt to ascend to see God permits of either success or failure. Clinically, when the patient is in a good mood, he succeeds in his dreams; when he is depressed, he fails. The outcome of the effort to overcome depression depends upon the patient's readiness, which is, in turn, determined by neurochemistry, endocrine contributions, and current environmental influence.

The reason that the *merkavah* paradigm is so cogent as well as common is that it is based upon the notion shared, I believe by almost all religions, that God is to be found above and his opponents below. The designated holy places of most religions are elevated places, hills and mountains, or else caves reproduced in temples.

My interpretation of the association of holiness with elevation is that the very small child finds ultimate salvation in his mother's arms, lifted to her shoulder. "Up, up, up!" is the usual cry when the child needs to be comforted. It is this elevation to mother's breast, face, and shoulders that is the original source—and subsequently the paradigm of all mood elevation.

The *hekhaloth* paradigm locates God inside a chamber, and that is where the mystical worshiper encounters him. Here, the mother's body is reproduced only symbolically. Centre stage is taken by the father's imago. I suspect that the earliest images of the parents are probably gender-neutral and the earliest impressions might be of a chimerical combination. The point I wish to make here is that the fantasy chamber, the *hekhal*, is duplicated in religious worship by the temple, the church, or even the cave. Both represent the cavity of the mother's body, the ultimate claustrum.

Since developmentally the *fons et origo* of comfort and beneficence is attachment to the mother's body, it is not surprising that attempts to regain good feeling in the presence of distress lie in the effort to return to that ur-experience, symbolically if not veridically. It is this principle that lies at the heart of the mystical experience. *Merkavah* and *hekhaloth* mysticism create the illusion of transport back to mother's body.

From this point of view, mood regulation may be regarded as the continuing effort to return to the situation of satisfying closeness or attachment to the image of the archaic parent—resisting the stresses of negative reality experience and of depressive inner pulls.

In this way the mystical endeavour can be employed in the service of apocalyptic mood regulation. But it is not only the mystical endeavour—it is the entire religious enterprise that takes us back to the effort to re-experience the earliest parental comfort. Therefore, mood oscillation and the apocalyptic complex in which it is projected out onto the outside world form one of the major archaic components of the religious instinct.

Conclusion

The sense of awe derives from the newborn's nondeclarative memory of his impression of his adult, giant parents. The tendency to mysticism derives from the infant's wish to undo the process of separation–individuation—that is, to merge back into the mother. Apocalyptic thinking is created by the externalization of early mood swings. Together, awe and mysticism create an affect that is generally described as religious. I adduce some evidence for the proposition that they are associated with temporal lobe function.

It will, no doubt, have occurred to the reader that not all of those individuals who have reported experiences of awe, mysticism, and apocalyptic thinking are religious in the conventional sense of attending religious services and complying with ritual, cultic rules.

What, then, can be the relation between these archaic proto-religious experiences and conventional religion?

First, let me note that the persisting affects associated with non-declarative memories leave a gap in the continuity of the conscious experience of the world. This gap is commonly filled by the image of a deity, usually given by the surrounding society, though sometimes created idiosyncratically. Many people, though, reject this image of the gods of their fathers and are left with their naked emotions and the sense that something is missing. It is the feeling that Romain Rolland described: "One may, he thinks, rightly call oneself religious on the ground of this oceanic feeling alone, even if one rejects every belief and illusion" (Freud, 1930a, p. 65).

These affects all subserve the attachment instincts, creating the urge to reinstate the earliest state of affairs. It is fulfilled by anaclitic clinging to parents in childhood, later by integrating oneself into a social group, finding a marital partner, and ultimately coming to depend, in one way or other, upon children and the wider family and community. To the extent that the community is a religious community, it is held together by a common belief system that includes the nature and name of the common deity and a mythology that attempts to satisfy childhood curiosity.

This is a possible framework for a religious system within which the archaic components to which I have drawn attention serve as primary motivation and earliest affective expression of the need for attachment. Individuals may accede to, or dissent from, any aspect of the frame, while retaining the central affects and being moved by them. One may have religious feelings without being formally observant.

9

Re-reading Freud on religion in Hindu India

Sudhir Kakar

> And there is the further difficulty that precisely in a judgment of this kind [on the future of civilization] the subjective expectations of the individual play a part which it is difficult to assess; and these turn out to be dependent on purely personal factors in his own experience.
>
> Sigmund Freud, *The Future of an Illusion* (1927c), p. 5

I first read *The Future of an Illusion* (Freud, 1927c) when I was 18. A youth who had grown up in provincial Indian towns, I had come to study mechanical engineering in Ahmedabad, a large city intimately associated with Gandhi and the Indian freedom struggle. It was here that I came across Freud's writings and took my first steps into the world of Western ideas and imagination. I cannot pretend that I understood everything I consumed so voraciously. I sensed, though, that in my inner world I was being gently guided away from my native Hindu–Indian imagination, full of myths and marvels, lighted by a romantic numinosum, into an iconoclastic way of seeing the world where, if one looked hard and deep enough, all gods have clay feet. The experience was exhilarating.

The Future of an Illusion was an important text in my personal "freedom struggle", also because its appraisal of religion neatly dovetailed with the assessment of my other youthful passion, which also held emancipatory promise: Marxism. Freud is pure Marx when he talks of civilization being imposed on a resisting majority by a minority that understood how to obtain possession of the means to power and coercion (p. 6) or when he talks of the economic basis of civilization, with its problems in acquisition and distribution of wealth, before discussing civilization's "mental assets" or "psychical inventory" of which religion is such an important part in reconciling men to their lot.

For someone who grew up at a time of Indian history when Western modernity—a catch-all term for political democracy, scientific rationalism, and philosophical individualism—was idealized by many as the most desirable future for our society, Freud's attack on all religion, including my Hindu heritage, was as welcome as the similar Marxian dismissal of religion as the opium of the masses. For many of us, intoxicated with the ideas of Western gurus, political freedom from colonialism had not yet translated into freedom from a colonized consciousness.

Decades later, no longer resonating to Nietzsche's (1949) call that every past is worth condemning, questioning my earlier idealizations of Western civilization and the Judeo–Christian tradition of which psychoanalysis, in spite of some differences in its image of man, is an integral part, I come back to Freud with some of the scepticism of the great sceptic himself. Re-reading *The Future of an Illusion* at a different stage of life and self-consciously as member of a non-Western cultural group, I am struck by how much of Freud's analysis of religion is inseparable from "personal factors in his own experience" and "subjective expectations" from his cultural–historical background. As a Hindu—or one who has wittingly donned the Hindu robe for the purposes of this essay, though not without some playful effort—I am not surprised. It is a tenet of Hindu philosophy that an individual "action" can only be understood in context of the culture of his country [*desha*], the historical era in which he lives [*kala*], the efforts required of him at his particular stage of life [*shrama*], and, lastly, on his innate psycho–biological traits [*guna*]. An individual can never know the configuration of all these factors, his experiential background, in any absolute sense.

This basic Hindu postulate is similar to the argument advanced by the philosopher Charles Taylor that our experiential background can never be articulated in a complete way, since any articulation "supposes a background. The very fashion in which we operate as engaged agents within such a background makes the total explication incoherent" (1995, p. 70).

If one replaces the Hindu doctrine of *guna*, which, in line with belief in rebirth, considers human development to be anchored in a succession of previous lives, with its Freudian counterpart—that is, *guna* being grounded in infancy, in our adult "pre-history" rather than a previous birth—then the traditional Hindu emphasis on the relativity of all human action, including the production of knowledge, is surprisingly modern. Its emphasis on relativity, though still rare in psychoanalytic writings (for some exceptions see Erikson, 1975; Stolorow & Atwood, 1992; Stolorow, Orange & Atwood, 2001), coincides with influential currents in modern Western philosophy, which also at least highlight the *desha-kala*, the cultural–historical embeddednes of human knowledge and understanding (Dilthey, 1976; Gadamer, 1975; Heidegger, 1927). And although psychoanalysis, both clinical and theoretical, often challenges some cultural–historical verities of its era—Freud's writings are an outstanding example—culture and history, *desha* and *kala*, operating silently in the background of our awareness, inevitably compel psychoanalysis to be *more* an artefact of its times than its critic (Zeddies, 2002).

Let me take an example from the beginning of *The Future of an Illusion,* where Freud sounds very much like a conservative, patrician Brahmin viewing the lower castes when he writes of the need for leaders of a superior quality:

> It is just as impossible to do without control of the mass by a minority as it is to dispense with coercion in the work of civilization. For masses are lazy and unintelligent; they have no love for instinctual renunciation, and they are not to be convinced by argument of its inevitability; and the individuals composing them support one another in giving free rein to their indiscipline. [1927c, pp. 7–8]

Here, using the four Hindu "coordinates" of action, the *desha* and *kala* of Freud's observation are fairly obvious: Europe between two

World Wars when extremist ideologues of the Left and Right were creating mass movements imbued with messianic fervour. Building on the classical notion of masses described by Gustave Le Bon—whose own ideas were, in turn, framed by the dread the French upper classes felt in relation to the revolutionary masses—Freud's reflections on mass psychology are coloured by the ideological concerns of the time: namely, the liberal fear of loss of individual autonomy in a collectivity and the socialist concern with how to make the desired collectivities more tolerable and tolerant. Moreover, Freud's strong anti-religious stance has also been related by scholars to the tradition of radical rationalism in which he had grown up (Loewald, 1977) as also to the cultural context of Freud's Vienna in which a conservative Catholic Church encouraged anti-Semitic policies that were finally to culminate in Nazism (Gay, 1988; McGrath, 1986; Schorske, 1979).

The individual coordinates of *The Future of an Illusion*, its *ashrama–guna* context, are more elusive. At a pinch, one can relate Freud's dismissal of religion as universal obsessional neurosis of humanity (p. 43) to his specific *ashrama* or stage of life, with its illness and deepening pessimism, especially when we know that his views were relatively more benign at earlier stages of life. In his introduction to Oscar Pfister's correspondence with Freud, Paul Roazen reminds us that a decade earlier, in his case history of the Wolf Man, Freud is much more appreciative of religion than in his consistently negative comments in *The Future of an Illusion* (Pfister, 1993). And as for the *guna*, personality traits arising from his "pre-history" which went into Freud's lack of musicality and his apathyy towards religion, it has been suggested that the latter was based on his need to overcome his fascination with the occult as also his need to defend himself against his love for his father (Ostow, 1989).

Ideas of God

From viewing *The Future of an Illusion* through a traditional Hindu methodological lens, let me go to a Hindu view of its vastly more important content. Here, I will only take up Freud's discussion on the psychological origin of the idea of God and the nature of illusion, which appear strange, if not incomprehensible, to a thoughtful Hindu who is otherwise in sympathy with Freud's project of a psychological deconstruction of religious ideas.

"Eighty years after you wrote *The Future of an Illusion,* I wonder if you would still adhere to its main conclusions", our imaginary Hindu (following the literary conceit often used by Freud) would begin: "I know that you called it 'childish' almost immediately after you wrote it" (Freud & Ferenczi, 1927, p. 375) and that later, in *Civilization and Its Discontents* (1930a, p. 74), you somewhat softened your severe stance by saying you were not talking about deepest sources of religion but with what a common man understands by his religion. Yet in all your writings on religion you do not retreat from two main conclusions: the idea of God as an enormously exalted father and the illusory nature of the religious belief system, 'so patently infantile, so foreign to reality' (Freud, 1930a, p. 74). I will thus respond to these two ideas without speculating on how you would have revised them, something you never hesitated to do in light of new observations and evidence.

"A major difficulty I have with *The Future of Illusion* is your emphasis on religious ideas and beliefs comprising the religion of the 'common man', whereas in Hinduism ritual and practice take precedence over belief, which is taken much less seriously than is the case with the so-called Abrahamic or Semitic religions of Judaism, Christianity, and Islam. A Hindu may believe in one God or many gods or be an atheist, but what makes him a Hindu are his ritual practices and adherence to rules rather than to doctrines. Ritual is prior to theological doctrine, historically and conceptually (Flood, 1998, p. 199), and Hindu religious identity does not depend on shared ideas and beliefs, but on rituals relating to rites of passage, worship at home or temple (*puja*), festivals and pilgrimages. In short, a Hindu *is* as a Hindu *does.*

"Hinduism's ideas of God have been shaped by many cross-currents throughout its 5000-year-old history. Over the centuries, the interaction and synthesis of these currents of belief has resulted in contemporary Hinduism with its varied teachings and diverse cults. 'Belief in stones and trees having souls (Animism, Pantheism) exists side by side with the belief in higher gods, the monotheistic worship of one god is as much possible as the polytheistic or demonical adoration of many gods, demons and spirits' writes the Indologist Axel

Michaels (1998); he continues: 'The religion is lived through ritualistic (Brahminism, Tantrism), devotional (Bhakti), spiritual–mystic (asceticism, Yoga, meditation) and heroic forms. . . . And yet to a large extent all these forms are peacefully practiced besides each other. One can almost say that religious post-modernism has been realized in India: "Anything goes"' (Michaels, 1998, pp. 17–18)."

It is thus difficult to have one definitive Hindu view of any religious idea. In the absence of a "master narrative", a *grand recit*, I can only give the contemporary ideas of god (or gods) in Hinduism while acknowledging that there are schools that, like Buddhism (which some Hindus would call the export version of Hinduism), ignore the existence of god altogether. In Upanishadic and Yogic mysticism, for instance, which date back to 600 BC and are considered by some the signature forms of Hindu religiosity, there is no trace of love or yearning for communion with God, which is considered the highest manifestation of spiritual mood in the Christian and Islamic mystical traditions."

Freud links the "birth of God" to two motives: one manifest, the other deep. The manifest motive is to defend against the superior, crushing forces of nature by humanizing them. Once humanized, men follow the infantile model of influencing adults in their environment by establishing relationships with them:

> We can apply the same methods against these violent supermen outside that we employ in our own society; we can try to adjure them, to appease them, and, by so influencing them, we may rob them of a part of their power. [Freud, 1927c, p. 17]

Freud's formulation of the manifest motive applies to the origins of ancient Hindu pantheon. Most—though not all—Vedic (ca 1800 BC) gods are nature gods and goddesses who can be appeased by offerings and worship, asked for help, or, as in case of the wrathful Rudra, be persuaded not to interfere with the human world. Today, the nature gods are rarely worshipped, although they are present in ancient invocations that accompany some of the religious rituals.

The manifest motive for the birth of God—to which Freud added a second one: the urge to rectify the painful shortcomings of civilization—is not a matter of dispute for a thoughtful Hindu. What he will respectfully contest is the validity of Freud's deeper motive: the universality of a father-complex—the fear of the father combined with the admiration and longing for him—that goes into the development of the idea of God.

"You are much more circumspect at the beginning of your enquiry into religion when, aware of the historical and cultural relativity of your arguments, you restrict them to 'our present-day white Christian civilization'" (Freud, 1927c, p. 20), our imaginary interlocutor will continue. "But as soon as you come to the deeper motive that conflates father and God, you observe no such limits—for instance, when you assert that 'the primal father was the original image of God, the model on which later generations have shaped the figure of God' (p. 42) or when you call religion the universal obsessional neurosis of humanity, which, 'like the obsessional neurosis of children, arose out of the Oedipus complex, out of the relation to father' (p. 43). Your whole construction of the idea of God arising from the constellation of the helpless child and the protective father who is also a source of danger, an ambivalence you claim is 'deeply imprinted in every religion', seems to be absent or at least insignificant in Hindu religious imagination; at best, it is but a minor theme in a grand symphony."

Indeed, iconographically, the only god represented with a grey beard and who may conceivably be equated with a protective father, the Creator Brahma, is a forgotten and neglected god today, who has but only one temple in India dedicated to his worship. In the three main Hindu traditions—Vaishnavism, Shaivism, and Shaktism, related, respectively, to the worship of Vishnu (and his incarnations), Shiva, and the many forms of the Great Goddess Maha Devi—it would be difficult, if not impossible, to locate the father in a Hindu's worshipped deity. This is not a question of monotheism versus pantheism, since most Hindus believe in the existence of one God although at the same time they feel free to worship God in different forms. In the Brihadraranyaka-Upanishad (ca. 900 BC), the sage Vidagdha asks another sage, Yajnavalkya, "How many gods are there?" "Three thousand and three, and three hundred and three", Yajnavalkya replies. But as Vidagdha keeps on repeating the question, the number of gods keeps on reducing: "thirty-six", "six", "three", "two", "one and a half", and, finally, "one" (Radhakrishnan, 1994, p. 235).

"If we just talk of the protective function that you ascribe to a father–god", Freud's Hindu opponent continues, "then in Hindu iconography this function is parental rather than fatherly. Whether in temples or coloured lithographs so easily available in India's bazaars, Hindu gods are generally not depicted alone but have their consorts by their sides. Very often, a deity is not invoked on its own but as part of a couple: Sitarama and not Sita and Rama, Radhakrishna and not Radha and Krishna. In the two main Hindu traditions of Vaishnavism and Shaivism, the feeling of helplessness and the looking for protection from God seem to be the last thing on a devotee's mind. Take Krishna, the incarnation of Vishnu and perhaps the most popular god, at least in north and central India: in Krishna's iconography and in his representation in religious poetry and song, he is either a toddler—with the child's attributes of freedom, spontaneity, and delight in self, which Hindus consider as divine attributes (Kakar, 1982, pp. 200–204)—or an eternal youth, a *puer aeternus,* with either his lover Radha at his side or playing the Divine Flute in middle of an admiring and often dancing circle of young women.

"In Shaivism, the god Shiva, originally the Destroyer of the Hindu trinity (Brahma is the Creator and Vishnu the Preserver), could have conceivably resembled the father–god of Judeo–Christian and Islamic religious traditions. But, Shiva, above all, is the untamed god who cannot be reduced to any single function. He is the Lord of the ascetics, but also the indefatigable lover whose sexual embrace with his consort Parvati lasted thousands of years. As Hari-Hara, he is half Vishnu and half Shiva; as the androgyne Ardhanarishwara, he is the 'Lord who is half woman'—Shiva and Parvati at the same time. Today, Shiva is not thought of as wrathful Deity charged with the periodic destruction of Creation, but as Shankara ['dispeller of doubt or difficulty'] or Shambhu ['benevolent']—that is, a friendly, sweet god, occasionally prone to excess.

"No, if it is ambivalence in relation to father that is a deep motive in the construction of God, then in Hinduism we have to look for this ambivalence in relation to the mother and to the Goddess, a motive that is upfront in the Shakta tradition. The innumerable village goddesses, all regarded as manifestations or aspects of the Great Goddess, Maha Devi, are earthy, mundane, attuned to the uncertainties and troubles, the desires and prayers of daily life (Kakar, 1982, p. 110). In comparison, the male gods are remote. The Great Goddess is an ambivalent figure: both the furious, bloodthirsty Kali with a lolling tongue and the gentle, benevolent Durga with breasts overflowing with maternal milk. It is these ferocious and protective forms—Wendy [Doniger] O'Flaherty (1980, p. 91) calls them 'goddesses of tooth' and 'goddesses of breast'—that are combined in the Great Goddess, in the primal mother, so to speak, rather than the primal father, which underlies the idea of Divine in the Shakta tradition.

"I believe that the mainstream attitude towards God in the three Semitic religions has misled you to generalize it to other religions of mankind. In devotional practice, besides the surrender, obedience, or filial love, which are the normal ways of approaching a father–god, Hindus seek to establish an intimacy with the Deity through other *bhavas* ['moods' or 'emotions'] that are congruent with the personality of the believer; in the Hindu world one size does not fit many. Some of the other attitudes towards God, for instance, are *sakhya,* the emotion of friendship, *madhurya,* the romantic and erotic feeling towards a lover, or *vatsalya,* the feeling of a mother towards her child: in other words, God as friend, lover, or child. The latter attitude towards the Divine, prominent in worship of child–Krishna, completely reverses the father–child accent you have placed on man's relationship to God. Indeed, a feeling of awe in relation to God and the degrees of fear associated with awe are rare in the Vaishnava or Shaiva traditions: "awe distances and separates rather than binds and joins" (Kakar, 1992, pp. 17–18).

In a further contrast with the Father–god of Abrahamic religions, the Hindu God is not only multifaceted human—father, mother, child, lover, friend—but also incorporates animals and birds in his divinity. Some of the animals are especially dear to the gods—the vehicles on which the gods travel and in whose worship they participate. For example, Indra rides on an elephant, Shiva on a bull, Yama on a buffalo, Durga on a tiger, Ganesha on a rat; among the birds, the goose is the vehicle of Brahma, the peacock that of Kartikeya. Monkeys are representative of Hanuman, while dogs are associated with Bhairva, an aspect of Shiva. The clear message is that God is immanent in all creation, human or animal. Indeed, the divinity even extends to some trees, such as the *pipal* [fig tree], or such plants as the *tulsi* [basil], which are associated with the gods and are widely worshipped.

Illusion and reality

With the advantage of hindsight, the "thoughtful Hindu" will say that Freud's ensnarement in the *desha-kala* web, in the "archaeology of knowledge" (Foucault, 1972) or the period systems of discourse that shackle what can be thought and expressed at a particular historical juncture, is nowhere more evident than in his blanket dismissal of illusion. For all his creativity, Freud was an heir to a European Christian world where illusion had long implied trickery and deception, a world where Satan was the arch-deceiver and where the literary use and weight of the word is illustrated, for instance, in *Macbeth* (III: v. 27–8) in the "illusion" of the "artificial sprites" that ensnare Macbeth (Turner, 2002). Whereas in an earlier era the malignant quality of illusion had been demonic, the Logos of science replacing that of theology in Freud's time led him to call it pathological. Religion is not only analogous to obsessional restrictions but comprises wishful illusions "such as we find in an isolated form nowhere else but in amentia, in a state of blissful hallucinatory confusion" (Freud, 1927c, p. 43).

"Hindus are much more positively inclined towards illusion", responds Freud's imaginary opponent. "They tend to associate illusion with playfulness, or even benevolent deception, rather than with malignancy. If you ask an orthodox Hindu about the nature of the world or why it was created, the answer would be, 'It is God's play [*leela*]'."

Since myth and metaphor are typically Hindu ways of viewing the world, a myth of child Krishna (an incarnation of Vishnu) and his human mother Yashoda conveys some of this quality Hindus associate with illusion:

> One day, Krishna's playmates reported to his mother that her son had been secretly eating mud. Yashoda scolded the child, who protested his innocence. "Mother", he said, "if you don't believe me you may look into my mouth." When the mother of God did so, she saw the whole universe in the little mouth. Motionless space, the four directions, the earth with its mountains, islands, and oceans, wind, fire, the milky way with the moon and the stars, water, sky, gods, the sense organs of the mind, the five elements of potential matter, the three qualities of creation, were all in Lord Krishna's mouth; and in it she saw her own village and herself. Yashoda was confused. Is this a dream

> or illusion made by God? Or is it a delusion of my own mind? Seeing his mother disturbed, Krishna closed his mouth. As soon as he did so, the vision was erased from Yashoda's memory, and, once more in grip of the maternal illusion, he was again her little boy. [Subramaniam, 1988, pp. 330–331]

In Vedic thought *maya*, generally translated as illusion, is identified as a particular power of the gods to create, a power later ascribed to magicians, artists, and, in certain Indian philosophies, to each one of us, at every moment of our lives (O'Flaherty, 1984, p. 118). In psychoanalysis, this equation of illusion with creativity is associated with the influential work of Winnicott (1953, 1970), which accorded "permission" to many later authors to view the role of illusion in religion in a non-pejorative and indeed positive light (Meissner, 1992; Pruyser, 1983; Rizzuto, 1979). Winnicott would have winced at Freud's anecdote about his grandson's matter-of-factness, in which Freud admires the child turning away in disdain from the narration of a fairytale when he was told it was not true (Freud, 1927c, p. 29).

It is not as if Hindus completely deny the dark side of illusion. The negative quality associated with *maya* has not been absent in Hindu philosophical thought or popular imagination. Based on the important work of the Indologist Wendy [Doniger] O'Flaherty (with its delightful title, *Dreams, Illusions and Other Realities*), let me summarize the Hindu doctrines of illusion and the way these philosophical constructions of his tradition have influenced the attitudes of the average Hindu.

The Vedic concept of *maya* as a kind of artistic power gradually led to its later connotations of magic, illusion, and deceit. In both cases, though, *maya* can best be translated as "transformation" (O'Flaherty, 1984, p. 118). In other words, some Indian philosophies regard *maya* as a positive fact of life to be embraced, while others will agree with Freud's evaluation and regard it as a negative fact, to be combated. Both attitudes towards illusion coexist in the Hindu mind. But how do Hindus draw a line between illusion and reality? Don't Hindus dismiss the whole of existence, the empirical world of our senses, as *maya*, as illusion? This commonly held view of what a Hindu believes is the nature of our world is misleading. Yes, there have been the extreme Hindu idealist philosophers (but more Buddhist ones) who gave an ontological status to the omnipotence of imagination, who felt it incumbent upon them to explain not why imagery is private but why reality is public (Beyer, 1973, p. 92). The ideas of these philosophers—Nagarjuna, Vasubandhu, and others—find strong echoes in the contemporary ideas of Marc Bohm and Ignacio Matte Blanco, who imply that imagination is the basis of reality (Arden, 1985). But an average Hindu does not really believe that "We are such stuff as dreams are made on" (Shakespeare's *The Tempest*, IV.i:156–157). In other words, for a Hindu to say

> that the universe is an illusion (*maya*) is not to say that it is unreal; it is to say, instead, that it is not what it seems to be, that it is something constantly being *made*. *Maya* not only deceives people about the things they think they know; more basically, it limits their knowledge to things that are epistemologically and ontologically second-rate. [O'Flaherty, 1984, p. 119]

"What Hindu theories about the 'softness' of reality do is to dissolve the very hard-and-fast line between illusion and reality that you make in *The Future of an Illusion*. For a Hindu, there are many different kinds of reality: of concrete experience, mystical visions, memories, dreams. Some are more real than others. As Wendy O'Flaherty (1984, p. 126) further remarks, 'These (realities) would have to be set out at various points on a spectrum that has no ends at all. A comparable, though different range of perceived realities exists in the West, but the traditional Western way has been to assign each phenomenon to one or other of the basic polar oppositions of hard and soft, real and unreal. This India refuses to do' (O'Flaherty, 1984, p. 126). Even Karl Popper, the most empirical-minded of modern philosophers who may be expected to sympathize with your views on illusion and reality, is more flexible on this question: 'Realism is essential to common sense. Common sense, or enlightened common sense' (Vishnu's dream, of course! One of the Hindu myths is that the world is Vishnu's dream and exists as long as he does not wake up. The world is real from the human perspective, but illusion from the viewpoint of God.) 'distinguishes between appearance and reality. . . . But common sense also realizes that appearances (say, a reflection in a looking glass) have a sort of reality; in other words, that there can be a surface reality—that is, an appearance—and a depth reality. Moreover, there are many sorts of real things' (Popper, 1979, p. 37)."

Concluding remarks

If Freud's imaginary opponent is wondering how the Master would have reacted to the Hindu take on *The Future of an Illusion*, I believe I can reassure him. Freud was certainly not dogmatic. We know he was ever willing to change his views in light of new evidence and was often a harsh critic of his own work, especially when it ventured out of the clinical into the cultural domain. "If experience should show—not to me, but to others after me, who think as I do—that we have been mistaken", he writes, "we will give up our expectations" (Freud, 1927c, p. 53). The *Future of an Illusion* is not a mistake but contains partial truths that cannot be universalized. From an Indian, Hindu perspective, its major deficiency lies in its basic premise: the importance Freud attaches to religious beliefs and ideas in his portrayal of religious man. Hinduism, though not indifferent to this aspect of religion, certainly considers it much less relevant than religious *experience*, whether in ritual, religious celebration, pilgrimage, or in the "profound" mystical experience to which Freud, in spite of his scepticism, paid respectful attention (Freud, 1930a). For a Hindu, it is the arresting, transformative moments in religious practice that constitute the core of religion. It is these religious moments that overcome what Yeats in his poem *Meru* (1956, p. 287) called the "desolation of reality". They are flashes that light up the narrow, mundane world of daily existence—a world that has always been inadequate to our experience and unequal to bear the burden of our hopes. Perhaps Freud the novelist ["In my mind I always construct novels" (Mahony, 1982, pp. 11–12)] and the artist ["I am really by nature an artist. . . . My books in fact more resemble works of imagination than treatises on pathology" (Papini, 1969)] rather than the positivist scientist of *The Future of an Illusion*, would have agreed.

And what of the young man at the beginning of this essay who had once welcomed *The Future of an Illusion* as an indispensable ally in his struggle to jettison the romantic "illusions" of his native Indian imagination and to move from the realm of *mythos* into that of *logos*? Older now, he continues to keep faith with Freud's ironic vision of human existence, although he is much less enamoured of the bargain he made when he was young.

10

How belief in God affects my clinical work

Neville Symington

God as the Infinite

Belief in God lies at the core of all religious denominations. Theravada Buddhism is an exception to this general rule, and for this reason it is sometimes described as a Philosophy rather than a Religion. My belief in God affects my clinical work, but how? What follows is a personal statement: it is the way this belief affects *my* work in the consulting-room. It contains no statement about how such a belief may affect someone else, nor is it a recommendation for other clinicians.

Mystics, such as Meister Eckhart and the author of *The Cloud of Unknowing* emphasize that the reality of God is obscured through the word *God*. The word conjures up in the mind an image that blinds me to the reality that the word *God* is supposed to designate. Thus the word makes the reality foggy. The way in which a word can disturb our understanding has been emphasized by Wilfred Bion, by the philosopher Frege, and also by G. K Chesterton, who said this:

> Atmosphere ought not to affect these absolutes of the intellect; but it does. . . . We cannot quite prevent the imagination from

> remembering irrelevant associations, even in the abstract sciences like mathematics. [Chesterton, 1933, p. 180]

God is one of the earliest words I learned in my childhood, along with *Jesus* and *Mum* and *Dad*. It has an almost tactile sense for me, and if this is an exaggeration, then it has at least a sensual quality, so that if someone said, *"Look, there is God"*, I would kneel down and worship a graven image. The author of the Book of Exodus has already tried to teach me that I cannot *see* God in that lovely passage:

> "You cannot see my face; for man shall not see me and live." And the Lord said, "Behold, there is a place by me where you shall stand upon the rock; and while my glory passes I will put you in a cleft of the rock, and I will cover you with my hand until I have passed by; then I will take away my hand, and you shall see my back; but my face shall not be seen." [*Exodus,* ch. 33, v. 20–23, revised standard version]

The word *Allah* obscures in a different way. It conjures up an image of the desert, a mosque, and Muslim worshippers dressed in white lying prostrate before an awesome presence way above the earth, with poor miserable humankind an insect in its sight. It embodies the idea of Fate, against which no human hand can be effective. Camus' *La Peste* swims into mind. So these images are conjured up by the word *Allah.*

The prophets' denunciation of idols was not only of images to false gods but images of *Yahweh.* They understood, following the lead given by the author of that passage from the Book of Exodus, that there can be no image of the infinite, again as G. K. Chesterton says,

> The imagination is supposed to work towards the infinite; though in that sense the infinite is the opposite of imagination. For the imagination deals with an image. And an image is in its nature a thing that has an outline and therefore a limit. [Chesterton, 1938, p. 107]

An image is of some finite thing, and words are codifications of images, so a word can never represent the infinite. Wilfred Bion used the term **O** to denote truth, ultimate reality, the infinite, or the godhead. I believe **O** stands for *Ontos,* which in Greek means

Being or Reality. Some authors think **O** stood for *Origin*. Bion's widow, Francesca, does not know what Bion meant to denote by the term. My supposition that it stood for *Ontos* in Bion's mind rests on two pieces of evidence: that his definition of **O**:

> I shall use the sign **O** to denote that which is the ultimate reality represented by terms such as ultimate reality, absolute truth, the godhead, the infinite, the thing-in-itself. [Bion, 1970, p. 26]

is precisely what *Ontos* means, and, secondly, that Bion used Greek letters to designate psychological realities. Also in *Elements of Psycho-Analysis* he says that container/contained is a manifestation of a central abstraction that is unknowable, which I shall quote later. In other words it, the unknowable, cannot be *imaged*. I know from my own experience that certain words designating this reality get in the way of making contact with it.

There are no images and therefore no words for this reality that we are trying to describe, so how are we to connect with it? There are certain words that *for me* do not interfere in the way that *God* and *Allah* do. *Brahman* is better for me: there are fewer images associated with this term, which comes from the Hindu tradition. So also the *THAT,* which comes from the same tradition. *Yahweh,* too, carries me into the imageless presence of the unknowable partly due to that lovely passage from Exodus. *Thou* under the influence of Martin Buber does the same.

I need, though, to reflect through a personal act of the intellect. Is there no signal that can direct me towards this act? Different people will approach it differently, but the way that led me to such an act is through reflecting on the *being-ness* of individual things. I can remember the day when the realization of *Being* took hold of me. I was 22 at the time and was attending four lectures a week for a year on the subject of Ontology. These lectures were being given by a philosopher who would come into the lecture hall, put a textbook on the podium, read a sentence, and then abandon the book and walk up and down talking about Being. I knew in my heart that here was a man who had a personal insight into Being. I think it was this personal assimilation of his that created an environment in which I also was able to grasp Being itself. I shall return to this point when addressing the clinical relevance of belief in Being.

Knowledge of God through an act of intellect

Can God be known through an act of intellect? The central belief of the Judaeo–Christian–Islamic tradition is that God intervened in history and revealed Himself to human beings, but the seers of the Upanishads had reached knowledge of *Brahman* without such an intervention. They arrived at it through the powers of their own reflective intellect. This reality can be grasped through contemplative reflection upon *Being*. Revelation could not occur unless the mind was capable of knowing God through a natural act of intellect. Belief is not a psychological act revealing what could not be known through an act of intellect but, rather, something that transforms what is known through it. Belief changes the nature of what is. It makes what issues from the intellect into a something that involves the whole of me. Belief gathers the disparate parts of me and anchors them into the unity of the act of intellect, which it also transforms. Belief also gathers me as an alienated individual into this unity, into *Being*, into *Brahman*, into *Yahweh*. It unites the disparate parts of myself into a unity and me, as an individual, into the one-ness of the world, of the universe. It *nothings* me or naughts me, as the anonymous author of *The Cloud of Unknowing* (McCann, 1952) puts it, and it ennobles me at the same moment.

I referred just now to a *personal act of intellect*. This is not an act of intelligence separated from my emotions. It is an act that grasps the *being-ness* of things without any contamination from what is taken in through the senses. So I differentiate *intellect* from intelligence. *Being-ness* has no colour, no sound, no touch, no smell, no taste, so the senses cannot apprehend it. The intellect devoid of the senses grasps it. This is what was grasped before Plato by Parmenides, who, shutting off his sensory information, declared that *being* constantly is and therefore all change must be an illusion. In this latter conclusion he was wrong, but I understand why he reached it.

All this is a preparation for my key point that belief in *Brahman* affects my clinical work in a profound way. This belief does two things: it gathers me into a singularity and focuses me upon *Brahman*, so it *naughts* me at the same time as gathering all the disparate parts of myself into one. These disparate parts of myself are what Jung called *complexes*:

> the so called unity of consciousness is an illusion. It is really a wish-dream. We like to think that we are one; but we are not, most decidedly not. We are not really masters in our own house. We live to believe in our will-power and in our energy and in what we can do; but when it comes to a real show-down we find that we can do it only to a certain extent, because we are hampered by those little devils the complexes. Complexes are autonomous groups of associations that have a tendency to move by themselves, to live their own life apart from our intentions. [Lecture III of the Tavistock Lectures, "The Symbolic Life"; in Jung, 1976, pp. 72–73]

This focus upon *Brahman* unites the *complexes* into a unity. This is because belief is an emotional action that draws all parts into the wake of its focus. This has two effects that are central to clinical work.

Of one thing I am certain: that only those things that I truly think and believe can effect change in the listener; these are things that I have made my own, things that belong to the heart. It is only when I speak like this that I connect with the psychotic part of the personality. That is one consequence of my belief in *Brahman*. The other is that my own hurt does not distort my perception of the other. In other words, I do not project onto the patient my own disowned parts. There are no disowned parts when there is a unity.

This unity, this unlimited being, both transcends myself and, at the same time, captures my inmost essence. In its transcendence it is the whole universe; in its immanence no part of me is outside its reality. I and this other one who is sitting with me in my consulting-room are one. This does not mean, of course, that the two are not separate, any more than when I say the universe is one that it is not composed of many forms.

I will now come down to earth. There is a certain kind of suffering that seems to be characteristic of our times. Here is someone in whom there is an absence that is so elemental that we find it difficult to grasp. If someone is lacking a leg, we can easily apprehend it; if his thinking is defective, we might discern it; if he lacks imagination, people will comment on it; but the suffering I am talking of is none of these. What is it, then, that is lacking? I call it an inner mirror. I will try to describe it.

Absence of subjectivity

A patient arrives. I shall call him Joshua. He is middle-aged and is worried at the prospect of retirement and death. Then he asks me, "Tell me, Neville, am I happy?" Now I am puzzled. When I reflect, I know that only I myself can answer that question of myself. I may not be sure whether I am happy or not, but I am certain that no one else can tell me. Marion Milner spoke of a patient who did not know whether she hated or loved and realized that the fluctuations between love and hate were so rapid, one microsecond in one state and one in the other, that she did not know whether she loved or hated. Now this may have been the case with Joshua, yet I do not think so. If I said to him, "So Joshua, one moment you are happy and the next you are not, so you don't know whether you are happy or not", he would reply, "Is that what you think, Neville? Is that it?" Slowly it begins to dawn on me that speaking words to him will always land me in the same dilemma with him. There is something lacking, and this is not something superficial but, rather, a little something, almost nothing, and yet it is the very essence of what makes me a human being. The analyst has to re-orientate his approach. There is a function in the personality that is undeveloped, and therefore a technique geared to promoting the development of this function has to be adopted. This was emphasized by that much-neglected philosopher, Maurice Blondel (1893, p. 98).[1] With this little something I am a human being rather than a computer. When a computer says, "I enjoyed the sandwiches", I know that those words indicate something completely different to when *I* say "I enjoyed the sandwiches", and yet I think Joshua's inner state is closer to the computer than to subjective experience. I know what I mean when I say "I enjoyed the sandwiches" and also when I say "I am very happy at the moment". Yet Joshua and I are both human beings, so his state of being cannot be entirely foreign to me. Can I dig into myself and find the computer? The answer to this is that I cannot, because if I find it, there is an *I* that has found it. The finding of it by my *I* is a transformation. "Finding" is the wrong word. There is a something that can only be seen when transformed. The way I speak about this is to say, I *realize* that I am happy, or I *realize* that I am sad, or I *realize* that I am disappointed, but the moment before the *realization* takes place, the state is not there. So I know by inference that I share with Joshua his computer-like state, but awareness I cannot have because awareness is knowledge that has become transformed. I have had many *realizations* in my life and I can argue against the position of someone who has not had a particular *realization,* but I cannot return to the unrealized state that I was in. I am changed. Now the question is this: where does *realization* come from? And the answer is that it comes from *Brahman*; it comes from God.

To understand this statement, it is necessary to analyse what we are doing when we are thinking. I have first to unpack that word "thinking" in order to define it. Those things that are closest to us, that are part of the fabric of our existence, are the most difficult to define. Ask me to explain what a horse is or what an atom is, and I can do it without too much difficulty; but ask me to define place or time or inner realities like feeling or thought, and it is much more difficult. So also it is difficult to analyse the process of thinking. First, it is an activity; second, it is an activity that is inner; third, it is an activity that is not bodily, though it may, as Rodin's famous sculpture suggests, have physical accompaniments that are suggestive of thought. Yet again, when Archimedes had his famous Eureka moment, it was as he was letting himself down into the bath in ancient Syracuse—not a manoeuvre that suggests profound thought. Then let us define the goal of this activity and then examine what instruments are needed in order to attain it. The goal is to transform a stimulus that strikes the human being from the outside into an activity whose sources is from within the organism. The transformation is from an *it* into an *I.* I need an instrument with which to achieve this. Of the many instruments that are available, they can be categorized under two headings: *Brahman,* or an idol. An idol is fashioned by the imagination via the senses; *Brahman* is grasped through the intellect. The author of *The Cloud of Unknowing* also wrote a treatise called *The Epistle of Privy Counsel,* where he describes it in this way:

> look that nothing remain in thy working mind but a naked intent stretching unto God, not clothed in any special thought of God, in himself, how he is in himself, or in any of his works, but only that he is as he is. Let him be so, I pray thee, and make

> him no otherwise. Seek no further in him by subtlety of wit; let that belief be thy ground. This naked intent, freely fastened and grounded in very belief, shall be nought else to thy thought and to thy feeling but a naked thought and a blind feeling of thine own being, as if though saidst thus unto God within thy meaning: "That that I am, Lord, I offer unto thee, without any looking to any quality of thy being, but only that thou art as thou art, without any more". [McCann, 1952, pp. 103–104]

I need to give some examples of idols in order to make clear the distinction that I am trying to make. If I try to explain mental phenomena upon the principle that all human motivation is governed by survival alone, if I try to explain mental phenomena on the assumption that the brain produces the mind, if I try to explain all mental phenomena on the basis that sense experience is the foundation of all knowledge, if I endow these as absolutes, then they are idols. They are anyway in error, although close to the truth. But an error that is close to the truth is the worst falsity. Chesterton endorsed this point when he said,

> falsehood is never so false as when it is very nearly true. [Chesterton, 1933, p. 105]

Freud's idolatry

In *The Future of an Illusion* what Freud describes as God is an idol. It is based on a sense image; in his case, it is the image of father. When the Old Testament prophets fulminated against the worship of idols, they meant an image of Yahweh rather than Yahweh himself. Freud starts, I believe accurately, saying that primitive human beings plagued, as we still are today, with earthquakes, storms, and diseases attributed these events to an animistic agency as a way of trying to control the uncontrollable. I shall quote him as he writes of it so eloquently:

> There are the elements, which seem to mock at all human control: the earth, which quakes and is torn apart and buries all human life and its works; water, which deluges and drowns everything in a turmoil; storms, which blow everything before

> them; there are diseases, which we have only recently recognized as attacks by other organisms; and finally there is the painful riddle of death, against which no medicine has yet been found, nor probably will be. With these forces nature rises up against us, majestic, cruel and inexorable; she brings to our mind once more our weakness and helplessness, which we thought to escape through the work of civilization. . . . Impersonal forces and destinies cannot be approached; they remain eternally remote. But if the elements have passions that rage as they do in our own souls, if death itself is not something spontaneous but the violent act of an evil Will, if everywhere in nature there are Beings around us of a kind that we know in our own society, then we can breathe freely, can feel at home in the uncanny and can deal by psychical means with our senseless anxiety. [Freud, 1927c, pp. 16–17]

In an aside I might say, I believe that a great deal that is given an intentional cause within psychoanalysis is in fact attributable, as Freud says here, to chance forces, rather than any act of human will.

However, Freud then goes on to fashion God upon this same model of a benign protector, which he dismisses along with the primitive animistic spirits and explicitly dismisses the understanding of god derived from the mystics. He has no idea of the conceptual development of the idea of god. Only a modicum of textual criticism of references to Yahweh in the Old Testament quickly reveals the difference between a primitive local storm god and the absolute or infinite. What Freud repudiates is just such a local deity expanded to become the god of the whole world, but his expansion of this god's power is not equalled with a deepening of the concept. He specifically says that he gives this animistic spirit the character of a father (Freud, 1927c, p. 17). Freud dismisses the purification of a sensual idolatrous image with these words:

> Philosophers stretch the meaning of words until they retain scarcely anything of their original sense. They give the name of "God" to some vague abstraction which they have created for themselves. [Freud, 1927c, p. 32]

What he dismisses with contempt may in fact be a true grasp of the absolute. With this sentence Freud dismisses, in one blow, the profound concept of god as conceptualized by Spinoza. And when Spinoza referred to god, he specifically said that he was not referring to the kind of god that was adored in Judeo–Christian worship. There is an ignorance here in Freud that is regrettable. What is clear is that he had no idea that there could be a knowledge of reality itself that was not derived from the senses. In this he was a faithful disciple of Locke. The idea that there was a faculty that directly grasped Being itself which was inherent in the thought of Aristotle, Aquinas, Spinoza, and more contemporary thinkers such as Van Steenberghen, Heidegger, and the School of Louvain, was dismissed by Freud. Reasoning is the only mental process that he allows, and what I refer to as the faculty of the intellect he categorizes as intuition or introspection, which is to be discarded. So he says:

> It is once again merely an illusion to expect anything from intuition and introspection; they can give us nothing but particulars about our own mental life. [Freud, 1927c, pp. 31–32]

He says here that they can give us *nothing but particulars about our own mental life.* This is such a serious error, although a very common one. The idea that through the intellect one cannot get to the reality outside oneself, to that greater reality of which one is a small part, is such individualistic and solipsistic viewpoint.

Now I must show how, when I use these as instruments to think with, I end by making the mental phenomenon to be moulded by the instrument rather than the other way around.

Clinical example

The woman started the session by saying,

> *"I hate coming today for a session."*

She was tormented because before the previous session I had seen her in the street, and she had hated that. She was terrified of me seeing her outside the consulting-room. She was a keen swimmer and went to a public piscina; she was panic-stricken at the thought that I might see her there one day. If that were to occur, I would look at her and consider her just as an object, a sexual object, and not as an independent human being. So when she started by saying:

> "*I hate having to come today.*"

I said,

> "*You are still full of anguish after the last session . . .*"

and she went straight on to say that in sexual intercourse she, Juliana, disappeared. Her own selfhood dissolved. Then she said that when her husband *looked* at her, it was the same for her as sexual intercourse. She further said that if she talked about sex, to me it was the same—that the talking about sex was the same as having sex. So I gave her this picture. I said that just after conception there was no differentiation in the *zygote* or *embryo* between legs, arms, eyes. She quickly interrupted me and said that she was just a ball, and that all was compressed within it. So talking to me about sex, having sexual intercourse with her husband, her husband looking at her, were all compressed together. So my interpretation here was based upon an image of her as a *zygote*, but where did this come from?

For many years I have had an interest in foetal development; I believe in Freud's theory of *fixation* where someone's emotional state is stuck at an earlier stage of development. So is that where my interpretation came from? I believe not. My mind was wandering as she spoke to me about the way different though related activities melted into an unshapely lump, so that sexual intercourse with her husband, her husband looking at her, and speaking to me about sex were one and the same thing for her. These experiences congealed into one formless mess of dough brought the image of a *zygote* to mind, but I remember searching for something that conformed to the way in which different though related realities were compacted. I might have instanced a hen's egg, or the way a silverfish curls up into a ball, or the way the grains of parmesan cheese melt into one lump under heat, or a minute nugget of China tea expands out into veritable plant in the drinking vessel; if I had said any of these images to her, it would, I believe, have brought the same reply from her—that is, that she was just compressed into a ball. It was my image that harmonized with her own experience; she paralleled my image with her own. What we are talking of here is a connection between the two of us. I was not, I believe, forcing her into a particular developmental model. The model I am thinking of is the one where we believe that what happens in infancy affects what occurs later in adult life. Although the *zygote* or *embryo* came most readily to mind, conditioned as I am by such a spreading out of ourselves from a source with no distinctions, yet it was the image of many separate though related things pressed together into a formless solidity that was the link of consonance between us. I am emphasizing that the image of the *embryo* was servant to . . . to what?—a series of interactions: sexual intercourse, her husband looking at her, and her talking to me about sexual matters. It was to this series that the image was servant.

Now let us say that I become excited by this image. I believe that all emotional activity finds its source in this early stage of foetal development. The next day she is talking about her son always talking about cricket, and I say that the way he turns everything into a game of cricket is a symbol for the way all things are joined up inside her, so that what happened in the last session is no different to what is happening now today in this session. Then, when she tells me that she is reading Chaucer in middle English and that some words are the same as those of today but others are not, I say that she is realizing that she is still an emotional foetus and that only certain things have developed further. Then she tells me that when she goes to sleep at night, she is frightened, and I say it is because she fears that she will be swallowed up by the womb of night and will be trapped there for ever, like an unborn foetus. If you are beginning to think that I have gone mad and that you had better have me committed to a psychiatric unit, then I think I must ask you to despatch a few of my colleagues there also. You can find instances of this little parody that I am offering in any psychoanalyst or psychotherapist who is "committed" to a particular school—object relations, self-psychology, intersubjectivist, or the relational school. If I resort to examples, the individuals from whom I quote will be insulted; but I ask you to consult a few clinical articles first from the object relations school, then from self-psychology, then from the intersubjectivist and finally the relational school, and see for yourselves whether what I have said finds verification.

Difference between God and an idol

An image that is right in one place is incorrect in another, so my being needs to be plastic, to be in a place that generates images, but the factory fashioning these images has of itself to be infinite. It has to be in a place that is beyond images. If it is itself an image, an idol, then it cannot fashion an image. A fashioner of images cannot itself be an image. Again Chesterton, that forgotten genius, put his finger on this point, which I have already quoted but will do so again:

> The imagination is supposed to work towards the infinite; though in that sense the infinite is the opposite of imagination. For the imagination deals with an image. And an image is in its nature a thing that has an outline and therefore a limit. [Chesterton, 1938, p. 107]

It is when the infinite is reduced to an image that we have not God but an idol, but the important point to note is that the idol is endowed with godly attributes—that is, it explains everything in terms of its own image. Again to repeat what is said above, Freud fell into this trap when he endowed an idol with divine quality. So the idea of a fixation point is extremely valuable and does explain, I believe, the way someone is emotionally fixed at an early stage of development. It is one of the tools available for the creator within, just as the colour blue is one of the available elements on the painter's palette. If, however, I have bowed my head to it in the belief that it is the only available colour or I have endowed it with properties that it does not have, then I will make poppies blue, a Labrador dog blue, a thunder-cloud blue. No doubt in our post-modern era I might find my painting winning prizes in many august places. Similarly if all my interpretations are based on the fixation point, I might find myself erected into the trauma expert and be asked to lecture at trauma conferences worldwide. I am making the point here that idols have a strong power to attract people to them. Those ancient Israelites of whose religious culture we are the inheritors kept sliding back to the worship of idols—but why? And why do we today make idols of, let us say, attachment theory, neuroscientific models of the mind, or mentalization? The reason is that in an idol I can hide myself. However, when I place the omnipotent, the omniscient, where it belongs—that is, in *Brahman*—then my own naked being, my smallness, my being as it actually is and not as I would like it to be stares out at me, and also I have to expand my mind.

Bion as mystic

The only psychoanalytic thinker who had what I am saying centre stage in his mind was Bion. So, for instance, after having formulated his model of container/contained which I referred to earlier, he says:

> I shall therefore close the discussion by assuming there is a central abstraction unknown because unknowable yet revealed in an impure form in statements such as "container or contained" and that it is to the central abstraction *alone* that the term "psycho-analytical element" can be properly applied [Bion, 1963, p. 7; emphasis added]

But why is it that I can hide myself within an idol but not within *Brahman*? It is because *Brahman is* me. It is the true me, the only me. There *is* a universe. It matters not a whistle how large or how small. I am part of it, and so are you. This is my essential being, my inner being, my outer being, and all my faculties are it. When I reflect on myself, I know my own finiteness: I know I am a limited being; I know that I was born at a particular moment and even without knowing the date of it or the day when I shall die; I can feel my circumscribed condition. I have never felt that I have always existed, and yet the universe and all that is in it simply is; it is uncaused; we simply cannot grasp it. I am not it, and yet I am. It is against this incomprehensible fact that I must be it. Again, the mystic who wrote *The Epistle of Privy Counsel* says:

> therefore come down into the lowest point of thy wit, the which some man holdeth by very proof that it is the highest, and think on the simplest manner, but by some man the wisest, not what thyself is, but that thyself is. [McCann, 1952, p. 105]

You can see that I am trying to distinguish between two angles on my own identity and this English mystic puts it clearly: "not *what* thyself is, but *that* thyself is". Sometimes conference organizers ask for details about myself, and I say that I am a psychoanalyst, that I once studied philosophy and theology, that I worked at the Tavistock, that I emigrated to Australia, that I am married. This is my *what-ness,* but that I exist is my *that-ness.* I only truly see myself when my *what-ness* is silhouetted against my *that-ness.* Idolatry is when I allow my *what-ness* to obliterate my *that-ness.* Our English mystic puts it thus:

> The which natural wit, be it never so subtle nor so holy, may be called (in comparison of this) but feigned folly formed in fantasy [McCann, 1952, p. 113]

The point about the idol is that it is an image which covers over the *THAT.* It arises from letting my *what-ness* blank out the *that-ness* of my being. The erection of the outer idol flows from the blanking out of the *that-ness* that is my very own being. In doing so, it shuts out who I am. The Old Testament prophets were complaining not of going after other gods but the making of an image of Yahweh, because the image blanks out the *that-ness.* It was not an image of other gods that they were complaining about, but the image of *the* God, Yahweh, of whom there can be no image.

So I need to explain why it is that the idol, the *what-ness,* prevents the psychoanalyst from seeing the person who is in front of me. My *that-ness* conditions the way I perceive the other: I see his or her *that-ness.* I see the other according to the lens through which I look. If I look through my *what-ness,* then my own self-illusion fills the radar screen and my own being, and that of the other is blotted out; if I look through my *that-ness,* I see the being of him or of her.

The *what-ness* is the object relations model, the self-psychology model, the intersubjectivist model, or the relational model. I have pretended that these *what-nesses* are *that-nesses.* I have built a golden calf. Only when I have broken it into bits can I see what is before me. The goal of psychoanalytic therapy is to know that which is. There is no insurance that I can achieve this, but the best recipe is a belief in *Brahman.*

Object-relations theory, self-psychology, the intersubjective or relational school are all *what-nesses*—if they are taken as being *that-ness,* then I shut my being into the prison of a *what-ness,* and I do the same with my patient; I fashion him into the mould of a *what-ness.* The guarantee that I shall meet the patient *as he is* and not as I want him to be, and my guiding star, is the *that-ness. That-ness,* **O**, God, *Brahman,* Ultimate Reality, the Infinite, Truth, or Yahweh are synonyms. Belief is that psychological act that gathers me into the unity denoted by any of these terms. This is the best guarantee I have that I meet the patient as he is and not a *"feigned folly formed in fantasy"*.

NOTES

1. If therefore the synthesis is something more than the immense multitude of its conditions, then there has to be in it something to contain and dominate this very immensity: a remainder that no doubt is as little as nothing and which the sciences take into account only to eliminate it. But it is this nothing which, from an interior viewpoint, is everything, since it is the invisible principle of the synthesis, the soul of all positive knowledge and of every efficacious operation."

Epilogue

Mary Kay O'Neil

> . . . it is either altogether beyond our powers, or at least very difficult, to attain certain knowledge about matters such as these. And yet a man would be a coward if he did not try with all his might to refute every argument about them, refusing to give up before he has worn himself out by examining them from all sides. For he must do one of two things: either he must learn, or discover, the truth about these matters, or if that is beyond his powers, he must take whatever human doctrine seems to him to be the best, and to offer the hardest resistance to refutation.
>
> Plato, in dialogue with Socrates

Freud was not a coward when he dared to write *The Future of an Illusion*, thereby challenging two shibboleths of civilization: God and organized religion. Nor were the authors of this volume cowards when they reflected on Freud's argument and accepted the challenge to support or refute his views and express their own. As *Salman Akhtar* proposes in the Introduction, Freud was not one-sided, as he is generally taken to be—Freud the Atheist was also Freud the Believer. Similarly, the contributors to this volume dared to consider the difficult and still controversial relationship between psychoanalysis and religion from many sides. Just as Freud approached this conundrum from within his time and place, so too do these psychoanalyst writers approach Freud's paper from within their contemporary world view and circumstances. The purpose of this Epilogue is to illustrate how psychoanalysts have grown from adherence to Freud's dogmatic stricture that theism and psychoanalysis are incompatible to the open-minded view that it is possible for psychoanalysis and religious belief to co-exist in a state of creative ambivalence.

The Future of an Illusion (1927c)—a transitional paper, as *Ethel Spector Person* suggests—leads into Freud's more complex consideration of culture in *Civilization and Its Discontents* (1930a). It is, in her view, Freud's way of leading into charting the interdigitation of culture and psyche. Person's deconstruction of Freud's paper presents his eight main arguments, defects and all. Having summarized what she believes Freud is trying to say, she states, from her "pragmatic" perspective, his argument's fatal flaw: Freud "comes perilously close to positioning it [psychoanalysis] as an alternative belief system to religion". To balance this view, Person acknowledges the ethicist Wallwork's important reading of "the sub-text in Freud's all-out attack on religion: his recognition 'that weakening the religious grounds for morality poses dangers to society and requires new rational justifications—the main task of ethics'".

Jonathan Lear, within his philosopher's framework, questions the validity of Freud's strong claim "that no one who properly understood psychoanalytic insights could legitimately find a way to embrace religious belief". He questions whether or not Freud's argument against religious belief fosters discrimination against those who are believers? Belief, illusion, reality, wishes as conscious and unconscious causes are used in Freud's rhetoric, leading to Lear's "diagnosis" that religion is "a manifestation in adult life of an infantile longing for a protective father—a powerful figure who was on one's side and who could ensure that the world was overall just." The "mercilessness" of Freud's view, according to Lear, is that the "great majority of mortals will never be able to rise above" this strongest of wishes of mankind and that only the educated could and should be able to see the "truth".

Lear challenges Freud's claim that "psychoanalytic validity implies that there is *no way* one can both (a) believe in the principles of psychoanalysis and live according to them *and* (b) live a life that embodies religious commitment". He proposes to impugn Freud's argument that it would be necessary either to show that it is psychoanalytically invalid to claim that religious belief is illusion or to establish that it is possible to believe in psychoanalytic principles and to live a religiously committed life. Indeed, Lear asserts that Freud does not offer a viable argument for either of these counterpoints.

Recognizing that these possibilities are difficult to argue and nearly impossible to validate, Lear turns to Maimonides to support the notion that there can be a psychoanalytic and religious engagement. "Maimonides basically agrees with Freud that the stories of the Torah are wishful—but he does so in the service of deepening religious belief, not debunking it." . . . "Contra Freud, Maimonides saw that there were sophisticated ways of living with these [Bible] stories other than forming straightforward empirical beliefs about their literal truth." Maimonides recognized that childish religious belief is illusion, but he also thought that this recognition was a step in overcoming idolatry, not religious commitment. Lear cuts through the dogmatic thrust of Freud's argument and raises the possibility of varying individual relationships between belief and psychoanalysis.

J. Anderson Thomson, Jr, a Darwinian fundamentalist and supporter of Freud's anti-religion argument—"its fierce wisdom, its insistence on an objective analysis of religion, and its rousing defence of science"—focuses upon the contemporary nightmare of religious belief gone awry. His scientifically supported argument that "Freud's seminal work on religion" can be examined within the context of today's knowledge leads to his view that Freud "was both prescient and wrong". Freud is noted as being wrong in several areas. For example: the need for the illusion of a powerful father (God) as a defence against the helplessness of childhood was Freud's lynchpin of religious formation, yet religious ideas arise from multiple natural capacities of the human mind. Freud proposed that the taboo against murder arose from the primal murder of the father and the displacement of man's need to project the father onto God's will in the form of the commandment—"Thou shall not kill". Now, it is thought that killing has been adaptive for most of evolutionary history. The fossil evidence of murder for genetic survival is overwhelming, and Darwin's thesis for the survival of the fittest holds sway. The genes of the killers were the genes that survived. There were also discrepancies in Freud's life. His psychoanalytic atheism was dogmatically imposed on his family. Martha, to her regret, was not allowed to keep Jewish religious observance. Ironically, the Christian holidays of Christmas and Easter were observed, albeit with secular practices.

For Thomson, however, Freud's errors pale in comparison to the soundness of his fundamental thesis that religion "arises from unconscious processes, captures adaptive structures of our psychology, and derails rationality." Thomson's conclusion leaves little doubt as to why he thinks Freud was prescient in calling into question the positive role of religious belief in human life. "Religion's usefulness now lies in the past. Its foundational texts are obvious fables. Religion is a man-made burden that remains the enemy of reason, science, and free inquiry (Hitchens, 2007). It has been and continues to be an accessory to ignorance, guilt, murder, genocide, bigotry, racism, apartheid, slavery, misogyny, genital mutilation, persecution of homosexuals, the spread of AIDS, the re-emergence of polio, opposition to the vaccine against cervical cancer, impeding child immunization, the obstruction of basic medical research, tyranny and suicide terrorism, to name only a few." In step with present-day writers (notably Dawkins, 2006, and Hitchens, 2007) Thomson argues for rationality based on evolutionary data and psychological investigation to replace religion.

Vamik D. Volkan offers his *lantern image,* with its transparent and opaque sides, to consider the relationship between psychoanalysis and religion and between religious fundamentalism and violence. The lantern is used to formulate a "metapsychology" based on the concept of the transitional object. With this image, Volkan elucidates the two sides of religious beliefs: the creative and the destructive. Creatively, to develop as a separate individual, the child turns the lantern this way and that, multiple times. When a child feels secure, outside reality is illuminated and perceived as separate: the mind is opened. In contrast, the insecure child turns the opaque side of the lantern towards a frustrating world and fosters a closed omnipotence. Normal development leads to the acceptance of the "not-me" world and adjustment to logical thinking. "Moments of rest" during which there is no need to differentiate between what is real and what is illusion, times when logical thinking need not be maintained, are other facets of this image. The need for these moments varies among individuals and groups; religious belief is one form of rest. The notion of "moments of rest" opens the possibility that religious experience can provide needed inner emotional support. Similarly, psychoanalysts travel between primary process (illusion) and secondary process (reality), and, within a secure space, are models for patients to reduce the anxiety associated with modifying psychic reality. Illusion—religious or psychoanalytic—and reality can co-exist productively. But what of the more regressive, restrictive, destructive side—that side of religious belief which leads to violence and which, Freud thought, destroys civilization? According to Volkan, religious fundamentalists are preoccupied with keeping the opaque side of the lantern turned against the real world that is perceived as threatening and frustrating. Volkan explores the meaning and unconscious motivations that make a person cling to closed and exaggerated religiosity. He also considers the danger of religious fundamentalist groups such as cults, as well as the global impact of violent destructiveness of movements like al-Qaeda.

Volkan ends with a challenge to the profession. If psychoanalysts are to understand extreme religious fundamentalism and how the psychology of large-group identity can manipulate people to engage in massive sadistic and masochistic deeds, the transparent side of the lantern needs to be turned to interdisciplinary collaboration. Moments of rest for the analyst come when what is learned from the outside world is reflected on and integrated into the inner world of psychoanalytic theory and practice.

George A. Awad's chapter—poignantly his last paper written just before his untimely death—focuses on the morality of the oppressed group. Calling on historical evidence and personal knowledge of Islam as a religion and a culture, he contests a cornerstone of Freud's argument. He does "not share Freud's disdain and contempt of the 'uneducated', 'suppressed' or 'oppressed' group." Nor does he share Freud's "valuation of the 'educated people and brain workers'". Awad contends that "all the originators and many of the followers of Radical Islam are 'educated people and brain workers'." His argument is strengthened by his focus (to avoid unsubstantiated generalizations) on one large group—the followers of the ideology of Sayyid Qutb, expressed by al-Qaeda—and one book—*Milestones*—which guides the groups' known ideology. The morality of radical Islamists is based exclusively on this interpretation of religion. A detailed description is offered of Qutb's ideology embedded in the minds of the radical Islamists and the formation of a new group that creates "historical truth" and of necessity isolates its members through submission and loss of individual identity in order to induct new recruits and preserve the purity of the group. Awad is careful to point out that Qutb's teachings are not representative of Islam as a whole, just as Lutheranism and Calvinism are not the only forms of Christianity; similarly, the followers of the extremist, the late Meir Kahane, do not represent all Jews.

In agreement with Hedges, Awad argues that fundamentalist dynamics are similar in any religion. Fundamentalists mirror each other in their obsessions, their intolerance of other beliefs or of disbelief, in waging war against artistic and cultural expression, silencing the media, subjugating women, promoting sexual repression, and expressing themselves through violence. Awad also supports Volkan's notion that Radical Islam turns to the lantern's opaque side, when he notes that submission only to what is in the Qur'an means cancelling centuries of great Arab–Islamic contributions to civilization. Awad concludes that young Muslim men may drift to religion to find meaning in a life to defend against an acute sense of inefficacy and insignificance. Although they may choose to adopt a certain ideology, they are also seduced by small group companionship and idealized, grandiose, and narcissistic teachings, which quell existential anxiety, demonize and dehumanize the other, obscure humanistic morality, and justify killing innocent people. The reader is convincingly led to the idea that recruits to al-Qaeda have lost or failed to develop the ability to reflect or mentalize—to have minds of their own.

In the *Future of an Illusion*, Freud expressed confidence, says Awad, that "religious irrationality could be replaced by reason, by a sensible social contract" and that the teaching of psychoanalysis could transform a culture rooted in illusion. *Moisés Lemlij* counters with his opinion that Freud was the victim of the same illusion of which he accused religious believers. To support this assertion, Lemlij offers a detailed account based on personal experience of political events that took place between 1960 and 2000 in Ayacucho, a region in the Peruvian Andean Highlands. "It was there and then that were concentrated the main development and activities of a terrorist political group, the Shining Path, whose structure and ideology had markedly religious features although they claimed an absolutely rational and material basis." From this terrible struggle, Lemlij attempts to understand the interrelationships of religion (the dream of reason turned to religious fanaticism), violence (massacre), and civilization (democratic, social, and economic devastation).

Lemlij traces the "religious war" that developed between the "Shining Path" and the evangelical churches. The complexities of this catastrophic war are best summarized in the author's words: "Both groups strove to win the minds and souls of the dispossessed and helpless. The Shining Path offered revolution, the evangelical churches offered paradise. The evangelicals considered the members of the Shining Path devils and the Anti-Christ. The Shining Path considered the evangelicals as traitors of the people. The Sacred texts were the Gospel and "Gonzalo Thought." The social structure of the area—the extended family, the peasant community, the rules of reciprocity, the age hierarchy, rituals, festivals, and the religious influences—contributed to the uprisings against the Shining Path. Lemlij asserts that "religion [in the form of extreme fundamentalism] is a disguised illusion of salvation that provokes catastrophes. . . . political ideologies that are the product of an idealization of reason are as perversely illusory as religions". He ends, if not pessimistically, at least with a cautionary note: "However advanced the world is, there will always be an Abimael, a bin Laden, a Torquemada, a Hitler, or a Stalin, who will appear at unexpected moments that produce a feeling that a final catastrophe approaches and that we need to cling to a hope of a new renaissance. Hence Freud's idea of substituting religious beliefs with scientific knowledge, of transforming a culture rooted in illusion for another based on a social contract inspired by reason, involves a constant and renewable struggle against the malevolent violence of narcissism."

It is not the believer or non-believer, the educated or un-educated who threaten civilization. Rather, the threat to civilization emanates from the unquestioning, isolated, and insecure mind.

Jennifer Bonovitz draws the reader away from these theoretical, philosophical, ideological, and political considerations to another aspect of the relationship between psychoanalysis and religion. Freud's core thesis that "the primal father was the original image of God, the model on which later generations have shaped the figure of God" reveals his "striking omission of the maternal in God". Bonovitz asserts that Freud blatantly excluded the positive life-giving, growth-promoting, maternal, sustaining functions of God. Nor did he consider the destructive derivative of the mother–child relationship in his construct of God. She questions the reason for this omission: "Was he disillusioned with mothers?" Empathically, she wonders whether the multiple traumatic losses of maternal figures with their sustaining, containing, self-affirming functions had contributed to Freud's "psychic blindness" regarding women and made it too painful for him to consider the maternal in God. Bonovitz draws the reader back to the core of psychoanalysis: our work with patients. Four clinical examples cut through the rigid separation of religion and psychoanalysis and open images of the maternal God emanating from Islamic, Hindu, Christian–Catholic religions: the creative presence of the Earth Goddess; the comforting function, in times of pain, of the soothing mother God; the inhibiting and controlling feared mother God, and the transformational God as in the transformational mother of infancy. Her lantern is turned to illuminate some of the forms and functions that the maternal aspects of God can take in analytic work. Bonovitz's clinical vignettes are moving and convincing.

It was a privilege to be able to include, posthumously, the deeply personal insights of *Mortimer Ostow.* Awe, mysticism, and apocalypse, drawn from within his rich Jewish religious tradition, are, for Ostow, three archaic determinants of the "religious instinct"—a metaphor for the human readiness to gather together to share in worship practices and belief in a parent-like supernatural Being. His grasp of psychodynamics and neuroscience and his clinical acumen all illuminate the sequential development of these three states of mind to expand understanding of the religious experience. He summarizes: "the sense of awe derives from the newborn's nondeclarative memory of his impression of his adult, giant parents. The tendency to mysticism derives from the infant's wish to undo the process of separation–individuation of early mood swings. Together, awe and mysticism create an affect that generally is described as religious . . .

and associated with temporal lobe function." While it is doubtful that any religious experience fails to include elements of awe and mysticism, both can occur outside a religious context, but they seldom do.

Apocalypse—meaning revelation to a divinely inspired sage or prophet—foretells of a dire future, with eventual reconciliation and rebirth. Apocalypse is ordinarily connected with religion. Ostow notes that "we possess a normal mechanism for mood regulation that strives towards but does not achieve homeostasis." He asserts that the sequence of anticipated death and destruction followed by rebirth are central to the understanding and regulation of intense mood. For example, for the person experiencing the mood oscillation of depression or bipolar illness, "fantasies of impending apocalyptic catastrophe can be seen to reflect the anticipation of a depressive crash, while dreams of rebirth and salvation project our psychic recovery: the internal homoeostatic correction."

In this chapter, Ostow does not directly address *The Future of an Illusion*. Nor does he agree with or challenge Freud's views. He expands understanding of religion and psychoanalysis by offering "a possible framework for a religious system within which the archaic components . . . serve as primary motivation and earliest affective expression of the need for attachment. Individuals may accede to, or dissent from, any aspect of the frame, while retaining the central affects and being moved by them. One may have religious feelings without being formally observant."

The Future of an Illusion was, for *Sudhir Kakar*, a gentle guide "away from my native Hindu–Indian imagination, full of myths and marvels, lighted by a romantic numinosum, into an iconoclastic way of seeing the world where . . . all gods have clay feet". Freud's treatise guided Kakar's youthful "struggles for freedom", his striving towards personal, cultural, and religious autonomy. At his later stage of life, in a different time and place, Freud's book has a different meaning for Kakar. He realizes that these shifts in meaning, like Freud's analysis of religion, are inseparable from "personal factors in his own experience" and "subjective expectations" from his cultural–historical background. As a Hindu, he is not surprised. "It is a tenet of Hindu philosophy that an individual 'action' can only be understood in the context of the culture of his country [*desha*], the historical era in which he lives [*kala*], the efforts required of him at his particular stage of life [*shrama*] and, lastly, on his innate psychobiological traits [*guna*].

Freud's *desha* and *karma* are obvious. Europe is between two World Wars and the concerns of the time—fear of loss of individual autonomy to the socialist collectivity and the anti-religious stance of radical rationalism—both inform and mould Freud's thesis. More elusive are Freud's *shrama* and *guna*. Illness and deepening pessimism lent negativity to Freud's earlier more appreciative view of religion, and his antipathy towards religion was probably based on his need to overcome his fascination with the occult and also his need to defend himself against his love for his father. Freud never retreats from "the idea of God as an enormously exalted father and the illusory nature of the religious belief system". Creatively, with his Hindu mind-set and myths, Kakar becomes Freud's imaginary opponent and outlines precepts of Hinduism that would give the "Master" pause for thought and perhaps revision: "A Hindu may believe in one God or many gods or be an atheist, what makes him a Hindu are his ritual practices and adherence to rules rather than to doctrines" . . . "In contrast to the Father–god of Abraham . . . the Hindu God (and Goddess) is not only multifaceted human—father, mother, child, lover, friend—but also incorporates animals and birds in divinity" . . . "Hindus are more positively inclined towards illusion". *Maya* (illusion or transformation) incorporates the creative part of life while recognizing its negative effects; and reality is constantly being made in many forms—concrete experience, mystical visions, memories, dreams—and some are more real than others.

Just as *The Future of an Illusion* gently guided Kakar to question his early views and later offered new meaning, so in a different time and place Freud the sceptic might well have been guided by Hindu tradition to appreciate the *religious experience,* just as he respected the *profound mystical experience.*

Bonovitz addresses Freud's great omission and brings the maternal back to religion and God. Maternally, she also provides the bridge to clinical applications of religion. *Ostow* and *Kakar* offer the reader more personal views of religion and psychoanalysis.

Neville Symington, with characteristic openness, offers a glimpse of how he integrated becoming a person and a psychoanalyst with his deeply personal thoughts on "How belief in God affects my clinical work". For Symington, belief in God does not emanate from the Judaeo–Christian–Islamic tradition wherein God revealed Himself to humans. Rather, his belief follows the tradition that created Brahman from a person's reflective intellect. "Belief gathers me as an alienated individual into this unity, into *Being*, into *Brahman*, into *Yahweh*. It unites the disparate parts of myself into a unity and me, as an individual, into the one-ness of the world." *Brahman* unites subjective complexities, and it is this unity, with no disowned parts, that allows him to relate to analysands as separate and distinct. He is highly critical of Freud's view: *"It is once again merely an illusion to expect anything from intuition and introspection; they can give us nothing but particulars about our own mental life"*, Bion's **O** and Blondel's *I* support Symington's views. Vignettes of small clinical moments, astutely selected, demonstrate the *I–Thou* relationship or the two *"I"* (*person*) relationship so essential to Symington's work. He brings the reader back to the dangers of adhering dogmatically to a psychoanalytic frame of reference rather than defining and using oneself as separate to understand the self of the other. "If I look through my *what-ness*, then my own self-illusion fills the radar screen and my own being, and that of the other is blotted out; if I look through my *that-ness*, I see the being of him or of her. He concludes: "Object-relations theory, self-psychology, the intersubjective or relational school are all *what-ness*—if they are taken as being *that-ness*, then I shut my being into the prison of a *what-ness*. The guarantee that I shall meet the patient *as he* and not as I want him to be and my guiding star is *that-ness*. *That-ness*, **O**, God, Brahman, Ultimate Reality, the Infinite, Truth, or Yahweh are synonyms. Belief is that psychological act that gathers me into the unity denoted by any of these terms. This is the best guarantee I have that I meet the patient as he is and not a '*feigned folly formed in fantasy.*'"

With these reflections on the clinical implications of belief in God and with his caution against strict adherence to a particular psychoanalytic theory, Symington addresses what Ethel Person referred to as Freud's fatal flaw when "he comes perilously close to positioning it as an alternative belief system to religion".

Dogmatic closure has yielded to open-minded expansion. Eight decades after Freud asserted that within psychoanalytic thought God and religious beliefs are to be replaced with rationality and scientific evidence, the contributors to this volume offer serious reflection on the shifts that have occurred both within psychoanalysis and within religion, as well as between them. Re-reading *The Future of an Illusion* and absorbing the thoughts of these contemporary psychoanalytic thinkers is indeed mind-expanding. Not only does each chapter offer food for thought, but their diverse contributions—whether from theoretical, philosophical, sociocultural, neuropsychological, clinical, or personal "spiritual" perspectives—are needed and timely.

In "Beyond Illusion: Psychoanalysis and the Question of Religious Truth", Blass (2004) concedes that within the last two decades psychoanalysis has rejected "Freud's reductionistic understanding of religion and his negative evaluation of it as an expression of infantile needs". She adds that "certain forms of religious belief and practice should be positively evaluated as a healthy development." This reconciliation between psychoanalysis and religion has had dual results. First, the four "untoward consequences" of Freud's view that Akhtar describes have been addressed within the profession and are exemplified within this volume: believer and non-believer psychoanalysts have re-opened theoretical controversy; the "religious" or "spiritual" minds of both patient and analyst are topics of creative discourse; the morality of the oppressed, the tendency to anthropomorphize nature, and the transformative role of the maternal in God have become areas for intra and inter psychic consideration; and, finally, the conflict between the ambivalent (conscious—secular and unconscious—religious) parts of Freud remains alive within psychoanalytic theory and practice. God and religion are clearly subjects for psychoanalysis. Second, this reconciliation has, as Blass proposes, blurred the fundamental differences between psychoanalysis and religion and thereby limited the needed dialogue that results from a concern with truth—the truth of religious and psychoanalytic claims.

Establishing the truth of these claims unequivocally is probably beyond human ability, but to continue the dialogue, to assert and attempt to refute beliefs (secular or religious), is well within human capacity. The views expressed by these psychoanalyst authors are especially timely, given the abundance of the many non-analyst writers who address the place of religion within contemporary society and culture (to cite a few recent examples, Dawkins, 2006; Hitchens, 2007; Lilla, 2007; Taylor, 2007). Gray, in his January 2008 essay, "Faith in Reason: Secular Fantasies of a Godless Age", concludes: "Despite the advance of science, humankind remains incurably religious, and the place of religion in society continues to be intractably contested. The belief that we are moving into a secular age looks evermore like an unwitting tribute to the perennial power of faith." Psychoanalysts must carry on the debate, as Freud would, from the particular vantage of psychoanalytic thought and practice, given its capacity to illuminate both religion's potential for providing solace and meaningful spiritual experiences and its potential for destructive contributions (e.g. extreme religious fundamentalism) to the contemporary world situation.

REFERENCES

Abram, J. (1997). *The Language of Winnicott: A Dictionary and Guide to Understanding His Work.* Northvale, NJ: Jason Aronson.

Abu-Rabi, I. M. (1996). *Intellectual Origins of Islamic Resurgence in the Modern Arab World.* Albany, NY: State University of New York Press.

Ad-Dab'bagh, Y. (2001). The median: Islamic faith and mental health. In: S. Akhtar & H. Parens (Eds.), *Does God Help? Developmental and Clinical Aspects of Religious Belief* (pp. 253–289). Northvale, NJ: Jason Aronson.

Akhtar, S. (1992). Tethers orbits, and invisible fences: Clinical, developmental, sociocultural, and technical aspects of optimal distance. In: S. Kramer & S. Akhtar (Eds.), *When the Body Speaks: Psychological Meanings in Kinetic Cues* (pp. 21–57). Northvale, NJ: Jason Aronson.

Akhtar, S. (2007). The trauma of geographic dislocation: Leaving, arriving, becoming, and being. In: M. T. Hooke & S. Akhtar (Eds.), *The Geography of Being* (pp. 165–190). London: IPA.

Akhtar, S., & Parens, H. (2001). Is God a subject for psychoanalysis? In: S. Akhtar & H. Parens (Eds.), *Does God Help? Developmental and Clinical Aspects of Religious Belief* (pp. 1–17). Northvale, NJ: Jason Aronson.

Alexander, R. (1987). *The Biology of Moral Systems.* New York: Aldine de Gruyter.

Allison, H. (1987). *Benedict de Spinoza: An Introduction.* New Haven, CT: Yale University Press.

Allman, W. F. (1994). *The Stone Age Present: How Evolution Has Shaped Modern Life—From Sex, Violence, and Language to Emotions, Morals, and Communities.* New York: Touchstone.

APA (1992). *Position Statement.* New York: American Psychoanalytic Association (available at http://www.apsa.org/ABOUTAPSAA/POSITIONSTATEMENTS/HOMOSEXUALITY/tabid/473/Default.aspx).

Arden, M. (1985). Psychoanalysis and survival. *International Journal of Psychoanalysis, 66*: 471–480.

Arlow, J. A. (1951). The consecration of the prophet. *Psychoanalytic Quarterly, 23:* 374–397.

Atran, S. (2002). *In Gods We Trust: The Evolutionary Landscape of Religion.* New York: Oxford University Press.

Atran, S. (2003). Genesis of suicide terrorism. *Science, 299* (7 March): 1534–1539.

Atran, S. (2006). The moral logic and growth of suicide terrorism. *The Washington Quarterly, 29* (2): 127–147.

Bach, S. (1977). Narcissistic state of consciousness. *International Journal of Psychoanalysis, 58*: 209–233.

Balint, M. (1968). *The Basic Fault: Therapeutic Aspects of Regression.* London: Tavistock Publications.

Balmer, R. (1989). *Mine Eyes Have Seen the Glory: A Journey into the Evangelical Subculture in America.* New York: Oxford University Press.

Baron-Cohen, S. (1995). *Mindblindness: An Essay on Autism and Theory of Mind.* Cambridge, MA: MIT Press.

Barrett, J. L. (2004). *Why Would Anyone Believe in God?* Walnut Creek, CA: Altamira Press.

Bear, D. M., & Fedio, P. (1977). Quantitative analysis of interictal behavior in temporal lobe epilepsy. *Archives of Neurology, 34*: 454–467.

Beyer, S. (1973). *The Cult of Tara: Magic and Ritual in Tibet.* Berkeley, CA: University of California Press.

Binswanger, L. (1956). *Erinnerungen an Sigmund Freud.* Bern: Francke Verlag.

Bion, W. R. (1963). *Elements of Psycho-Analysis.* London: Heinemann; reprinted London: Karnac, 1989.

Bion, W. R. (1965). *Transformations.* London: Heinemann.

Bion, W. R. (1970). *Attention and Interpretation.* London: Tavistock Publications.

Bion, W. R. (1992). *Cogitations.* London: Karnac.

Blass, R. B. (2004). Beyond illusion: Psychoanalysis and the question of religious truth. *International Journal of Psychoanalysis, 85*: 615–634.

Blondel, M. (1893). *Action.* Notre Dame, IN: University of Notre Dame Press, 1984.

Blos, P. (1979). *Adolescence Passage.* New York: International Universities Press.

Bollas, C. (1979). The transformational object. *International Journal of Psychoanalysis, 60*: 97–107.

Bowlby, J. (1982). *Attachment and Loss, Vol. 1: Attachment.* New York: Basic Books.

Boyer, P. (1994). *The Naturalness of Religious Ideas: A Cognitive Theory of Religion.* Berkeley, CA: University of California Press.

Boyer, P. (2001). *Religion Explained: The Evolutionary Origins of Religious Thought.* New York: Basic Books.

Brinich, P. (1982). Rituals and meanings: The emergence of mother–child communication. *Psychoanalytic Study of the Child, 37*: 3–13.

Brook, J. A. (1992). Freud and splitting. *International Review of Psychoanalysis, 19*: 335–350.

Burkett, W. (1996). *Creation of a Sacred: Tracks of Biology in Early Religions.* Cambridge, MA: Harvard University Press.

Buss, D. (2005). *The Murderer Next Door: Why the Mind Is Designed to Kill.* New York: Penguin.

Buss, D., & Duntley, J. D. (2000). "Is the Mind Made for Murder?" Paper presented at the annual meeting of the Human Behavior and Evolution Society, Amherst, MA.

Cartwright, N. (1983). *How the Laws of Physics Lie.* Oxford: Oxford University Press.

Cartwright, N. (1989). *Nature's Capacities and Their Measurement.* Oxford: Oxford University Press.

Cartwright, N. (1999). *The Dappled World: A Study in the Boundaries of Science.* Cambridge: Cambridge University Press.

Chagnon, N. A. (1988). Life histories, blood revenge, and warfare in a tribal population. *Science, 239*: 985–992.

Chesterton, G. K. (1933). *St. Thomas Aquinas.* London: Hodder & Stoughton.

Chesterton, G. K. (1938). *Autobiography.* London: Hutchinson & Co.

Clark, R. (1980). *Freud: The Man and the Cause.* New York: Random House.

Cohn, N. (1970). *The Pursuit of the Millennium.* New York: Oxford University Press.

Cordovero, M. (1558). *Tomer Devorah,* trans. L. Jacobs. New York: Sephor-Herman Press, 1960.

Davidson, D. (1984). Radical interpretation. In: *Inquiries into Truth and Interpretation* (pp. 125–139). Oxford: Oxford University Press.

Dawkins, R. (1976). *The Selfish Gene.* New York: Oxford University Press.

Dawkins, R. (1985). *The Blind Watchmaker: Why the Evidence of Evolution Reveals a World Without Design.* New York: Houghton Mifflin.

Dawkins, R. (2004). *The Ancestor's Tale: A Pilgrimage to the Dawn of Evolution.* New York: Houghton Mifflin.

Dawkins, R. (2006). *The God Delusion.* New York: Houghton Mifflin.

Degregori, C. I. (1993). *Qué difícil es ser Dios. Ideología y violencia política en Sendero Luminoso.* Travaux de l'IFEA 77. Bogota: Sociedad antropológica de Colombia.

Degregori, C. I. (1996). Cosechando tempestades. Las rondas campesinas y la derrota de Sendero Luminoso en Ayacucho. In: C. I. Degregori, J. Coronel, P. Del Pino, & O. Starn (Eds.), *Las rondas campesinas y la derrota de Sendero Luminoso.* Lima: IEP.

Del Pino, P. (1996). Tiempos de guerra y de dioses. Ronderos, evangélicos y senderistas en el valle del río Apurímac. In: C. I. Degregori, J. Coronel, P. del Pino, & O. Starn (Eds.), *Las rondas campesinas y la derrota de Sendero Luminoso.* Lima: IEP.

Dennett, D. (1997). Appraising grace. *The Sciences* (Jan/Feb).

Dennett, D. (2005). *Breaking the Spell: Religion as a Natural Phenomenon.* London: Viking.

Dilthey, W. (1976). The types of world view and their development in metaphysical systems. In: *Dilthey: Selected Writings,* ed. H. P. Rickman. Cambridge: Cambridge University Press.

Drassinower, A. (2003). *Freud's Theory of Culture: Eros, Loss, and Politics.* Lanham, MD: Rowman & Littlefield.

Duverger, M. (1968). *The Study of Politics,* trans. R. Wagoner. London: Thomas Y. Crowell, 1980.

Eigen, M. (1981). The area of faith in Winnicott, Lacan and Bion. *International Journal of Psychoanalysis, 62*: 413–433.

Einstein, A. (1950). *The World as I See It.* New York: Citadel Press, 1971.

El Diario (1986). "La entrevista del siglo." Available at http://www.eldiariointernacional.com/Descarga/Entrevista/Entrevista.htm

Elorza, A. (2004). Religión y violencia. *Diario El País* (Madrid), 16 April.

Erikson, E. H. (1950). *Childhood and Society.* New York: W. W. Norton.

Erikson, E. H. (1956). The problem of ego identification. *Journal of the American Psychoanalytic Association, 4*: 56–121.

Erikson, E. H. (1959). *Identity and the Life Cycle.* New York: International Universities Press.

Erikson, E. H. (1966). Ontogeny of ritualization. In: R. M. Loewenstein, L. M. Newman, M. Schur, & A. Solnit (Eds.), *Psychoanalysis: A General Psychology* (pp. 601–621). New York: International Universities Press.

Erikson, E. H. (1975). On the nature of psycho-historical evidence. In: *Life History and the Historical Moment.* New York: W. W. Norton.

Fitzpatrick-Hanly, M. (1992). *The Modernist Madonna: Semiotics of the Mater-*

nal Metaphor by Jane Silverman Van Buren, 1989 [Book review]. *International Review of Psychoanalysis, 19*: 113–117.

Flood, G. (1998). *An Introduction to Hinduism.* Cambridge: Cambridge University Press.

Folger, T. (2004). Foreword. In: S. Pinker (Ed.), *The Best American Science and Nature Writing 2004.* New York: Houghton Mifflin.

Foucault, M. (1972). *The Archaeology of Knowledge,* trans. A. Sheridan Smith. London: Tavistock Publications.

Freeman, T. (2004). *Men, Women and Kabala: A Handbook from the Masters.* New York: Class One Press.

Freud, E. L. (Ed.) (1960). *Letters of Sigmund Freud.* New York: Basic Books.

Freud, S. (1899a). Screen memories. *Standard Edition, 3.*

Freud, S. (1900a). *The Interpretation of Dreams. Standard Edition, 4–5.*

Freud, S. (1901b). *The Psychopathology of Everyday Life. Standard Edition, 6.*

Freud, S. (1905c). *Jokes and Their Relation to the Unconscious. Standard Edition, 8.*

Freud, S. (1907b). Obsessive actions and religious practices. *Standard Edition, 9*: 116.

Freud, S. (1908d). "Civilized" sexual morality and modern nervous illness. *Standard Edition, 9.*

Freud, S. (1908e [1907]). Creative writers and day-dreaming. *Standard Edition, 9.*

Freud, S. (1910c). *Leonardo da Vinci and a Memory of His Childhood. Standard Edition, 11*: 63–137.

Freud, S. (1912–13). *Totem and Taboo. Standard Edition, 13*: 1.

Freud, S. (1914c). On narcissism: An introduction. *Standard Edition, 3.*

Freud, S. (1915b). Thoughts for the times on war and death. *Standard Edition, 14.*

Freud, S. (1916–17). *Introductory Lectures on Psycho-Analysis. Standard Edition, 15–16*: 3–232.

Freud, S. (1920g). *Beyond the Pleasure Principle. Standard Edition, 18.*

Freud, S. (1921c). *Group Psychology and the Analysis of the Ego. Standard Edition, 18*: 65–143.

Freud, S. (1923b). *The Ego and the Id. Standard Edition, 19.*

Freud, S. (1924c). The economic problem of masochism. *Standard Edition, 19.*

Freud, S. (1927c). *The Future of an Illusion. Standard Edition, 21*: 5–56.

Freud, S. (1927e). Fetishism. *Standard Edition, 21.*

Freud, S. (1930a). *Civilization and Its Discontents. Standard Edition, 21*: 64–145.

Freud, S. (1939a). *Moses and Monotheism. Standard Edition, 23*: 1–137.

Freud, S. (1940b [1938]). *An Outline of Psychoanalysis. Standard Edition, 23*: 141–207.

Freud, S., & Ferenczi, S. (1927). Letter from Sigmund Freud to Sándor Ferenczi, 23 October 1927 (pp. 326–327). In: *The Correspondence of Sigmund Freud and Sándor Ferenczi, Vol. 3, 1920–1933*. Cambridge, MA: Harvard University Press, 2000.

Fromm, E. (1942). *The Fear of Freedom*. London: Routledge & Kegan Paul.

Fuller, D. (1947). *The Confessions of St. Augustine*. Grand Rapids, MI: Zondervan.

Gadamer, H. G. (1975). *Truth and Method*. New York: Crossword.

Galison, P. (1987). *How Experiments End*. Chicago: University of Chicago Press.

Galison, P. (1997). *Image and Logic: A Material Culture of Microphysics*. Chicago: University of Chicago Press.

Gay, P. (1987). *A Godless Jew: Freud, Atheism, and the Making of Psychoanalysis*. New Haven, CT: Yale University Press.

Gay, P. (1988). *Freud: A Life for Our Time*. New York: W. W. Norton.

George, N., Dolan, R. J., Fink, G. R., Russell, C., & Driver, J. (1999). Contrast polarity and face recognition in the human fusiform gyrus. *Nature Neuroscience, 2* (6): 574–580.

Geuss, R. (1999). Nietzsche and genealogy. In: *Nature, Culture and History* (pp. 1–28). Cambridge: Cambridge University Press.

Gloor, P., Olivier, A., Quesney, L. F., Andermann, F., & Horowitz, S. (1982). The role of the limbic system in experiential phenomena of temporal lobe epilepsy. *Annals of Neurology, 12*: 129–144.

Goldman, D. (1993). *In Search of the Real: The Origins and Originality of D. W. Winnicott*. Northvale, NJ: Jason Aronson.

Gorritti, G. (1994). Shining Path's Stalin and Trotsky. In: D. S. Palmer (Ed.), *Shining Path of Peru*. New York: St. Martin's Press.

Gray, J. (2008). Faith in reason: Secular fantasies of a godless age. *Harper's Magazine, 316* (January, No. 1892).

Greenacre, P. (1970). The transitional object and the fetish: With special reference to the role of illusion. *International Journal of Psychoanalysis, 51*: 447–456.

Grotstein, J. (2001). God and the unconscious: Eternal antonymies or long-lost twins? In: S. Akhtar & H. Parens (Eds.), *Does God Help? Developmental and Clinical Aspects of Religious Belief* (pp. 321–359). Northvale, NJ: Jason Aronson.

Guthrie, S. G. (1993). *Faces in the Clouds: A New Theory of Religion*. New York: Oxford University Press.

Guzmán, A. (1976). El problema campesino y al guerra popular. *Bandera Roja* (August, No. 46).

Hacking, I. (1981). *Scientific Revolutions.* Oxford: Oxford University Press.

Hacking, I. (1983). *Representing and Intervening: Introductory Topics in Philosophy of Natural Science.* Cambridge: Cambridge University Press.

Haddad, Y. (1983). Sayyid Qutb: Idealogue of Islamic revival. In: J. Esposito (Ed.), *Voices of Resurgent Islam* (pp. 67–98). New York: Oxford University Press.

Hardin, H. (1987). On the vicissitudes of Freud's early mothering: Early environment and loss. *Psychoanalytic Quarterly, 56*: 628–644.

Harris, S. (2004). *The End of Faith: Religion, Terror and the Future of Reason.* New York: W. W. Norton.

Harris, S. (2006). *Letter to a Christian Nation.* New York: Knopf.

Hartung, J. (1995). Love thy neighbor: The evolution of in-group morality. *Skeptic, 3* (4): 86–99.

Hauser, M. (2006) *Moral Minds: How Nature Designed Our Universal Sense of Right and Wrong.* New York: Ecco.

Hedges, C. (2006). *American Fascists: The Christian Right and the War on America.* New York: Free Press.

Heidegger, M. (1927). *Being and Time.* New York: Harper & Row, 1962.

Hitchens, C. (2007). *God Is Not Great: How Religion Spoils Everything.* New York: Twelve, Hachette Book Group.

Holy Qur'an (1946). Birmingham: Islamic Propagation Centre International.

Hopper, E. (2003). *Traumatic Experience in the Unconscious Life of Groups. The Fourth Basic Assumption: Incohesion: Aggregation/Massification or (ba) I: A/M.* London: Jessica Kingsley.

Horton, P., & Sharp, S. (1984). Language, solace, and transitional relatedness. *Psychoanalytic Study of the Child, 39*: 167–194.

Humphrey, N. (1996). *Leaps of Faith: Science, Miracles, and the Search for Supernatural Consolation.* New York: Copernicus.

Humphrey, N. (2002). What shall we tell the children? [Amnesty International Lecture, 1997.] In: *The Mind Made Flesh: Frontiers of Psychology and Evolution.* New York: Oxford University Press.

Ideele (1996). La masacre de Lucanamarca. *Revista del Instituto de Defensa Legal (Lima)* (November).

Isbell, B. J. (1994). Shining Path and peasant responses in rural Ayacucho. In: D. S. Palmer (Ed.), *Shining Path of Peru.* New York: St. Martin's Press.

Jung, C. G. (1937). Psychology and religion. In: *The Collected Works, Vol. 11: Psychology and Religion.* Princeton, NJ: Princeton University Press, 1969.

Jung, C. G. (1976). *The Collected Works, Vol. 18: The Symbolic Life.* Princeton, NJ: Princeton University Press.

Kakar, S. (1982). *The Inner World: A Psychoanalytic Study of Childhood and Society in India.* Delhi & New York: Oxford University Press.

Kakar, S. (1992). *The Analyst and the Mystic.* Chicago: University of Chicago Press.

Kakar, S. (2003). Seduction and the Saint. *Annual of Psychoanalysis, 31*: 197–209.

Kakar, S. (2007). *The Analyst and the Mystic: Psychoanalytic Reflections on Religion and Mysticism.* New Delhi: Penguin.

Katalikkiren, P. (2008). *Islam and the Divine Feminine.* Retrieved July 2008 from http://www.crescentlife.com/spirituality/divine_feminine.htm

Khachadourian, R. (2007). A reporter at large. Azzam the American: The making of an Al Qaeda homegrown. *The New Yorker*, 22 January.

Kirkpatrick, L. A. (1999). Towards an evolutionary psychology of religion and personality. *Journal of Personality, 67*: 921–949.

Kirkpatrick, L. A. (2004). *Attachment, Evolution, and the Psychology of Religion.* New York: Guilford Press.

Kirov, G., Kemp, R., Kirov, K., & David, A. S. (1998). Religious faith after psychotic illness. *Psychopathology, 31*: 234–245.

Kriegman, D., & Kriegman, O. (1998). "War and the Evolution of the Human Propensity to Form Nations, Cults, and Religions." Paper presented at the Association for Politics and the Life Sciences Annual Conference, Boston, MA (3 September).

Kuhn, T. S. (1962). *The Structure of Scientific Revolutions.* Chicago: University of Chicago Press.

Kuhn, T. S. (1987). *Black-Body Theory and Quantum Discontinuity, 1894–1912.* Chicago: University of Chicago Press.

Kuhn, T. S. (1997). *The Essential Tension: Selected Studies in Scientific Tradition and Change.* Chicago: University of Chicago Press.

Kurtz, S. (1992). *All the Mothers Are One: Hindu India and the Cultural Reshaping of Psychoanalysis.* New York: Columbia University Press.

Laor, N. (1989). Psychoanalytic neutrality toward religious experience. *Psychoanalytic Study of the Child, 44*: 211–230.

Lear, J. (2005). Morality and religion. In: *Freud* (pp. 192–219). New York: Routledge.

Lear, J. (2007). Working-through the end of civilization. *International Journal of Psychoanalysis, 88*: 291–308.

Lehmann, H. (1983). Reflections on Freud's reaction to the death of his mother. *Psychoanalytic Quarterly, 52*: 237–249.

Lewis, B. (1990). The roots of Moslem rage. *The Atlantic Monthly,* September 20, pp. 47–60.

Lilla, M. (2007). *The Stillborn God: Religion, Politics, and the Modern West.* London: Alfred A. Knopf.

Loewald, H. W. (1953). Psychoanalysis and modern views on human existence and religious experience. *Journal Pastoral of Care, 7*: 1–15.

Loewald, H. W. (1977). Review of *The Freud/Jung Letters. Psychoanalytic Quarterly, 46*: 514–527.

Loewald, H. W. (1978). *Psychoanalysis and the History of the Individual.* New Haven, CT: Yale University Press.

Lotto, D. (2001). Freud's struggle with misogyny: Homosexuality and guilt in the dream of Irma's injection. *Journal of the American Psychoanalytic Association, 49*: 1289–1313.

Mahony, P. (1982). *Freud as a Writer.* New York: International Universities Press.

Maimonides, M. (1963). *The Guide for the Perplexed,* trans. S. Pines. Chicago: University of Chicago Press.

Marty, M. E., & Appleby, R. S. (Eds.) (1995). *Fundamentalism Comprehended.* Chicago: University of Chicago Press.

Mayer, J. F. (1998). "Apocalyptic millennialism in the West: The case of Solar Temple." Paper read at The Critical Incident Analysis Group (CIAG), University of Virginia, Charlottesville, VA (13 November).

McCann, J. (Ed.) (1952). *The Cloud of Unknowing and Other Treatises.* London: Burns Oates.

McDermott, T. (2005). *Perfect Soldiers.* New York: HarperCollins.

McGrath, W. J. (1986). *Freud's Discovery of Psychoanalysis.* Ithaca, NY: Cornell University Press.

Meissner, W. (1984). *Psychoanalysis and Religious Experience.* New Haven, CT: Yale University Press.

Meissner, W. (1986). *Thy Kingdom Come: Psychoanalytic Perspectives on the Messiah and the Millennium.* New Haven, CT: Yale University Press.

Meissner, W. (1987). *Life and Faith: Psychological Perspectives on Religious Experience.* Washington, DC: Georgetown University Press.

Meissner, W. (1992). Religious thinking as transitional conceptualization. *Psychoanalytic Review, 79*: 175–196.

Meissner, W. (2001). So help me God! Do I help God or does God help me? In: S. Akhtar & H. Parens (Eds.), *Does God Help? Developmental and Clinical Aspects of Religious Belief* (pp. 75–126). Northvale, NJ: Jason Aronson.

Michaels, A. (1998). *Hinduismus.* Munich: C. H. Beck.

Milgram, S. (1974). *Obedience to Authority.* New York: Harper & Row.

Millones, L. (2005). La nostalgia de un pasado glorioso. Ayacucho 1919–1959. In: H. Tomoeda & L. Millones (Ed.), *Pasiones y desencuentros en la cultura andina.* Lima: Congreso del Perú.

Modell, A. (1970). The transitional objects and the creative art. *Psychoanalytic Quarterly, 39*: 240–250.

Moloney, J. (1954). Mother, God, and superego. *Journal of the American Psychoanalytic Association, 2*: 120–151.

Moore, E., & Fine, B. (1990). *Psychoanalytic Terms and Concepts*. New Haven, CT: Yale University Press.

Moses-Hrushovski, R. (2000). *Grief and Grievance: The Assassination of Yitzhak Rabin*. London: Minerva Press.

Nadler, S. (1999). *Spinoza: A Life*. Cambridge: Cambridge University Press.

Nadler, S. (2001). *Spinoza's Heresy*. Oxford: Clarendon Press.

Neri, C. (2005). What is the function of faith and trust in psychoanalysis? *International Journal of Psychoanalysis, 86*: 79–97.

Nesse, R., & Lloyd, A. (1992). The evolution of psychodynamic mechanisms. In: J. Barkow, L. Cosmides, & J. Tooby (Eds.), *The Adapted Mind*. New York: Oxford University Press.

Nicholi, A. M. (2002). *The Question of God: C. S. Lewis and Sigmund Freud Debate God, Love, Sex, and the Meaning of Life*. New York: Free Press.

Nietzsche, F. (1949). *The Use and Abuse of History*. Indianapolis, IN: Bobbs Merrill.

Ochs, C. (1977). *Behind the Sex of God*. Boston, MA: Beacon Press.

O'Flaherty, W. (1980). *Women, Androgynes and Other Mythical Beasts*. Chicago: University of Chicago Press.

O'Flaherty, W. (1984). *Dreams, Illusions and Other Realities*. Chicago: University of Chicago Press.

Ostow, M. (1957). The erotic instinct: A contribution to the study of instincts. *International Journal of Psychoanalysis, 38*: 1–20.

Ostow, M. (1958). The death instinct: A contribution to the study of instincts. *International Journal of Psychoanalysis, 39*: 1–12.

Ostow, M. (1989). A Godless Jew. *International Journal of Psychoanalysis, 16*: 119–121.

Ostow, M. (1995). *Ultimate Intimacy: The Psychodynamics of Jewish Mysticism*. London: Karnac.

Ostow, M. (2001). Three archaic contributions to the religious instinct: Awe, mysticism, and apocalypse. In: S. Akhtar & H. Parens (Eds.), *Does God Help? Developmental and Clinical Aspects of Religious Belief* (pp. 197–233). Northvale, NJ: Jason Aronson.

Ostow, M. (2006). *Spirit, Mind and Brain: A Psychoanalytic Examination of Spirituality and Religion*. New York: Columbia University Press.

Panksepp, J. (1998). *Affective Neuroscience: The Foundations of Human and Animal Emotions*. New York: Oxford University Press.

Papini, G. (1969). A visit to Freud. *Review of Existential Psychology and Psychiatry, 9*: 130–134.

Pedahzur, A. (2005). *Suicide Terrorism*. Malden, MA: Polity Press.

Penfield, W., & Jasper, H. (1954). *Epilepsy and the Functional Anatomy of the Human Brain.* Boston, MA: Little, Brown.

Penfield, W., & Kristiansen, K. (1951). *Epileptic Seizure Patterns.* Springfield, IL: Charles C Thomas.

Person, E. (2001). Knowledge and authority: The godfather fantasy. *Journal of the American Psychoanalytic Association, 49*: 1133–1155.

Pfister, O. (1993). The illusion of a future: A friendly disagreement with Prof. Sigmund Freud. *International Journal of Psychoanalysis, 74*: 557–558.

Pieper, J. Z. T. (2004). Religious coping in highly religious psychiatric inpatients. *Mental Health, Religion, and Culture, 7*: 349–363.

Pinker, S. (1997). *How The Mind Works.* New York: W. W. Norton.

Pinker, S. (2002). *The Blank Slate: The Modern Denial of Human Nature.* New York: Viking.

Popper, K. (1979). *Objective Knowledge: An Evolutionary Approach.* Oxford: Oxford University Press.

Portocarrero, G. (1998). *Razones de sangre.* Lima: Pontificia Universidad Católica del Perú.

Pruyser, P. (1983). *The Play of the Imagination: Toward a Psychoanalysis of Culture.* New York: International Universities Press.

Qutb, S. (1966). *Milestones.* Kuwait: Al Faisal Press, 1989.

Radhakrishnan, S. (1994). *The Principal Upanishads.* New Delhi: Harper Collins.

Rahman, F. (1979). *Islam.* Chicago: University of Chicago Press.

Rao, D. (2001). God playing psychoanalyst: Some lessons from the Bhagavad Gita. In: S. Akhtar & H. Parens (Eds.), *Does God Help? Developmental and Clinical Aspects of Religious Belief* (pp. 177–195). Northvale, NJ: Jason Aronson.

Rao, D. (2005). Manifestations of God in India: A transference pantheon. In: S. Akhtar (Ed.), *Freud Along the Ganges: Psychoanalytic Reflections on the People and Culture of India* (pp. 271–308). New York: Other Press.

Reddy, S. (2001). Psychoanalytic reflections on the sacred Hindu text, the Bhagavad Gita. In: S. Akhtar & H. Parens (Eds.), *Does God Help? Developmental and Clinical Aspects of Religious Belief* (pp. 153–175). Northvale, NJ: Jason Aronson.

Reddy, S. (2005). Psychoanalytic process in a sacred Hindu text: The Bhagavad Gita. In: S. Akhtar (Ed.), *Freud Along the Ganges: Psychoanalytic Reflections on the People and Culture of India* (pp. 309–333). New York: Other Press.

Ridley, M. (2000). *Genome: The Autobiography of a Species in 23 Chapters.* New York: HarperCollins.

Rizzuto, A.-M. (1979). *The Birth of the Living God: A Psychoanalytic Study*. Chicago, IL: University of Chicago Press.

Rizzuto, A.-M. (1998). *Why Did Freud Reject God? A Psychodynamic Interpretation*. New Haven, CT: Yale University Press.

Rizzuto, A.-M. (2001). Does God help? What God? Helping whom? The convolutions of divine help. In: S. Akhtar & H. Parens (Eds.), *Does God Help? Developmental and Clinical Aspects of Religious Belief* (pp. 21–51). Northvale, NJ: Jason Aronson.

Rubin, J. B. (2005). Psychoanalytic and Buddhist history and theory. In: S. Akhtar (Ed.), *Freud Along the Ganges: Psychoanalytic Reflections on the People and Culture of India* (pp. 335–358). New York: Other Press.

Sageman, M. (2004). *Understanding Terror Networks*. Philadelphia, PA: University of Pennsylvania Press.

Sapolsky, R. (2005). *Monkeyluv: And Other Essays on Our Lives as Animals*. New York: Scribner.

Sayers, J. (1991). Freud, feminism, and religion. In: S. M. Stein (Ed.), *Beyond Belief: Psychotherapy and Religion* (pp. 146–161). London: Karnac.

Schafer, R. (1992). *Retelling a Life: Narration and Dialogue in Psychoanalysis*. New York: Basic Books.

Schorske, C. E. (1979). *Fin-de-siècle Vienna: Politics and Culture*. New York: Knopf.

Scott Palmer, D. (2005). Terror en el nombre de Mao. Revolución y respuesta en Perú [Terror in the name of Mao: Revolution and response in Peru]. In: *El Perú y sus estudiosos. Tercer Congreso Internacional de Peruanistas, Nagoya, Japón, 2005*. Lima: UNMSM.

Šebek, M. (1994). Psychopathology of everyday life in the post-totalitarian society. *Mind and Human Interaction, 5*: 104–109.

Sen, A. (2005). *The Argumentative Indian: Writings on Indian History, Culture, and Identity*. London: Penguin.

Shafii, M. (1985). *Freedom from the Self: Sufism, Meditation, and Psychotherapy*. New York: Human Sciences Press.

Siassi, S., & Siassi, G. (2008). Islam, women, and sex. In: *The Crescent and the Couch: Cross-Currents between Islam and Psychoanalysis*. Northvale, NJ: Jason Aronson.

Sivan, E. (1985). *Radical Islam: Medieval Theology and Modern Politics*. New Haven, CT: Yale University Press.

Smith, H. (1973). Foreword. In: [Anon.] *The Way of a Pilgrim*, trans R. M. French. San Francisco: HarperCollins.

Sokolowski, R. (1990). Religion and psychoanalysis: Some phenomenological contributions. In: J. H. Smith & S. A. Handelman (Eds.), *Psycho-*

analysis and Religion (pp. 1–17). Baltimore, MD: Johns Hopkins University Press.

Solms, M. (1997). *The Neuropsychology of Dreams: A Clinico-Anatomical Study.* Mahwah, NJ: Lawrence Erlbaum Associates.

Spence, D. (1982). *Narrative Truth and Historical Truth: Meaning and Interpretation in Psychoanalysis.* New York: W. W. Norton.

Spinoza, B. (1992). *Ethics: Treatise on the Emendation of the Intellect,* trans. S. Shirley. Indianapolis, IN: Hackett.

Spinoza, B. (2001). *Theological–Political Treatise,* trans. S. Shirley. Indianapolis, IN: Hackett.

Squire, L. R., & Kandel, E. R. (1999). *Memory: From Mind to Molecules.* New York: Scientific American Library, Freeman.

Sterba, R. (1934). The fate of the ego in analytic therapy. *International Journal of Psychoanalysis, 15*: 117–126.

Stolorow, R., & Atwood, G. (1992). *Contexts of Being.* Hillsdale, NJ: Analytic Press.

Stolorow, R., Orange, D., & Atwood, G. (2001). World horizons: A post-Cartesian alternative to the Freudian unconscious. *Contemporary Psychoanalysis, 37*: 43–61.

Stringer, C., & Andrews, P. (2005). *The Complete World of Human Evolution.* London: Thames & Hudson.

Stringer, C., & McKie, R. (1996). *African Exodus: The Origins of Modern Humanity.* New York: Henry Holt.

Subramaniam, K. (1988). *Srimad Bhagavatam.* Bombay: Bharatiya Vidya Bhavan.

Taylor, C. (1995). *Philosophical Arguments.* Cambridge, MA: Harvard University Press.

Taylor, C. (2007). *A Secular Age.* Boston, MA: Harvard University Press.

Thomson, J. (2001). Does God help me or do I help god or neither? Discussion of Meissner's chapter, "So help me God! Do I help God or Does God help me?" In: S. Akhtar & H. Parens (Eds.), *Does God Help? Developmental and Clinical Aspects of Religious Belief.* Northvale, NJ: Jason Aronson.

Thomson, J. A. (2006). "We Few, We Happy Few, We Band of Brothers (and Occasional Sister!): The Dynamics of Suicide Terrorism." Paper presented at the Eighteenth Biennial Congress, International Society of Human Ethology, Detroit, MI (31 July).

Turner, J. F. (2002). A brief history of illusion. *International Journal of Psychoanalysis, 83*: 1063–1082.

Vallabhaneni, M. R. (2005). Advaita Vedanta, psychoanalysis, and the self.

In: *Freud Along the Ganges: Psychoanalytic Reflections on the People and Culture of India*, ed. S. Akhtar, pp. 359–393.

Van Buren, J. (1989). *The Modernist Madonna: Semiotics of the Maternal Metaphor.* Bloomington, IN: Indiana University Press.

Volkan, V. D. (1976). *Primitive Internalized Object Relations: A Clinical Study of Schizophrenic, Borderline and Narcissistic Patients.* New York: International Universities Press.

Volkan, V. D. (1979). The glass bubble of a narcissistic patient. In: J. LeBoit & A. Capponi (Eds.), *Advances in Psychotherapy of the Borderline Patient* (pp. 405–431). New York: Jason Aronson.

Volkan, V. D. (1980). Narcissistic personality organization and "reparative" leadership. *International Journal of Group Psychotherapy, 30*: 131–152.

Volkan, V. D. (1981). *Linking Objects and Linking Phenomena: A Study of the Forms, Symptoms, Metapsychology and Therapy of Complicated Mourning.* New York: International Universities Press.

Volkan, V. D. (1997). *Bloodlines: From Ethnic Pride to Ethnic Terrorism.* New York: Farrar, Straus, & Giroux.

Volkan, V. D. (2004). *Blind Trust: Large Groups and Their Leaders in Times of Crises and Terror.* Charlottesville, VA: Pitchstone Publishing.

Volkan, V. D. (2006). *Killing in the Name of Identity.* Charlottesville, VA: Pitchstone Publishing.

Volkan, V. D., & Kayatekin, S. (2006). Extreme religious fundamentalism and violence: Some psychoanalytic and psychopolitical thoughts. *Psyche & Geloof, 17*: 71–91.

Waelder, R. (1960). *Basic Theory of Psychoanalysis.* New York: International Universities Press.

Walker, B. (1983). *The Woman's Encyclopedia of Myths and Secrets.* New York: Harper & Row.

Wallwork, E. (2007). Ethics in psychoanalysis. In: E. S. Person, A. M. Cooper, & G. O. Gabbard (Eds.), *APPI Textbook of Psychoanalysis* (pp. 281–295). Arlington, VA: American Psychiatric Publishing.

Weber, E. (1999). *Apocalypses: Prophecies, Cults, and Millennial Beliefs through the Ages.* Cambridge, MA: Harvard University Press.

Weinberg, S. (2006). Presentation at Beyond Belief: Science, Reason, Religion and Survival Symposium, Salk Institute, San Diego, California, Session 1 (5 November). Video available at http://thesciencenetwork.org/programs/beyond-belief-science-religion-reason-and-survival/session-10-1

Wessinger, C. (1999). *How the Millennium Comes Violently: From Jonestown to Heaven's Gate.* New York: Seven Bridges Press.

Williams, B. (2002). Genealogy. In: *Truth and Truthfulness: An Essay in Genealogy* (pp. 20–40). Princeton, NJ: Princeton University Press.

Winnicott, D. W. (1946). Some thoughts on the meaning of the word democracy. In: *The Family and Individual Development.* London: Tavistock Publications, 1965.

Winnicott, D. W. (1953). Transitional objects and transitional phenomena. In: *Through Paediatrics to Psycho-Analysis* (pp. 229–242). London: Hogarth Press, 1975; reprinted London: Karnac, 1984.

Winnicott, D. W. (1960). String: A technique of communication. In: *The Maturational Processes and the Facilitating Environment: Studies in the Theory of Emotional Development* (pp. 153–157). London: Hogarth Press, 1965; reprinted London: Karnac, 1984.

Winnicott, D. W. (1963). Morals and education. In: *The Maturational Processes and the Facilitating Environment: Studies in the Theory of Emotional Development.* London: Hogarth Press, 1965; reprinted London: Karnac, 1984.

Winnicott, D. W. (1967). The location of cultural experience. *International Journal of Psychoanalysis, 48*: 368–372.

Winnicott, D. W. (1970). Living creatively. In: *Home Is Where We Start From.* Harmondsworth: Penguin, 1986.

Winnicott, D. W. (1971). Creativity and its origins. In: *Playing and Reality* (pp. 65–85). London: Tavistock.

Wittgenstein, L. (1978). *Philosophical Investigations.* Oxford: Blackwell.

Wrangham, R. W. (1999). Evolution of coalitionary killing. *Yearbook of Physical Anthropology, 42*: 1–30.

Wrangham, R. W., & Peterson, D. (1996). *Demonic Males: Apes and the Origins of Human Violence.* Boston: Houghton Mifflin.

Yeats, W. B. (1956). *The Collected Poems of W. B. Yeats.* New York: Macmillan.

Zaehner, R. (1966). *Hinduism.* New York: Oxford University Press.

Zeddies, T. J. (2002). Behind, beneath, above, and beyond. *Journal of the American Academy of Psychoanalysis, 30*: 211–229.

INDEX

For Product Safety Concerns and Information please contact our EU representative GPSR@taylorandfrancis.com Taylor & Francis Verlag GmbH, Kaufingerstraße 24, 80331 München, Germany